QUICK *from* SCRATCH

Bow Ties with Salami and Artichoke Hearts, page 101

QUICK *from* SCRATCH

REAL FOOD FOR BUSY WEEKNIGHTS

American Express Publishing Corporation
New York

Editorial Director: Judith Hill
Assistant Editors: Jacqueline Bobrow and Susan Lantzius
Copy & Production Editor: Terri Mauro
Wine Editor: Richard Marmet
Art Director: Nina Scerbo
Photographer: Melanie Acevedo
Food Stylist: Deborah Mintcheff
Prop Stylists: Edward Kemper Design
Illustrator: Karen Scerbo
Production Manager: Yvette Williams-Braxton

Vice President, Books and Information Services: John Stoops
Marketing Director: Mary V. Cooney
Marketing/Promotion Manager: Roni Stein
Operations Manager: Doreen Camardi
Business Manager: David Geller

Cover Photos: (Front) Lime-Marinated Chicken Breasts, page 219, with Corn Salad, page 255
(Back, clockwise from top left) Lentil Soup with Six Vegetables, page 23; Beef, Green-Bean, and Cherry-Tomato Stir-Fry, page 151; BLT Burritos, page 55; Cod Cakes with Scallions and Herbs, page 163; Pears and Prunes Poached in Spiced Red Wine, page 279; Roasted Asparagus with Hazelnut Sauce, page 237

AMERICAN EXPRESS PUBLISHING CORPORATION
©1996 American Express Publishing Corporation

LIBRARY OF CONGRESS CATALOGING-IN-PUBLICATION DATA
Quick from scratch : real food for busy weeknights.
p.   cm.
Includes index.
ISBN 0-916103-31-5
1. Quick and easy cookery. I. Food & wine (New York, N.Y.)
TX833.5.Q533   1996
641.5'55—dc20   96-6203
CIP

Published by American Express Publishing Corporation
1120 Avenue of the Americas, New York, New York 10036

Manufactured in the United States of America

CONTENTS

MAIN DISHES

SIDE DISHES

Shrimp and Watercress Stir-Fry with Lemon Garlic Sauce, page 141

FOREWORD

If I'm not working late or going out to dinner, this is my weeknight scenario: I get home and I want to prepare something Interesting, with a capital "I." Breakfast for dinner used to hold some appeal, but that phase has definitely passed. Now I want to try something new—but I don't want to try my patience. I usually don't bother making a meal that starts with a first course and ends with dessert. The main course and side dishes are the only recipes I concern myself with.

As it turns out, Judith Hill, the editor of FOOD & WINE Books and an extraordinary cook, eats just the same way, and her staff does, too. This collective demand for practical recipes that deliver good flavor in no time flat inspired *Quick from Scratch*. Don't look for menus here, or how-to photos. The 215 recipes in this volume, which range from Soft Polenta with Meat Ragù, page 117, to Shrimp and Watercress Stir-Fry with Lemon Garlic Sauce, page 141, are completely delicious and so simple that you'll feel like you're cheating.

Quick from Scratch is the cookbook I've been waiting for, the one that answers the question "What am I going to make for dinner?" without insulting my culinary IQ. Enjoy! And remember, you don't need to tell anyone it was so fast and easy.

DANA COWIN
Editor in Chief
FOOD & WINE Magazine

Lemon Risotto with Asparagus and Shiitake Mushrooms, page 131

INTRODUCTION

This book is dedicated to Tuesday night. You know—that point when you've plunged into the week, you have a million things on your schedule, and Friday seems a long time away. You get home late and want to relax over a decent dinner and a glass of wine, but simply do not have hours to cook.

This book is also dedicated to a certain kind of person, a cook who's as busy as any of us but still manages to avoid falling into the microwaving-frozen-products routine—who sets a premium on real food made with fresh ingredients. In short, the person we believe our reader to be.

In fact, we think our readers are a lot like us. We, too, get home from work late, and good food is a priority for all of us who contributed to this book. The recipes reflect the way we cook on week-nights ourselves. As we were developing these recipes, at every test-kitchen tasting, Jackie Bobrow, Susan Lantzius, and I asked each other, "Would you make this? On Tuesday night?"

JUDITH HILL
Editorial Director
FOOD & WINE Books

Vietnamese Noodle Salad with Vegetables and Beef, page 79

WINE INTRODUCTION

Quick from Scratch is about the ease with which we can incorporate good food into our busy week-day lives without a great deal of fuss. The wines suggested for each recipe have been chosen in the same spirit. These might not be the wines that connoisseurs pay huge sums to swirl, sip, slurp, and swoon over. Those wines have their place, but they certainly don't fit into our everyday lives or make sense for our budgets.

For the most part, the wines recommended here are moderately priced, widely available, and meant to accompany and enhance, rather than dominate, a meal. They are also, unless otherwise noted, wines that are meant to be drunk young (so try to find the most recent vintage). Finally, to avoid a time-consuming search for specific producers or vintages, recommendations are phrased in terms of broad categories (California chardonnay) rather than specific bottles (a 199X vintage of Y Chardonnay from Z Vineyard).

These wines are drinks to refresh us at the end of a hectic day at work. They are beverages that make our food taste better and that increase the enjoyment of our meals. And they are bottles that we can recork if we don't finish in one night and still enjoy the following evening without worrying about them becoming undrinkable (as many of the more expensive, older wines often do). In short, these wines are meant to be no big deal. Rather, they are wines that can be woven into our lives as seamlessly as can the recipes in this book.

RICHARD MARMET

SOUPS & STEWS

Chicken Soup with Butternut Squash and Shiitakes, page 19

"SOUP OF THE EVENING, BEAUTIFUL SOUP!" Lewis Carroll was referring to soup as the first in a string of courses; whereas nowadays, a large serving of soup often comprises the whole meal. Still, the same spirit is there: soup feels comforting, restoring, nourishing. It's the perfect thing after a hard day. And stews have much the same effect. The soups and stews in this chapter are quick, with long-simmered taste. They're doubly practical for weeknight meals because most of them just get better as they sit. We always make enough for two nights and enjoy them even more the second time.

Wellfleet Clam Stew

Slightly piquant clam broth brimming with potatoes and fresh clams, this delicious hearty soup is a treat in both warm and cold weather. A sprinkling of parsley, lemon juice, and Parmesan cheese is an unusual, and we think exceptional, finishing touch. Serve with crusty bread.

WINE RECOMMENDATION

Shellfish, garlic, pepper, lemon—it's a lot to ask a wine to deal with! Look for a Muscadet de Sèvre-et-Maine from France. It has lively enough acidity to stand up to the dish, and it also happens to be a classic shellfish wine.

SERVES 4

- 2 tablespoons olive oil
- 1 onion, chopped
- 2 scallions including green tops, chopped
- 8 large cloves garlic, peeled
- 2 pounds baking potatoes (about 4), peeled and cut into $\frac{1}{2}$-inch pieces
- 1 quart bottled clam juice
- 1 large tomato, chopped
- $\frac{1}{2}$ cup dry vermouth or dry white wine
- $\frac{1}{2}$ teaspoon dried red-pepper flakes
- $\frac{1}{4}$ teaspoon salt, more if needed
- 3 dozen littleneck clams, scrubbed
- $\frac{1}{4}$ teaspoon fresh-ground black pepper
- $\frac{1}{2}$ teaspoon grated lemon zest
- 4 teaspoons lemon juice
- $\frac{1}{4}$ cup grated Parmesan cheese
- $\frac{1}{3}$ cup chopped flat-leaf parsley

1. In a large pot, heat the oil over moderate heat. Add the onion and scallions and cook, stirring occasionally, until beginning to brown, about 5 minutes. Add the garlic and cook, stirring, for 1 minute.

2. Stir in the potatoes, clam juice, tomato, vermouth, red-pepper flakes, and salt. Top with the clams. Bring to a boil over moderately high heat and cook, covered, until the clams begin to open, about 5 minutes. Remove the open clams and continue to cook, uncovering the pot as necessary to remove the clams as soon as their shells open, about 5 minutes longer. Discard any clams that do not open. Cover the clams loosely with aluminum foil to keep warm. Continue cooking, partially covered, until the potatoes are tender, about 5 minutes longer. Taste the broth for salt, and if necessary, add more.

3. To serve, put the clams back into the pot and add the black pepper and lemon zest. Cover and simmer until the clams are warm through, about 1 minute. Do not overcook or the clams will be tough. Ladle into bowls and sprinkle with the lemon juice, Parmesan, and parsley.

—Jim Flint

SHRIMP GAZPACHO

Whole shrimp, cubes of avocado, and garlic croûtes embellish this quintessential cold summer soup, turning it into a refreshing supper.

WINE RECOMMENDATION
Gazpacho is nice with any number of refreshing white wines, but try echoing the soup's origins with a Spanish white such as Rueda or the more expensive alvariño.

SERVES 4

1½ pounds medium shrimp
1¼ pounds cucumbers, peeled and seeded
1½ pounds tomatoes (about 3), peeled
  1 large green bell pepper, quartered
  1 small onion, quartered
  2 cloves garlic, 1 chopped, 1 cut in half
  3 cups canned tomato juice
¼ cup red-wine vinegar
  4 tablespoons olive oil
½ teaspoon Tabasco sauce
     Salt
¼ teaspoon fresh-ground black pepper
  4 thick slices country bread
  1 avocado, preferably Hass, diced

1. In a pot of boiling, salted water, cook the shrimp until just done, about 2 minutes. Drain, let cool, and shell.

2. Set aside about a quarter of the cucumbers and a third of the tomatoes. Put the rest in a food processor. Add the bell pepper, onion, and the chopped garlic, and puree with the tomato juice, vinegar, 3 tablespoons of the oil, the Tabasco sauce, 1½ teaspoons salt, and the black pepper.

3. Cut the reserved vegetables into small dice. Add the vegetables and shrimp to the soup.

4. Heat the broiler. Put the bread on a baking sheet and broil, turning once, until crisp and brown on the outside but still slightly soft in the center, about 3 minutes. Rub one side of the bread with the cut sides of the garlic halves and brush with the remaining 1 tablespoon oil. Sprinkle the bread with a pinch of salt. Cut each bread slice in half.

5. Ladle the soup into bowls. Top with the avocado and serve with the garlic croûtes.

SHRIMP, TOFU, AND SPINACH SOUP

Cubes of tofu and leaves of spinach simmer with shiitake mushrooms and whole shrimp in a gingery, Asian-flavored broth. Serve this soup with a pair of chopsticks as well as a spoon, or cut the tofu and shrimp into smaller pieces.

 WINE RECOMMENDATION
A white wine with quite high acidity will work best with the spinach and pungent Asian ingredients. The classic French shellfish wine, Muscadet de Sèvre-et-Maine, fills the bill and, of course, goes nicely with the shrimp as well.

SERVES 4

1   2-ounce package cellophane noodles (bean threads)

1   tablespoon cooking oil

1   tablespoon grated fresh ginger

3   cloves garlic, minced

½   teaspoon curry powder

1½ quarts Chicken Stock, page 303, or canned low-sodium chicken broth

3   tablespoons Asian fish sauce (nam pla or nuoc mam)*

2   teaspoons soy sauce

1½ teaspoons sugar

¾   teaspoon Asian sesame oil

⅛   teaspoon salt

⅛   teaspoon dried red-pepper flakes

¼   pound shiitake mushrooms, stems removed and caps cut into thin slices

½   pound spinach, stems removed, leaves washed and cut into 1½-inch pieces (about 5 cups)

4   scallions including green tops, cut into 1-inch pieces

½   pound firm tofu, cut into 1-inch cubes

½   pound medium shrimp, shelled, or any firm white fish cut into 1-inch chunks

1½ tablespoons lemon juice

*Available at Asian markets and some supermarkets

1. Put the noodles in a medium bowl, cover with hot water, and leave to soften, about 15 minutes. Drain and cut into 4-inch pieces.

2. In a large pot, heat the oil over moderate heat. Add the ginger and garlic and cook, stirring, for 2 minutes. Add the curry and cook 30 seconds longer. Add the stock, fish sauce, soy sauce, sugar, sesame oil, salt, and red-pepper flakes. Bring to a boil. Add the sliced mushrooms, reduce the heat, and simmer for 4 minutes.

3. Add the spinach, scallions, and tofu, and simmer just until the spinach wilts, about 1 minute. Add the shrimp and noodles and cook until just done, about 2 minutes. Stir in the lemon juice.

CHICKEN SOUP WITH BUTTERNUT SQUASH AND SHIITAKES

Butternut squash is in season during the autumn, just the time of year when you want to start serving warming soup for dinner. The small amount of cream, just a tablespoon per person, enriches the flavor deliciously. However, you can omit it if you prefer. Shiitakes have a distinctive flavor, but if they're not your favorite, try a different wild mushroom, or use plain white ones.

WINE RECOMMENDATION

The mild, supple soup matches nicely with a favorite full-bodied chardonnay from either California or Washington State.

SERVES 4

- 2 tablespoons cooking oil
- ½ pound shiitake mushrooms, stems removed and caps sliced
- 1¾ teaspoons salt
- 2 onions, chopped
- 2 ribs celery, chopped
- 3 cloves garlic, minced
- 4 skinless chicken thighs
- 5 cups Chicken Stock, page 303, or canned low-sodium chicken broth
- 1 tablespoon chopped fresh tarragon, or 1 teaspoon dried
- 1 ¾-pound piece butternut squash, peeled, seeded, and cut into approximately ½-inch pieces
- 2 tablespoons chopped flat-leaf parsley
- ¼ cup heavy cream (optional)

1. In a large pot, heat 1 tablespoon of the oil over moderately high heat. Add the sliced mushrooms and ¼ teaspoon of the salt and cook, stirring occasionally, until brown, about 5 minutes. Remove.

2. Reduce the heat to moderately low. Add the remaining 1 tablespoon oil to the pot. Add the onions and celery. Cook, covered, for 4 minutes. Add the garlic and cook 1 minute longer.

3. Add the chicken, stock, dried tarragon, if using, and the remaining 1½ teaspoons salt. Bring to a boil. Reduce the heat and simmer for 10 minutes. Add the squash and simmer until the chicken and squash are done, 15 to 20 minutes longer. Remove the chicken from the soup. Cut the meat off the bone and then into 1-inch pieces. Skim any fat from the surface of the soup. Return the chicken to the soup. Add the mushrooms, parsley, fresh tarragon, if using, and cream, and heat through.

CHICKEN AND ORECCHIETTE SOUP WITH FENNEL AND SPINACH

Now that most supermarkets have salad bars, you can buy spinach already washed and stemmed. You'll only need ¾ pound. We like the combination of fennel and spinach, but you can substitute virtually any vegetable that you like.

WINE RECOMMENDATION
Fennel is best with a white wine that has plenty of acidity and personality, such as a sauvignon blanc. Try one from the Alto Adige region of northern Italy.

SERVES 4

¾ cup orecchiette

2 tablespoons olive oil

1 small fennel bulb (about ¾ pound), cut into thin slices

2 onions, chopped

1 rib celery, chopped

2 cloves garlic, minced

1 quart Chicken Stock, page 303, or canned low-sodium chicken broth

1 cup canned tomatoes with their juice, chopped

1½ teaspoons chopped fresh rosemary, or ½ teaspoon dried, crumbled

¼ teaspoon dried red-pepper flakes

1¼ teaspoons salt

2 boneless, skinless chicken breasts (about ⅔ pound in all)

⅛ teaspoon fresh-ground black pepper

½ pound spinach, stems removed, leaves washed and cut into 1½-inch pieces (about 5 cups)

¼ cup grated Parmesan cheese, plus more for serving

1. In a pot of boiling, salted water, cook the orecchiette until just done, about 15 minutes. Drain.

2. Meanwhile, in a large pot, heat 1 tablespoon of the oil over moderate heat. Add the fennel, onions, celery, and garlic. Cook, stirring occasionally, until golden brown, about 8 minutes. Add the stock, tomatoes, rosemary, red-pepper flakes, and 1 teaspoon of the salt. Bring to a boil. Reduce the heat and simmer until the vegetables are tender, about 10 minutes.

3. In a small frying pan, heat the remaining 1 tablespoon oil over moderate heat. Season the chicken breasts with the remaining ¼ teaspoon salt and the black pepper. Sauté the chicken for 5 minutes. Turn and sauté until browned and just done, about 4 minutes longer. Cut the chicken into ¾-inch pieces.

4. Add the spinach to the soup and cook for 4 minutes. Stir in the orecchiette, chicken, and Parmesan cheese. Serve with additional Parmesan.

WHITE-BEAN SOUP WITH TINY MEATBALLS

Keep a few cans of beans on your kitchen shelf; they can be transformed into an infinite variety of satisfying dishes. Here, tiny meatballs float in a hearty white-bean and tomato soup.

WINE RECOMMENDATION
Beans and ground beef find a great match in a simple, fruity red wine. Try a grenache or a moderately priced pinot noir from California.

SERVES 4

- 1 tablespoon olive oil
- 1 onion, chopped
- 1 carrot, chopped
- 3 cloves garlic, minced
- ¾ teaspoon dried rosemary, crumbled
- 3 cups Chicken Stock, page 303, or canned low-sodium chicken broth
- 1 cup canned crushed tomatoes
- ½ cup dry white wine
- 1 bay leaf
- 2 teaspoons salt
- ½ pound ground beef
- 2 tablespoons chopped flat-leaf parsley
- 4 teaspoons dry bread crumbs
- 2 tablespoons grated Parmesan cheese, plus more for serving
- Fresh-ground black pepper
- 1 19-ounce can white beans, preferably cannellini, drained and rinsed (about 2 cups)

1. In a large pot, heat the oil over moderately low heat. Add the onion, carrot, garlic, and rosemary. Cover and cook, stirring occasionally, until the vegetables are soft, about 10 minutes. Add the stock, tomatoes, wine, bay leaf, and 1½ teaspoons of the salt. Bring to a boil. Reduce the heat and simmer for 25 minutes.

2. Meanwhile, make the meatballs: In a medium bowl, mix the ground beef, parsley, bread crumbs, Parmesan, the remaining ½ teaspoon salt, and ⅛ teaspoon pepper until thoroughly combined. Shape into twenty-five tiny meatballs.

3. Add the beans and meatballs to the soup. Cover and simmer until the meatballs are just done, 5 to 7 minutes longer. Remove the bay leaf. Stir in ¼ teaspoon pepper. Serve with additional Parmesan.

LENTIL SOUP WITH SIX VEGETABLES

If there can be such a thing as a light lentil soup, this is it—a delectable brothy version with chunky vegetables and leafy escarole.

WINE RECOMMENDATION
Hearty, wholesome, and just a bit peppery, this soup is a fine match with a full-bodied but easygoing white wine, such as a pinot blanc from Alsace in France.

SERVES 4

2	tablespoons olive oil
2	onions, cut into 1-inch pieces
2	carrots, cut into 1-inch pieces
2	ribs celery, cut into 1-inch pieces
6	cloves garlic, peeled
1	pound lentils (about 2⅓ cups)
2½	quarts water
1	teaspoon dried rosemary, crumbled
2¼	teaspoons salt
¼	teaspoon dried red-pepper flakes
¼	teaspoon fresh-ground black pepper
1	fresh red bell pepper, or 1 bottled roasted red pepper
1	head escarole, torn into 2-inch pieces (about 2 quarts)

1. In a large pot, heat the oil over moderately high heat. Add the onions, carrots, celery, and garlic. Cook, stirring occasionally, until lightly browned, about 5 minutes.

2. Add the lentils, water, rosemary, salt, red-pepper flakes, and black pepper. Bring to a boil, reduce the heat, and simmer until the lentils are tender, about 40 minutes.

3. Meanwhile, if using a fresh bell pepper, roast it over an open flame or broil, turning with tongs, until charred all over, about 10 minutes. When the pepper is cool enough to handle, pull off the skin. Remove the stem, seeds, and ribs. Cut the pepper into 1-inch pieces. If using a bottled roasted pepper, cut it into 1-inch pieces. Add the roasted pepper to the soup.

4. Stir the escarole into the soup and simmer until wilted, 3 to 4 minutes.

—KATHERINE ALFORD

CORNED-BEEF AND CABBAGE SOUP

Don't reserve corned beef solely for sandwiches. Here it's stirred into a caraway-flavored tomato broth. Serve the soup with thick slices of fresh rye bread for a satisfying meal.

WINE RECOMMENDATION
This cabbage-laden soup, with its forceful caraway taste, will go nicely with a light, fruity red wine, such as a Corbières or a Coteaux du Languedoc, both from the South of France.

SERVES 4

1 tablespoon cooking oil

1 onion, chopped

1 carrot, chopped

2 cloves garlic, minced

1½ tablespoons caraway seeds

1 potato (about ½ pound), peeled and cut into ½-inch chunks

5 cups Chicken Stock, page 303, or canned low-sodium chicken broth

2 tablespoons tomato paste

1 bay leaf

¾ teaspoon salt

½ pound green cabbage, shredded (about 2 cups)

½ pound sliced corned beef, cut into approximately ½-inch pieces

¼ teaspoon fresh-ground black pepper

2 tablespoons chopped flat-leaf parsley

1. In a large pot, heat the oil over moderately low heat. Add the onion, carrot, garlic, and caraway seeds. Cover and cook, stirring occasionally, until the vegetables begin to soften, about 5 minutes.

2. Add the potato, stock, tomato paste, bay leaf, and salt. Bring to a boil. Reduce the heat and simmer until the potato is tender, about 15 minutes. Add the cabbage and cook for 10 minutes. Stir in the corned beef and pepper and bring back to a simmer. Remove the bay leaf. Stir in the parsley.

VARIATION

For a borscht-like soup, add one 15-ounce can of small whole beets, drained and quartered, along with the corned beef.

Moules a la Mariniere

We know that this traditional dish is really neither a soup nor a stew, but we were so convinced that it belonged in this book that we made a place for it here. Not only are mussels delicious and inexpensive, they take only about 3 minutes to cook.

WINE RECOMMENDATION
A great choice to enliven this intensely flavored classic is a light, tart Muscadet de Sèvre-et-Maine from the mouth of the Loire Valley in France.

SERVES 4

- 4 pounds mussels, scrubbed and debearded
- 2 tablespoons butter
- 1 small onion, minced
- 1 clove garlic, minced
- ½ teaspoon dried thyme
- ½ cup dry white wine
- 3 tablespoons chopped flat-leaf parsley

1. Discard any mussels that have broken shells or that don't clamp shut when tapped. In a large pot, melt the butter over moderately low heat. Add the onion, garlic, and thyme and cook, stirring occasionally, for 3 minutes.

2. Add the wine and mussels. Cover and bring to a boil over high heat. Cook, shaking the pot occasionally, just until all of the mussels open, about 3 minutes. Discard any mussels that do not open. Stir in the parsley and serve in large bowls with crusty bread.

Variations

■**Moules à la Crème:** Cook the mussels as directed. Remove them from the pot with a slotted spoon. Add 1 cup heavy cream to the pot and bring to a boil. Boil until the mixture just begins to thicken, about 3 minutes. Add the parsley and mussels.

■**Mussels with Coconut Milk, Scallions, and Cilantro:** In a large pot, heat 1 tablespoon oil over moderately high heat. Add 5 chopped scallions including green tops and ¼ teaspoon dried red-pepper flakes. Cook for 1 minute. Add ¼ cup rice- or white-wine vinegar, ¼ cup water, and the mussels. Cook as directed. Remove the mussels from the pot with a slotted spoon. Stir in ½ cup canned unsweetened coconut milk and simmer 3 minutes. Add ⅓ cup chopped cilantro or fresh parsley, 1 tablespoon lime juice, ¼ teaspoon salt, and the mussels.

SMOKY PORK CHILI

When you make chili with quick-cooking pork tenderloin instead of a tougher cut of meat, the entire stew is ready in under an hour. Grated cheese is our topping of choice, but add sour cream, chopped onion, cilantro leaves, or a combination, as you like.

WINE RECOMMENDATION
Match the down-home appeal of this slightly spicy chili with an easygoing, fruity red wine, such as a grenache or mourvedre from California or Washington State.

SERVES 4

- 3 strips bacon, cut crosswise into ¼-inch slices
- 1½ pounds pork tenderloin, cut into ¾-inch pieces
- 1 tablespoon cooking oil
- 2 onions, chopped
- 4 cloves garlic, minced
- 2 teaspoons paprika
- 2 teaspoons ground cumin
- 1 teaspoon ground coriander
- ¼ teaspoon cayenne
- 1¼ teaspoons salt
- 2 cups canned tomatoes with their juice, chopped
- 1½ cups Chicken Stock, page 303, or canned low-sodium chicken broth
- 1 tablespoon tomato paste
- 1 19-ounce can kidney beans, drained and rinsed (about 2 cups)
- 3 ounces cheddar cheese, grated (about ¾ cup)

1. In a large pot, cook the bacon until crisp. Remove with a slotted spoon and drain on paper towels. Add about half of the pork to the pot and cook over moderate heat until the meat begins to brown, about 3 minutes. Remove. Repeat with the remaining pork. Remove.

2. Add the oil to the pot. Reduce the heat to low. Stir in the onions and garlic. Cover and cook, stirring occasionally, until the onions are soft, about 10 minutes. Stir in the paprika, cumin, coriander, cayenne, and salt. Cook, stirring, for 1 minute.

3. Add the tomatoes with their juice, the stock, and the tomato paste. Bring to a boil. Reduce the heat and simmer, partially covered, for 15 minutes. Add the beans and cook 5 minutes longer. Stir in the pork tenderloin with any accumulated juices and the bacon and cook until the meat is just done, about 5 minutes longer. Serve topped with the cheese.

TWO-BEAN CHILI WITH SMOKED HAM

Although handy canned beans are often too soft because they overcook in the canning process, they're just fine in the right setting, such as this spicy chili. Serve it as suggested with sliced avocado, sour cream, and lime, or topped with chopped onion and grated cheese.

WINE RECOMMENDATION

Bean dishes such as this do very well with light, fruity, slightly chilled red wines. Try a bottle of Coteaux du Languedoc from southern France, or a Beaujolais.

SERVES 4

1 tablespoon cooking oil

1 onion, chopped

1 red or green bell pepper, chopped

3 cloves garlic, minced

2 teaspoons ground cumin

1 teaspoon ground coriander

1 ½-pound piece smoked ham, such as Black Forest, cut into ½-inch pieces

1½ cups Chicken Stock, page 303, or canned low-sodium chicken broth

1½ cups canned tomatoes with their juice, chopped

2 tablespoons tomato paste

1 teaspoon dried oregano

½ teaspoon dried thyme

¼ teaspoon cayenne

½ teaspoon salt

1 19-ounce can black beans, drained and rinsed (about 2 cups)

1 19-ounce can pinto beans, drained and rinsed (about 2 cups)

1 avocado, preferably Hass, sliced (optional)

½ cup sour cream (optional)

1 lime, cut into wedges (optional)

1. In a large saucepan, heat the oil over moderately low heat. Add the onion, bell pepper, and garlic. Cover and cook, stirring occasionally, until the vegetables are soft, about 10 minutes. Add the cumin and coriander and cook, stirring, for 1 minute.

2. Stir in the ham, stock, tomatoes with their juice, the tomato paste, oregano, thyme, cayenne, and salt. Bring to a boil. Reduce the heat, cover, and simmer for 15 minutes. Add the black and pinto beans, bring to a simmer, and cook 5 minutes longer. Serve topped with the sliced avocado and sour cream and put the lime wedges alongside.

INDIAN CHILI

Chili made with Indian spices and ground lamb may seem a bit exotic, but it's just as homey and comforting as old-fashioned beef chili—and it cooks for less than half an hour.

WINE RECOMMENDATION
A versatile wine choice for Indian dishes is gewürztraminer. A bottle from the Alsace region in France is preferable for its acidity, but there are also versions from California and Washington State that are worth exploring.

SERVES 4

- 1 tablespoon cooking oil
- 2 onions, chopped
- 3 cloves garlic, minced
- 1 pound ground lamb
- 1 28-ounce can (about 3½ cups) crushed tomatoes
- 1 tablespoon curry powder
- 1½ teaspoons salt
- Pinch cayenne, more to taste
- 2 15-ounce cans black beans, drained and rinsed (about 3⅓ cups in all)
- ¼ cup plain yogurt, for serving (optional)

1. In a large saucepan, heat the oil over moderately low heat. Add the onions and garlic and cook, stirring occasionally, until the onions are translucent, about 5 minutes.

2. Add the lamb and cook, breaking up the meat with a fork, until it is no longer pink, about 3 minutes. Stir in the tomatoes, curry powder, salt, and cayenne, and bring to a boil. Reduce the heat and simmer, stirring occasionally, for about 15 minutes.

3. Add the beans and cook, stirring occasionally, for 5 minutes longer. Ladle the chili into bowls and top each serving with a dollop of yogurt.

—JUDITH SUTTON

VARIATIONS

■ **Beef:** If you're not a fan of lamb, use ground beef instead.

■ **Kidney Bean:** You can replace the black beans with red kidney beans, if you prefer.

PORK-TENDERLOIN AND SWEET-POTATO STEW

Onion wedges, lots of garlic, and a little white wine give character to this new-style stew. Serve it with bread—corn bread would be especially good.

WINE RECOMMENDATION

A light, fruity red wine with plenty of acidity is a great match for the slightly sweet flavor of this stew. Try a gamay- or cabernet-franc-based wine from France's Loire Valley.

SERVES 4

- 1 tablespoon cooking oil
- 4 small onions, cut lengthwise into quarters
- 5 cloves garlic, minced
- 1 tablespoon flour
- ½ cup dry white wine
- 1 pound sweet potatoes, peeled and cut into ½-inch chunks
- 1 28-ounce can (about 3½ cups) tomatoes, drained and chopped
- 2 cups Chicken Stock, page 303, or canned low-sodium chicken broth
- 1 teaspoon dried thyme
- 1 bay leaf
- ¾ teaspoon salt
- 1½ pounds pork tenderloin, cut into 1½-inch cubes
- ¼ teaspoon fresh-ground black pepper
- 3 tablespoons chopped flat-leaf parsley

1. In a large pot, heat the oil over moderate heat. Add the onions. Cover and cook, stirring occasionally, until softened, about 7 minutes. Stir in the garlic and cook for 1 minute. Add the flour and cook, stirring, for 1 minute longer.

2. Add the wine and bring to a boil, scraping the bottom of the pan to dislodge any brown bits. Add the sweet potatoes, tomatoes, stock, thyme, bay leaf, and salt. Cover and simmer for 20 minutes.

3. Add the pork. Cover and simmer until the meat is just done, about 10 minutes. Remove the bay leaf. Stir in the pepper and parsley.

—PAUL GRIMES

QUICK STEAK STEW WITH MUSHROOMS

Mildly spiced with paprika and chili powder and packed with sirloin, shiitake mushrooms, carrots, and green beans, this stew's guaranteed to satisfy.

WINE RECOMMENDATION
Match this thick stew with a dense red wine, such as a Gigondas or an older Cornas from the Rhône Valley in France.

SERVES 4

3½	tablespoons cooking oil
1½	pounds sirloin steak, cut into approximately 1½-inch cubes
1	tablespoon butter
1	onion, chopped
½	pound shiitake mushrooms, stems removed and caps cut in half
½	pound white mushrooms, cut in half
2	cloves garlic, minced
1	tablespoon flour
1½	tablespoons paprika
1½	teaspoons chili powder
2½	cups Chicken Stock, page 303, or canned low-sodium chicken broth
3	carrots, cut into ½-inch pieces
1	red bell pepper, cut into ½-inch pieces
1	teaspoon Dijon mustard
1½	teaspoons salt
¼	teaspoon dried thyme
1	bay leaf
½	pound green beans, cut into 1½-inch lengths
2	tablespoons chopped flat-leaf parsley
¼	teaspoon fresh-ground black pepper

1. In a large, heavy pot, heat 1½ tablespoons of the oil over moderately high heat. Add half the steak. Brown on all sides, about 6 minutes, and remove. The meat should be medium rare. Repeat with the remaining meat. Remove.

2. Add the remaining 2 tablespoons oil and the butter to the pot and reduce the heat to moderately low. Add the onion and cook, stirring occasionally, until translucent, about 5 minutes. Increase the heat to moderately high. Add the halved shiitake and white mushrooms. Cook, stirring, until well browned, about 5 minutes. Stir in the garlic. Reduce the heat, add the flour, and cook, stirring, for 1 minute. Add the paprika and chili powder and cook, stirring, for 30 seconds. Add the stock, carrots, bell pepper, mustard, salt, thyme, and bay leaf.

3. Bring to a simmer and cook, partially covered, for 10 minutes. Add the green beans and simmer just until tender, about 8 minutes.

4. Add the meat with any accumulated juices, the parsley, and the black pepper, and bring to a simmer. Cook until the steak is just warmed through, about 5 minutes for medium rare or 1 to 2 minutes longer for meat that is cooked through. Remove the bay leaf.

LENTIL STEW WITH SPINACH AND SAUSAGE

Here's real sustenance for a winter's night. Hearty, whole-grain bread would be right with this stew.

WINE RECOMMENDATION
The earthy taste of lentils (and other beans) is perfect with a rich but simple white wine. Try a pinot blanc or the fuller-flavored pinot gris from the region of Alsace in France.

SERVES 4

1½ pounds kielbasa or Italian sausage

1 tablespoon cooking oil

1 onion, chopped

1 carrot, chopped

2 cloves garlic, minced

¾ teaspoon dried thyme

1½ cups lentils

3 cups Chicken Stock, page 303, or canned low-sodium chicken broth

1¼ teaspoons salt

½ pound spinach, stems removed, leaves washed and cut into approximately ½-inch strips (about 5 cups)

1. If using kielbasa, cut it into serving portions. Prick the sausage in a few places with a fork. In a large pot, heat the oil over moderate heat. Add the sausage and cook, turning, until browned, about 8 minutes. Remove the sausage. Pour off all but 1 tablespoon fat from the pan.

2. Reduce the heat to moderately low. Put the onion, carrot, garlic, and thyme in the pan and cook, stirring occasionally, until the onion is translucent, about 5 minutes.

3. Add the lentils, stock, and salt, and bring to a boil. Reduce the heat and simmer, partially covered, until the lentils are almost done, about 30 minutes.

4. Add the sausage. Cover and simmer until the lentils are tender, about 10 minutes. Stir in the spinach and continue simmering, covered, until the spinach is done, about 4 minutes longer.

CHICKEN-BREAST VARIATION

Omit the sausage. Heat 1 tablespoon cooking oil in the pot. Season 4 boneless, skinless chicken breasts with ¼ teaspoon salt and ⅛ teaspoon pepper. Brown well on both sides, about 6 minutes in all. Remove. Add another tablespoon oil to the pan and cook the vegetables and lentils as directed. Slice the chicken and add with the spinach.

PORK AND SAUSAGE WITH BLACK BEANS

Spicy sausage, chunks of pork, and black beans are a winning combination in this thick and hearty Latin American stew. Because it's made with tenderloin and canned beans, there's no need for long simmering. Plain boiled rice is an ideal accompaniment.

WINE RECOMMENDATION

The Latin flavor here is best matched with a light, fruity red wine, such as a grenache from California, or with a Mexican beer.

SERVES 4

 2   tablespoons cooking oil

 1   pound hot Italian sausage or chorizo

1½   pounds pork tenderloin, cut into 1½-inch cubes

 1   onion, chopped

 3   cloves garlic, minced

 1   cup canned crushed tomatoes

 1   7-ounce jar pimientos, drained and chopped

 2   tablespoons chopped cilantro (optional)

 1   bay leaf

1½   cups Chicken Stock, page 303, or canned low-sodium chicken broth

 ½   teaspoon salt

 2   15-ounce cans black beans, drained and rinsed (about 3⅓ cups in all)

 ⅛   teaspoon fresh-ground black pepper

1. In a large pot, heat ½ tablespoon of the oil over moderate heat. Add the sausage and cook, turning, until browned, about 8 minutes. Remove and cut into 1-inch pieces.

2. Add 1 tablespoon of the oil to the pot and raise the heat to moderately high. Add about half of the pork to the pot and cook until the meat begins to brown, about 3 minutes. Remove. Repeat with the remaining pork. Remove.

3. Add the remaining ½ tablespoon oil to the pot and reduce the heat to moderately low. Add the onion and cook, stirring occasionally, until translucent, about 5 minutes. Add the garlic and cook, stirring, for 30 seconds. Add the tomatoes, pimientos, cilantro, and bay leaf. Cook, stirring frequently, for 5 minutes.

4. Add the sausage, the pork tenderloin with any accumulated juices, the stock, and the salt. Bring to a boil, reduce the heat, and simmer, partially covered, for 15 minutes. Remove the bay leaf.

5. Meanwhile, puree 1 cup of the beans and a little of the liquid from the simmering stew in a food processor or blender. Stir the pureed and whole beans and the pepper into the stew and continue cooking for 5 minutes.

SANDWICHES, *etc.*

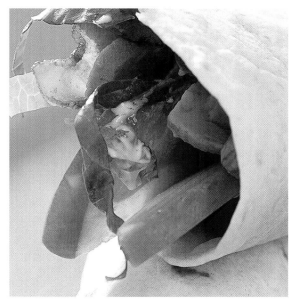

BLT Burritos, page 55

IF YOU HAVE A BIG, HEARTY SANDWICH at lunch, chances are you won't want one again at night. But we find that the traditional sandwich lunch is giving way to lighter fare. We still love substantial sandwiches as much as ever, and therefore serve them for dinner ourselves at least once a week. The ones in this chapter are easy, yet original and satisfying. We've interpreted the sandwich category rather broadly to include quesadillas, fajitas, and burritos.

Grilled-Vegetable Sandwiches with Fresh Mozzarella and Pesto Mayonnaise

We call for a large round loaf of bread for these sandwiches. If only long loaves of standard diameter are available, use the same filling to make six sandwiches and serve three halves per person.

WINE RECOMMENDATION
Full-flavored pesto makes a forceful, acidic white wine, such as a sauvignon blanc from Italy, a good choice.

SERVES 4

- 1 eggplant (about 1¼ pounds), cut lengthwise into ¼-inch slices
- 3 zucchini, cut lengthwise into ¼-inch slices
- 1 tablespoon olive oil
- ½ teaspoon salt
- ⅛ teaspoon fresh-ground black pepper
- ¾ cup mayonnaise
- 3 tablespoons store-bought pesto
- 8 thick slices from a large round loaf of country bread
- ½ pound salted fresh mozzarella, sliced
- 1 large tomato, sliced

1. Light the grill or heat the broiler. In a large shallow bowl, toss the eggplant and zucchini with the oil, salt, and pepper. If using the broiler, arrange the vegetables in a single layer on two baking sheets; cook in batches. Grill or broil, turning once, until the vegetables are lightly browned and tender, 10 to 12 minutes.

2. In a small bowl, combine the mayonnaise and pesto. Spread the mayonnaise on the bread. Sandwich the grilled vegetables, mozzarella, and tomato between the slices of bread.

—Judith Sutton

Variations

- Substitute Gouda or provolone for the mozzarella.

- Use slivered sun-dried tomatoes along with or instead of the fresh tomato.

SOFT-SHELL-CRAB SANDWICHES

Soft-shell-crab lovers will adore this sandwich. The crabs are sautéed until crisp and golden and then sandwiched in a toasted roll with bacon, arugula or watercress, peppery mayonnaise, and a squeeze of lemon. What a great way to celebrate the soft-shell season, which lasts from spring through late summer.

WINE RECOMMENDATION
The rich, luscious taste and texture of these sandwiches is delightful with a white Mâcon or other white made from chardonnay grapes from Burgundy's Côte Chalonnaise.

SERVES 4

- 8 strips bacon
- 6 tablespoons mayonnaise
- ½ teaspoon Tabasco sauce
  Salt
- 4 large, crusty rolls, cut in half
- 2 tablespoons olive oil
- 1 tablespoon butter
- 4 large soft-shell crabs, cleaned
- ⅛ teaspoon fresh-ground black pepper
- 1½ tablespoons flour
- 1 tablespoon lemon juice
- 2 bunches arugula (about 4 ounces in all), stems removed, or 1 bunch watercress (about 5 ounces), tough stems removed

1. In a large frying pan, fry the strips of bacon until crisp. Drain on paper towels and break each strip in half. Pour off the fat from the pan.

2. In a small bowl, combine the mayonnaise, Tabasco sauce, and a pinch of salt.

3. Put the rolls on a baking sheet, cut-side up, and toast under the broiler. Spread both sides of the rolls with the mayonnaise.

4. Heat the oil and butter in the frying pan over moderately high heat. Season the crabs with ½ teaspoon salt and the pepper. Dust the crabs with the flour and shake off the excess. Put the crabs in the pan, upside down. Cook for 3 minutes. Turn, reduce the heat to moderate, and cook until golden brown, about 3 minutes longer. Sprinkle with the lemon juice. Remove from the heat.

5. Sandwich the crabs, bacon, and arugula in the rolls.

CRISP-CHICKEN-BREAST SANDWICHES WITH SPINACH AND GINGER CREAM

A gingery sour-cream spread works as a great foil for the crisp, golden-brown chicken and fresh spinach.

WINE RECOMMENDATION
The ginger flavor really comes through in this sandwich and should be matched with a full-bodied but mild-mannered white, such as a pinot blanc from the region of Alsace in France.

SERVES 4

¼ cup sour cream

¼ cup mayonnaise

1 scallion including green top, minced

1¾ teaspoons grated fresh ginger

1⅛ teaspoons salt

1 baguette, cut into four 6-inch lengths, each split horizontally

¾ cup dry bread crumbs

¼ teaspoon fresh-ground black pepper

4 boneless, skinless chicken breasts (about 1⅓ pounds in all)

2 eggs, beaten to mix
  Cooking oil, for frying

3 ounces spinach (about 1¾ cups), stems removed and leaves washed and dried

1. In a small bowl, combine the sour cream, mayonnaise, scallion, ginger, and ⅛ teaspoon of the salt. Spread the ginger cream on each piece of baguette.

2. Combine the bread crumbs, the remaining 1 teaspoon salt, and the pepper.

3. Dip each chicken breast into the eggs and then into the bread-crumb mixture. Shake off any excess bread crumbs.

4. In a large frying pan, heat about ¼ inch of oil over moderate to moderately low heat. Add the chicken breasts and cook, turning once, until golden and just done, about 12 minutes. Drain on paper towels. Sandwich the chicken and spinach between pieces of baguette.

Focaccia with Chicken, Goat Cheese, and Roasted Red Peppers

Focaccia makes a great sandwich. It's increasingly available, but if you can't find it, use thick slices of country bread.

WINE RECOMMENDATION

An Italian wine makes sense given the obvious culinary influences in this sandwich, and a sauvignon blanc is always the perfect accompaniment to goat cheese. Try one from the Alto Adige region in northern Italy.

SERVES 4

- 4 boneless, skinless chicken breasts (about 1⅓ pounds in all)
- 4 tablespoons olive oil
  Salt and fresh-ground black pepper
- 2 teaspoons red-wine vinegar
- ¼ teaspoon Dijon mustard
- 1 10-inch round or 8-by-10-inch rectangle of focaccia, cut into quarters
- 6 ounces mild goat cheese, such as Montrachet, at room temperature
- 1 cup bottled roasted red peppers, drained
- 2 ounces greens, such as arugula, watercress, or leaf lettuce (about 3 cups)

1. Coat the chicken with 1 tablespoon of the oil. Season with ¼ teaspoon salt and ⅛ teaspoon pepper. Heat a grill pan over moderate heat. Cook the chicken for 5 minutes. Turn and cook until browned and just done, about 4 minutes longer. Let cool. Cut each breast in half horizontally to make two thin pieces. Alternatively, heat the tablespoon of oil in a large frying pan and season, cook, and cut the chicken as directed.

2. In a small bowl, whisk together the vinegar, mustard, ⅛ teaspoon salt, and a pinch of pepper. Add the remaining 3 tablespoons oil slowly, whisking.

3. Arrange the focaccia on a work surface. Cut each piece in half horizontally. Brush the cut surfaces of each piece with the vinaigrette.

4. Spread the bottoms of the focaccia with the goat cheese and top with the roasted red peppers. Sprinkle with a pinch each of salt and pepper. Add the chicken and greens and cover with the top piece of focaccia.

GOAT-CHEESE AND CHICKEN QUESADILLAS WITH GUACAMOLE

A puree of jalapeño, scallion, and cumin flavors the chicken in these quesadillas. Serve them with sour cream. You can make the salsa, opposite page, in place of the guacamole, or use both.

WINE RECOMMENDATION
A wine needs a lot of flavor to work with this dish, and a California sauvignon blanc (the classic pairing with goat cheese) is one of the few wines that have enough. Your favorite beer would also do fine.

SERVES 4

- ½ cup lightly packed cilantro or parsley with thick stems removed
- 1 jalapeño pepper, seeds and ribs removed, cut into quarters
- 1 scallion including green top, cut into quarters
- 1 tablespoon ground cumin
- ½ cup olive oil
- 2 tablespoons plus 1 teaspoon lime or lemon juice
- 1¾ teaspoons salt
- 4 boneless, skinless chicken breasts (about 1⅓ pounds in all)
- 2 avocados, preferably Hass
- 1 onion, chopped
- ¼ cup warm water
- 12 6-inch flour tortillas
- ½ pound mild goat cheese, such as Montrachet, at room temperature
- ½ cup sour cream, for serving

1. In a blender or food processor, puree the cilantro, jalapeño, and scallion with the cumin, ¼ cup of the oil, 1 tablespoon of the lime juice, and ¾ teaspoon of the salt until very smooth. Alternatively, chop the cilantro, jalapeño, and scallion very fine and mix them with the other ingredients.

2. In a medium frying pan, heat 1 tablespoon of the oil over moderate heat. Add the chicken breasts and cook until browned, about 5 minutes. Turn and cook until almost done, about 3 minutes longer. Cover the pan, remove from the heat, and let sit 5 minutes. Reserve any pan juices. Cut the chicken into ½-inch pieces.

3. Meanwhile, peel the avocados and mash them with a fork, leaving some small chunks. Stir in the remaining 4 teaspoons lime juice and 1 teaspoon salt.

4. Heat 1 tablespoon of the oil in the frying pan. Add the onion and cook, stirring occasionally, until translucent, about 5 minutes. Stir in the chicken with any pan juices, the cilantro puree, and the water.

5. Heat the broiler. Brush one side of the tortillas with the remaining 2 tablespoons

oil. Spread the goat cheese on the other side of each tortilla. Arrange six of the tortillas, cheese-side up, on two baking sheets. Top with the chicken mixture and a second tortilla, cheese-side down.

6. Broil the quesadillas in two batches, turning once, until golden, about 1½ minutes per side. With a spatula, gently press the tortillas together and then cut them in half. Serve with a dollop of sour cream and the guacamole.

HOMEMADE SALSA

When tomatoes are in season, this quick salsa is a refreshing alternative to guacamole.

MAKES 1½ CUPS

- 1   pound tomatoes, seeded and chopped
- 1   jalapeño pepper, ribs and seeds removed, minced
- 2   tablespoons finely chopped red onion
- 2   tablespoons cooking oil
- 2   teaspoons lemon or lime juice
- ½   teaspoon salt

Stir together all of the ingredients.

AEGEAN PITA PIZZA

Classic ingredients of the eastern Mediterranean—dill, mint, cucumbers, tomatoes, and feta cheese—are layered with ground beef on a toasted pita for a quick and original dish, something between a pizza and a sandwich.

WINE RECOMMENDATION
Although a beef "pizza" suggests red wine, the Mediterranean flavors here work better with white. The perfect compromise: a chilled rosé from France's Provence region.

SERVES 4

- 1/3 cup pine nuts
- 2 tablespoons olive oil
- 4 cloves garlic, minced
- 6 scallions including green tops, sliced
- 1 1/2 pounds ground beef
- 3/4 teaspoon dried oregano
- 1 1/2 tablespoons chopped fresh mint, or 1 1/2 teaspoons dried
- 2 tablespoons chopped fresh dill, or 1 1/2 teaspoons dried
- 1/4 teaspoon ground allspice
- 2 1/4 teaspoons salt
- 1/2 teaspoon fresh-ground black pepper
- 4 plum tomatoes, diced
- 1 cucumber, peeled, seeded, and cut into 1/4-inch dice
- 1 tablespoon lemon juice
- 1/2 cup black olives, such as Niçoise or Kalamata, pitted
- 6 pitas
- 5 ounces feta cheese, crumbled (about 1 1/4 cups)

1. In a medium frying pan, toast the pine nuts over moderately low heat, stirring frequently, until golden brown, about 4 minutes. Remove. Or toast the pine nuts in a 350° oven for 6 minutes.

2. In the frying pan, heat 1 tablespoon of the oil over moderate heat. Add the garlic and scallions and sauté for 1 minute. Add the beef, oregano, mint, 1 tablespoon of the fresh or 3/4 teaspoon of the dried dill, the allspice, and 1 1/4 teaspoons of the salt. Cook until the meat loses its pink color, 3 to 4 minutes. Add the pine nuts and 1/4 teaspoon of the pepper.

3. In a medium bowl, combine the tomatoes, cucumber, lemon juice, the remaining dill, the olives, and the remaining 1 teaspoon salt and 1/4 teaspoon pepper.

4. Heat the broiler. Put the pitas on a baking sheet. Toast under the broiler until one side is lightly browned, about 1 minute. Flip the pitas. Spoon the beef mixture onto the pitas, leaving a 1/2-inch border. Sprinkle with the feta cheese and broil until the cheese is melted and beginning to brown.

5. Cut the pitas in half. Top with the cucumber salad and a drizzle of the remaining oil. Serve one and a half pitas per person.

—KATHERINE ALFORD

ROAST-BEEF SANDWICHES WITH HORSERADISH SLAW

Horseradish is a delicious accompaniment to roast beef. Here we've added the pungent condiment to coleslaw for a new take on a classic overstuffed deli sandwich. You can serve the slaw on its own, but beware—it's quite spicy. You may want to cut back a bit on the horseradish.

WINE RECOMMENDATION
Go for a gutsy, gulpable red wine with plenty of fruit to serve alongside this hearty roast-beef sandwich. Try a Corbières or Faugères from the Languedoc-Rousillon region of France.

SERVES 4

1½	tablespoons white-wine vinegar
3	tablespoons bottled horseradish
2	tablespoons Dijon mustard
¼	teaspoon salt
⅛	teaspoon fresh-ground black pepper
4½	tablespoons olive oil
¾	pound green cabbage (about ¼ head), shredded (about 3 cups)
1	small onion, cut into paper-thin slices
	Mayonnaise, for spreading (optional)
8	slices rye bread
1	pound sliced roast beef

1. In a large bowl, whisk together the vinegar, horseradish, mustard, salt, and pepper. Add the oil slowly, whisking. Add the cabbage and onion and toss. If you have time, cover and set aside at room temperature for 30 minutes.

2. Spread mayonnaise on the bread. Sandwich the roast beef and slaw between the slices of bread.

—JUDITH SUTTON

VARIATIONS

■ The sandwiches are also good with baked ham, pastrami, or corned beef in place of the roast beef.

■ Add ½ teaspoon dried dill to the slaw.

STEAK-AND-CHEESE SANDWICHES WITH BALSAMIC MAYONNAISE

Sirloin steak, provolone cheese, and balsamic mayonnaise raise Philadelphia's famed steak-and-cheese sandwich to a new level. For an even shorter preparation time, use rare roast beef from your supermarket deli.

WINE RECOMMENDATION
This rich and robust sandwich will be best with a refreshingly fruity, simple red, such as a Beaujolais-Villages from France. Beer would also be delicious.

SERVES 4

- 1 tablespoon cooking oil
- 2 large onions (about 2 pounds), cut into thin slices
- 1¼ teaspoons salt
  Fresh-ground black pepper
- 1½ pounds sirloin steak, about 1 inch thick
- 6 tablespoons mayonnaise
- 1 teaspoon balsamic vinegar
- 6 ounces sliced provolone cheese
- 4 large, crusty rolls, cut in half

1. In a large frying pan, heat the oil over moderate heat. Add the onions, 1 teaspoon of the salt, and ¼ teaspoon pepper. Cover and cook, stirring occasionally, until the onions are soft, about 10 minutes. Uncover the pan and continue cooking, stirring occasionally, until the onions are golden, about 5 minutes longer. Leave them in the pan.

2. Heat the broiler. Sprinkle the steak with ⅛ teaspoon pepper and the remaining ¼ teaspoon salt. Broil the steak for about 5 minutes. Turn the meat and cook to your taste, about 5 minutes longer for medium rare. Transfer to a carving board and let rest in a warm spot for about 10 minutes. Cut on the diagonal into very thin slices.

3. In a small bowl, combine the mayonnaise and vinegar. Reheat the onions. Leave the onions in the pan and divide them into four portions. Top each portion with a quarter of the cheese. Cover and heat gently just until the cheese melts, about 2 minutes.

4. Spread the mayonnaise on one side of each roll. Divide the steak among the rolls. With a spatula, transfer the onions and cheese to the sandwiches. Cover with the tops of the rolls.

VARIATIONS

■ For a vegetarian version, meaty portobellos can replace the steak. Remove the stems from four 6-ounce mushrooms. Brush the caps with 2 tablespoons olive oil and season with ½ teaspoon salt and ¼ teaspoon fresh-ground black pepper. Broil until just done, about 5 minutes per side. Cut each mushroom into three slices and use in place of the steak.

■ Replace the provolone with your favorite cheese. Virtually any one will work. If you're a blue-cheese fan, stir 2 ounces crumbled blue cheese (about ½ cup) into the onions when rewarming and let the cheese melt just until it's creamy. Omit the balsamic vinegar. Or divide the onions as directed and top them with 6 ounces of sliced ripe Brie or Camembert. Cheddar and Gruyère would be good, too.

■ Use 1½ pounds of skirt steak, cut into two pieces, in place of the sirloin. Season the steak and broil for 3 minutes. Turn and cook to your taste, 3 to 4 minutes longer, depending on the thickness, for medium rare.

TEST-KITCHEN TIP

The best way to keep bread such as baguettes, country loaves, or rolls for several days is to freeze them. Be sure to wrap the loaves airtight. Take the bread out of the freezer several hours before you plan to serve it and defrost uncovered. Rolls will take less time. Do not use a microwave oven unless you like eating slices of sponge.

JERK-STEAK SANDWICHES WITH CHUTNEY

With spicy skirt steak, red onion, arugula or watercress, and sweet-hot mango chutney all stacked in a crusty roll, this Jamaican-style-beef sandwich delivers lots of flavor and assures satisfaction.

WINE RECOMMENDATION
The spices and strong flavors here make an ice-cold beer the best accompaniment. If it must be wine, choose a light, slightly chilled Beaujolais from France or a gamay from California.

SERVES 4

- 3 scallions including green tops, cut in quarters
- 2 cloves garlic, chopped
- ¼ cup cooking oil
- 1 tablespoon lime juice
- 4 teaspoons soy sauce
- 1 tablespoon plus ½ teaspoon Tabasco sauce
- 1 tablespoon dried thyme
- 1 tablespoon five-spice powder*
- 2 teaspoons ground allspice
- 1½ teaspoons salt
- 1 teaspoon fresh-ground black pepper
- 1½ pounds skirt steak, cut into two pieces
- ¼ cup mayonnaise
- 4 large, crusty rolls, cut in half
- ¾ cup bottled mango chutney
- 1 red onion, cut into thin slices

- 2 bunches arugula (about 4 ounces in all), stems removed, or 1 bunch watercress (about 5 ounces), tough stems removed

*Available at Asian markets and some supermarkets, or see page 197 for homemade

1. Light the grill or heat the broiler. In a blender or food processor, puree the scallions and garlic with the oil, lime juice, soy sauce, 1 tablespoon of the Tabasco, the thyme, five-spice powder, allspice, salt, and pepper.

2. Put the steak in a large, shallow glass dish or stainless-steel pan. Rub the meat with the spice mixture. Marinate 10 minutes. In a small bowl, combine the mayonnaise with the remaining ½ teaspoon Tabasco. Spread the mayonnaise on the bottom halves of the rolls and the chutney on the top halves.

3. Grill or broil the steaks for 3 minutes. Turn and cook to your taste, 3 to 4 minutes longer, depending on the thickness, for medium rare. Transfer to a carving board and leave to rest in a warm spot for 5 minutes. Cut diagonally across the grain into thin slices. Sandwich the meat, onion, and arugula in the rolls.

Fajitas with Chimichurri Sauce

Warm flour tortillas, sliced skirt steak, browned onions, and pungent Chimichurri Sauce make a superb combination. In Argentina, Chimichurri is often served with pork, lamb, and organ meats as well as steak.

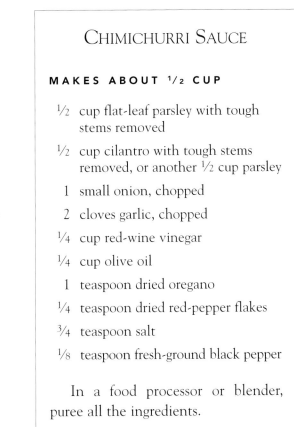 **WINE RECOMMENDATION** The Argentine influence in the sauce is reason enough to give that country's red wines a try with this dish. Look for a cabernet sauvignon, merlot, or malbec from Argentina's Mendoza region.

SERVES 4

2 tablespoons olive oil

3 onions, cut into thin slices

¾ teaspoon salt

8 6-inch flour tortillas

1 pound skirt steak, cut into 2 pieces

¼ teaspoon fresh-ground black pepper

   Chimichurri Sauce

1. In a large frying pan, heat 1 tablespoon of the olive oil over moderately high heat. Add the onions and ½ teaspoon of the salt and cook, stirring occasionally, until browned, about 8 minutes.

2. Heat the oven to 350°. Stack the tortillas and wrap them in aluminum foil. Warm in the oven for about 15 minutes.

3. Light the grill or heat the broiler. Coat the steaks with the remaining 1 tablespoon oil. Sprinkle with the remaining ¼ teaspoon salt and the pepper. Grill or broil the steaks for 3 minutes. Turn the meat and cook to your taste, 3 to 4 minutes longer, depending on the thickness, for medium rare. Let rest in a warm spot for 5 minutes. Cut the steaks diagonally across the grain into thin slices.

4. Roll the steak slices, onions, and Chimichurri in the tortillas.

Chimichurri Sauce

MAKES ABOUT ¹/₂ CUP

½ cup flat-leaf parsley with tough stems removed

½ cup cilantro with tough stems removed, or another ½ cup parsley

1 small onion, chopped

2 cloves garlic, chopped

¼ cup red-wine vinegar

¼ cup olive oil

1 teaspoon dried oregano

¼ teaspoon dried red-pepper flakes

¾ teaspoon salt

⅛ teaspoon fresh-ground black pepper

In a food processor or blender, puree all the ingredients.

Corned-Beef and Carrot-Ginger-Slaw Sandwiches

Grated carrots are spiced with fresh ginger and tossed with mayonnaise for a creamy, slightly sweet and hot slaw—the perfect match for salty corned beef.

WINE RECOMMENDATION
The corned beef and carrots here will go nicely with either a beer or a bottle of assertive sauvignon blanc from California.

SERVES 4

6	tablespoons mayonnaise
2	tablespoons cooking oil
1	tablespoon red-wine vinegar
1½	tablespoons grated fresh ginger
¼	teaspoon salt
¼	teaspoon fresh-ground black pepper
6	carrots, grated (about 3½ cups)
1	pound sliced corned beef
8	lettuce leaves
8	slices rye bread

1. In a medium bowl, whisk together the mayonnaise, oil, vinegar, ginger, salt, and pepper. Stir in the carrots.

2. Sandwich the corned beef, slaw, and lettuce between slices of the bread.

Variations

■ Use pastrami, sliced ham, or roast beef in place of the corned beef.

■ Serve the sandwiches hot. Heat the corned beef, wrapped in aluminum foil, in a 350° oven for about 20 minutes. Toast the bread.

Spiced-Lamb Sandwiches with Yogurt Sauce

A warm pita stuffed with crisp ovals of ground lamb makes a savory sandwich with a Middle Eastern accent. Yogurt sauce and refreshing cubes of cucumber reinforce the lineage.

WINE RECOMMENDATION
These spicy handfuls will be ideal with a light, very fruity, slightly chilled red wine, such as a Beaujolais-Villages from France.

SERVES 4

1½ pounds ground lamb

6 tablespoons grated onion

6 tablespoons chopped flat-leaf parsley

1 clove garlic, minced

1½ tablespoons lemon juice

¾ teaspoon ground coriander

1 teaspoon paprika

¾ teaspoon cayenne

2¾ teaspoons salt

1½ cups plain yogurt

4 pitas

2 tablespoons cooking oil

1 cucumber, peeled, seeded, and cut into ½-inch dice

1. In a medium bowl, combine the ground lamb, onion, parsley, garlic, lemon juice, coriander, ½ teaspoon of the paprika, ¼ teaspoon of the cayenne, and 1½ teaspoons of the salt. Shape the meat into sixteen ovals.

2. In a small bowl, combine the yogurt, the remaining ½ teaspoon paprika and ½ teaspoon cayenne, and 1 teaspoon of the salt.

3. Brush the pitas with 1 tablespoon of the oil and sprinkle with the remaining ¼ teaspoon salt. Put the pitas on a baking sheet.

4. In a large frying pan, heat the remaining 1 tablespoon oil over moderately high heat. Add the meat and cook until brown on all sides, about 6 minutes. Lower the heat, cover the pan, and cook until done, about 4 minutes longer. If necessary, brown the meat in two batches, then return all of it to the pan, cover, and continue cooking until done.

5. Meanwhile, heat the broiler. Toast the pitas under the broiler until beginning to brown, about 1 minute per side.

6. Cut the pitas in half. Stuff each half with lamb, cucumber, and some of the yogurt sauce. Serve the additional sauce alongside.

Mushroom and Black Forest Ham Sandwiches with Lemon Parmesan Sauce

Rustic and yummy open-faced sandwiches made with thick slices of country bread combine old-fashioned satisfaction with contemporary flare.

WINE RECOMMENDATION
A lively, fruity red wine, such as a Corbières from southern France or a Chianti Classico from Italy, will cut through the slight smokiness of the Black Forest ham and the richness of the mayonnaise and cheese.

SERVES 4

1	fresh red bell pepper, or 1 bottled roasted red pepper
¾	pound mushrooms, cut into thin slices
2½	teaspoons lemon juice
½	teaspoon salt
¾	cup grated Parmesan cheese
¾	cup mayonnaise
¾	teaspoon grated lemon zest
¼	teaspoon fresh-ground black pepper
6	¾-inch-thick slices country or sourdough bread
¾	pound sliced Black Forest ham

1. If using a fresh bell pepper, roast it over an open flame or broil, turning with tongs until charred all over, about 10 minutes. When the pepper is cool enough to handle, pull off the skin. Remove the stem, seeds, and ribs. Cut the fresh or bottled pepper into thin strips.

2. In a medium bowl, toss the mushrooms with 1½ teaspoons of the lemon juice and ¼ teaspoon of the salt. In another bowl, whisk together the cheese, mayonnaise, lemon zest, the remaining 1 teaspoon lemon juice and ¼ teaspoon salt, and the black pepper.

3. Heat the broiler. Cut the bread slices in half so that you have twelve pieces. Put the bread on a baking sheet and toast under the broiler on one side. Flip the slices over and spread with a thin layer of the cheese sauce. Layer each piece of bread with ham, roasted pepper, and mushrooms. Spread the remaining sauce evenly on top of each sandwich.

4. Broil the sandwiches until golden brown. Serve three halves per person.

BLT BURRITOS

Crisp, salty bacon and smooth, mellow avocado are a terrific combination. Here the two are rolled into flour tortillas with sliced tomato, romaine lettuce, and a spicy mayonnaise.

WINE RECOMMENDATION
What could be better than a cold Mexican beer with this sandwich? If you prefer wine, try a fruity rosé made from one of the typical Rhône Valley grape varieties, such as mourvedre or grenache.

SERVES 4

1¼ pounds bacon

 ½ cup mayonnaise

 ¼ teaspoon Worcestershire sauce

 ¼ teaspoon Tabasco sauce

 ½ teaspoon lime juice

  8 6-inch flour tortillas

  3 cups shredded romaine lettuce (about 5 leaves)

1½ avocados, preferably Hass, sliced lengthwise

  2 tomatoes, cut in half and then sliced

 ¼ teaspoon salt

1. In a large frying pan, cook the bacon until crisp. Drain on paper towels. In a small bowl, combine the mayonnaise, Worcestershire sauce, Tabasco sauce, and lime juice.

2. Heat the oven to 350°. Stack the flour tortillas and wrap them in aluminum foil. Warm the tortillas in the oven for about 15 minutes.

3. Spread the tortillas with the mayonnaise. Put the lettuce, avocados, and tomatoes on one end and sprinkle with the salt. Top with the bacon and roll up.

—PETER KLEIN
EL TEDDY'S

VARIATION

At El Teddy's, chef Klein uses chipotle chiles in adobo sauce in the mayonnaise for these burritos. The chiles are sold in cans and are available at some supermarkets and most Spanish markets. Replace the Worcestershire sauce, Tabasco sauce, and lime juice with 1½ teaspoons chopped chipotles in adobo sauce.

TEST-KITCHEN TIP

Not everyone has a microwave, so we've written the recipe to heat the tortillas in a standard oven. If you do have a microwave, by all means use it; the tortillas will stay even more pliable and easy to roll. Follow the directions on the package, or wrap the tortillas in plastic and heat at high for about 1 minute. Turn and heat for about 30 seconds longer.

CHEESE-AND-SALAMI-SALAD SANDWICHES

You'll have your meal in hand with this crusty, garlic-rubbed baguette stuffed with meat, cheese, and a tangy salad.

WINE RECOMMENDATION
A simple, fairly innocuous white wine from Italy will pair up just fine with this sandwich. Look for a Soave Classico or a Verdicchio.

SERVES 4

- 6 ounces Gruyère cheese, cut into 1-by-¼-inch sticks
- 6 ounces sliced hard salami or *soppressata*, cut into 1-by-¼-inch sticks
- ¼ cup chopped red onion
- 3 tablespoons chopped flat-leaf parsley
- 2 tablespoons red-wine vinegar
- 1½ tablespoons olive oil
- ¼ teaspoon salt
- ¼ teaspoon fresh-ground black pepper
- 1 baguette, cut into four 6-inch lengths
- 2 cloves garlic, cut in half
- 1 bunch arugula (about 2 ounces), stems removed, or 4 large leaves lettuce

1. In a medium bowl, combine the cheese, salami, onion, parsley, vinegar, oil, salt, and pepper.

2. Cut each piece of baguette in half lengthwise. Toast the bread, cut-side up, under the broiler, and rub the cut side of each piece with garlic. Sandwich the salad and arugula between pieces of baguette.

VARIATIONS

- Add 1 teaspoon capers to the cheese salad.

- Use fresh mozzarella, plain or smoked, in place of the Gruyère cheese.

- Put a slice of tomato in each sandwich.

OPEN-FACED MORTADELLA SANDWICHES WITH BLACK OLIVES AND CAPERS

A tasty spread of minced olives, capers, onion, and garlic complements the rich mortadella and bubbling-hot mozzarella.

WINE RECOMMENDATION
A good wine for this Mediterranean-flavored dish, with its black olives, garlic, and capers, is a rosé or white from the Provence region of France.

SERVES 4

1 cup black olives, pitted and minced

½ cup capers, minced

2 tablespoons minced red onion

1 clove garlic, minced

3 tablespoons olive oil

1 tablespoon red-wine vinegar

¼ teaspoon fresh-ground black pepper

8 slices country bread

½ pound sliced mortadella

½ pound mozzarella cheese, grated

1 tablespoon chopped flat-leaf parsley

1. In a medium bowl, combine the olives, capers, onion, garlic, 1 tablespoon of the oil, the vinegar, and the pepper.

2. Heat the broiler. Put the bread on a baking sheet and broil, turning once, until crisp and brown on the outside but still slightly soft in the center, about 3 minutes

in all. Brush one side of the bread with the remaining 2 tablespoons oil.

3. Spread the olive mixture on the bread. Top with the mortadella, mozzarella, and parsley. Broil until the cheese melts, 1 to 2 minutes.

TIME-SAVER

Use ¼ cup bottled tapenade (black-olive paste) in place of the olives.

SALADS

Spinach and Red-Cabbage Salad
with Smoked Trout and Apples, page 61

THE MAIN-DISH SALAD PHENOMENON HAS GROWN beyond summer-supper status. Salad has become the casserole of the '90s: a simple meal-in-a-dish that accommodates fresh and leftover ingredients with equal aplomb. We're in a bigger hurry than we were in the '50s, the height of the American casserole, and salad ingredients require little or no cooking time; we like the idea of eating more vegetables now, and salads are the answer again. About half of the recipes here use deli or leftover meats, canned tuna, or cheese. The others call for quick-cooking meat, chicken, or fish. All you need add to the menu is bread—or breadsticks, which are great to keep on hand.

Spinach and Red-Cabbage Salad with Smoked Trout and Apples

A profusion of complementary ingredients makes a marvelous salad of many flavors and textures. To save time, replace the spinach with 6 ounces of the pre-washed mix of greens, labeled mesclun, now available in many supermarkets.

WINE RECOMMENDATION

Choose a white wine with an ample dose of acidity (to cut the smokiness of the trout and the richness of the nuts) and plenty of personality (to balance the leafy ingredients). Try a chenin blanc from the Loire Valley in France, such as a Vouvray.

SERVES 4

1¼ cups pecan pieces

4 fillets smoked trout, or 2 whole smoked trout

1 pound spinach, stems removed and leaves washed (about 9 cups)

½ pound red cabbage, shredded (about 2 cups)

3 heads Belgian endive, cut crosswise into 1-inch pieces

2 Golden Delicious apples, peeled, cored, and cut into 2-inch matchstick strips

1 red onion, chopped fine

2 tablespoons chopped flat-leaf parsley

Sherry Balsamic Vinaigrette

1. In a medium frying pan, toast the pecans over moderately low heat, stirring frequently, until golden brown, about 5 minutes. Or toast them in a 350° oven for about 8 minutes.

2. If using whole trout, remove the skin and lift each fillet off the bone. Break the fillets into 1-inch chunks.

3. In a large bowl, combine the trout with the pecans, spinach, cabbage, Belgian endive, apples, onion, and parsley. Add the vinaigrette and toss.

Sherry Balsamic Vinaigrette

MAKES ABOUT ¾ CUP

¼ cup balsamic vinegar

1 teaspoon Dijon mustard

1 tablespoon dry sherry

½ teaspoon salt

½ teaspoon fresh-ground black pepper

½ cup olive oil

In a small bowl, whisk together all the ingredients but the oil. Add the oil slowly, whisking.

SWORDFISH-AND-POTATO SALAD

Potato salad becomes a meal when you add moist chunks of meaty swordfish.
A creamy shallot dressing complements both elements.

WINE RECOMMENDATION This hearty fish salad works well with a light, refreshing white wine, such as a pinot grigio from Italy or a bottle of Entre-Deux-Mers (a blend of sauvignon blanc and semillon) from the Bordeaux region of France.

SERVES 4

1½ pounds boiling potatoes, cut into 1-inch pieces

1½ pounds swordfish steaks, about 1 inch thick

1 tablespoon olive oil

½ teaspoon salt

¼ teaspoon fresh-ground black pepper
   Shallot Dressing

2 tablespoons chopped flat-leaf parsley

1 head Boston lettuce, separated into leaves

1. Put the potatoes in a medium saucepan of salted water. Bring to a boil and simmer until tender, about 10 minutes. Drain the potatoes, return to the pan, and cover to keep warm.

2. Meanwhile, heat the broiler. Coat the fish with the oil and sprinkle with the salt and pepper. Broil the fish for 3 minutes. Turn and cook until golden brown and just done, 2 to 3 minutes longer. Cut into 1-inch chunks.

3. Reserve ¼ cup of the dressing. In a large bowl, toss the potatoes with the remaining dressing. Gently fold the swordfish and the parsley into the potatoes.

4. Line four plates with the lettuce leaves. Mound the salad in the center of each plate and drizzle with the reserved dressing.

—SUSAN SHAPIRO JASLOVE

SHALLOT DRESSING

MAKES ABOUT 1 CUP

⅓ cup white-wine vinegar

1 large shallot, minced

1 tablespoon grainy mustard

½ teaspoon salt

½ teaspoon fresh-ground black pepper

½ cup olive oil

¼ cup mayonnaise

In a medium bowl, whisk together the vinegar, shallot, mustard, salt, and pepper. Add the oil slowly, whisking. Whisk in the mayonnaise.

Sourdough Panzanella with Tuna, White Beans, and Rosemary

Crunchy bread cubes are the primary ingredient in this satisfying Italian salad. You can use any crusty white bread you like. We prefer sourdough; it's hardly traditional, but it is good.

WINE RECOMMENDATION

A light, dry, and refreshing white wine will work best with this salad. Try a Verdicchio from the Marches region of Italy or a Soave Classico from Italy's Veneto region.

SERVES 4

- 1 10-ounce loaf sourdough bread, cut into 1-inch cubes (about 5 cups)
- 1 19-ounce can white beans, preferably cannellini, drained and rinsed (about 2 cups)
- 2 6-ounce cans tuna packed in oil, drained and flaked
- 1 large tomato, cut into ¾-inch chunks
- 1 small red onion, chopped fine
- 3 tablespoons chopped flat-leaf parsley
   Rosemary Vinaigrette
- ½ large head romaine lettuce, cut crosswise into 1-inch strips (about 5 cups)

1. Heat the oven to 250°. Put the bread on a baking sheet and bake until crisp on the outside, about 15 minutes. Let cool.

2. In a large bowl, toss the bread, beans, tuna, tomato, onion, parsley, and vinaigrette. Let sit 5 minutes. Toss in the lettuce and serve.

Rosemary Vinaigrette

MAKES ABOUT 1 CUP

- ¼ cup red-wine vinegar
- 1 teaspoon Dijon mustard
- 1 teaspoon lemon juice
- 1 tablespoon chopped fresh rosemary, or 1 teaspoon dried, crumbled
- 1 clove garlic, minced
- ½ teaspoon salt
- ¼ teaspoon fresh-ground black pepper
- ¾ cup olive oil

In a small bowl, whisk together all the ingredients but the oil. Add the oil slowly, whisking.

Shrimp Variation

Use 1 pound of medium shrimp in their shells in place of the tuna. Cook in boiling, salted water until just done, about 2 minutes. Drain, let cool, and peel.

SALAD NICOISE WITH GRILLED TUNA

While you can use canned tuna, as is traditional in this popular Provençal salad, we've gilded the lily with grilled tuna steaks. Whichever you choose, this salad is great for hot summer days.

WINE RECOMMENDATION
A seamless pairing would be a rosé from Provence in France, often made from grenache and mourvedre grapes. Also, look for California rosés using the same varietals.

SERVES 4

- 4 tuna steaks, about 1 inch thick (about 1½ pounds in all)
- ¾ cup plus 1 tablespoon olive oil
- 1 teaspoon salt
- ½ teaspoon fresh-ground black pepper
- ¼ cup red-wine vinegar
- 1½ teaspoons Dijon mustard
- 1 pound new potatoes, cut into quarters
- ½ pound green beans, cut crosswise in half
- 1 head Boston lettuce, torn into bite-size pieces (about 1½ quarts)
- 1 large tomato, cut into wedges
- 4 hard-cooked eggs, cut in half
- 1 green bell pepper, cut into ¼-inch rings (optional)
- ¼ cup black olives, such as Niçoise or Kalamata
- 1 2-ounce tin anchovy fillets, drained
- 3 tablespoons chopped flat-leaf parsley

1. Light the grill. Coat the tuna with the 1 tablespoon oil. Season with ½ teaspoon of the salt and ¼ teaspoon of the pepper. Grill the tuna, turning once, until done to your taste, about 8 minutes for medium. Let cool.

2. In a small bowl, whisk together the vinegar, mustard, and the remaining ½ teaspoon salt and ¼ teaspoon pepper. Add the ¾ cup oil slowly, whisking.

3. Put the potatoes in a medium saucepan of salted water. Bring to a boil and simmer until tender, about 12 minutes. Drain the potatoes and toss with 3 tablespoons of the dressing. Let cool.

4. In a medium saucepan of boiling, salted water, cook the beans until just done, about 5 minutes. Drain. Rinse with cold water and drain thoroughly. Toss with 3 tablespoons of the dressing.

5. To serve, toss the lettuce with ⅓ cup of the dressing. Mound on four plates. Arrange the potatoes, beans, tomato, eggs, and bell pepper around the lettuce. Top the lettuce with the tuna, olives, and anchovies. Drizzle the remaining vinaigrette over the tuna and vegetables and sprinkle with the parsley.

CHICKPEA SALAD WITH SHRIMP AND FETA CHEESE

Here's a Mediterranean-style salad you can put together in no time. The chickpeas are tossed with herbs, red onion, and cherry tomatoes, mounded on a bed of watercress, and then topped with the shrimp and feta.

WINE RECOMMENDATION

If your wine store carries Greek wines, use this dish as an excuse to explore a *dry* white from that country. If not, choose a light, acidic white such as a vinho verde from Portugal.

SERVES 4

- ⅔ cup plus 1 tablespoon olive oil
- 1 clove garlic, minced
- 16 large shrimp (about 1 pound), shelled
- 2 teaspoons salt
  Fresh-ground black pepper
- ¼ cup red-wine vinegar
- 1 teaspoon Dijon mustard
- 3 19-ounce cans chickpeas, drained and rinsed (about 1½ quarts)
- 1 small red onion, chopped
- 3 cups cherry tomatoes, cut in half
- 3 tablespoons chopped fresh tarragon or flat-leaf parsley
- 1 tablespoon lemon juice
- 2 bunches watercress (about 10 ounces in all), tough stems removed
- ¼ pound feta cheese, crumbled (about 1 cup)

1. Heat a grill pan or large, heavy frying pan until hot. In a small bowl, combine the 1 tablespoon oil and the garlic. Toss the shrimp with the garlic oil and season with ¼ teaspoon of the salt and ⅛ teaspoon pepper. Cook the shrimp, turning once, until just done, about 4 minutes in all. Let cool.

2. In a large bowl, whisk together the vinegar, mustard, ½ teaspoon of the salt, and ¼ teaspoon pepper. Add the remaining ⅔ cup oil slowly, whisking.

3. Reserve 2 tablespoons of the dressing. Add the chickpeas, onion, tomatoes, tarragon, lemon juice, the remaining 1¼ teaspoons salt, and ¼ teaspoon pepper to the remaining dressing and toss.

4. Toss the watercress with the reserved 2 tablespoons dressing. Put the watercress on plates and top with the chickpea salad. Arrange the shrimp on top of the salad and scatter the cheese over all.

Cobb Salad

Happily, this old California favorite is experiencing a renaissance and turning up all across the country.

WINE RECOMMENDATION
Acidity counts for a lot in wine/salad matches. Try one of the more acidic American whites, such as a dry riesling from California or Washington State.

SERVES 4

1 tablespoon olive oil

4 boneless, skinless chicken breasts (about 1⅓ pounds in all)

¼ teaspoon salt

⅛ teaspoon fresh-ground black pepper

8 slices bacon

1 head romaine lettuce, cut into ½-inch pieces (about 1½ quarts)

2 avocados, preferably Hass, cut into ½-inch dice

¾ pound tomatoes (about 3 medium), seeded and cut into ½-inch dice

¼ pound blue cheese, crumbled (about 1 cup)

Lemon-Shallot Vinaigrette

1. In a large frying pan, heat the oil over moderate heat. Season the chicken with the salt and pepper and cook for 5 minutes. Turn and cook until browned and just done, about 4 minutes longer. Let cool. Cut into ½-inch chunks. In the same pan, fry the bacon until crisp. Drain on paper towels. Cool and then crumble.

2. In a large salad bowl, spread the lettuce in an even layer. Arrange the bacon in a strip on one side of the bowl, followed by strips of chicken, avocado, tomato, and finally cheese. Toss the salad with the dressing at the table.

Lemon-Shallot Vinaigrette

MAKES ABOUT 1 CUP

6 tablespoons lemon juice (from about 2 lemons)

¾ teaspoon Dijon mustard

2 shallots, minced

1 clove garlic, minced

2 tablespoons chopped flat-leaf parsley

2 teaspoons chopped fresh thyme, or ¾ teaspoon dried

¾ teaspoon salt

¾ teaspoon fresh-ground black pepper

½ cup olive oil

In a small bowl, whisk together all the ingredients but the oil. Add the oil slowly, whisking.

Grilled Vegetable and Chicken Salad with Parmesan Croutes

Mixed greens topped with grilled zucchini, red peppers, green beans, and chicken make an appetizing summer salad. Try balsamic in place of the red-wine vinegar, if you prefer. You can simplify the salad by serving bread in place of the croûtes.

WINE RECOMMENDATION Match the liveliness of this salad with a light and refreshingly crisp white wine, such as an ugni blanc from the Côtes de Gascogne region of southwestern France.

SERVES 4

- ⅔ cup olive oil
- 1 tablespoon chopped fresh thyme, or 1 teaspoon dried
- 4 boneless, skinless chicken breasts (about 1⅓ pounds in all)
- 1 teaspoon salt
- ½ teaspoon fresh-ground black pepper
- 2 small zucchini, cut lengthwise into ⅛-inch slices
- 1 red bell pepper, cut into 1½-inch pieces
- ¼ pound green beans
- 2 tablespoons red-wine vinegar
- ½ teaspoon Dijon mustard
- 2 tablespoons chopped fresh basil
- 2 quarts mixed salad greens (about 6 ounces)

  Parmesan Croûtes, opposite page

1. Light the grill. In a small bowl, combine ⅓ cup of the oil and the thyme. Coat the chicken with 1 tablespoon of the thyme oil. Sprinkle with ¼ teaspoon of the salt and ⅛ teaspoon of the pepper. Grill the chicken over moderately high heat for about 4 minutes. Turn and cook until just done, about 5 minutes. Remove, cool, and cut diagonally into ¼-inch slices.

2. In a large bowl, toss the zucchini, red pepper, and green beans with the remaining thyme oil, ½ teaspoon of the salt, and ¼ teaspoon of the pepper. Grill the vegetables over moderately high heat, turning, until just done, about 4 minutes per side for the zucchini and 4 to 6 minutes per side for the red peppers and beans. Remove and let cool.

3. In a small bowl, whisk together the vinegar, mustard, and the remaining ¼ teaspoon salt and ⅛ teaspoon pepper. Add the remaining ⅓ cup oil slowly, whisking. Add the basil.

4. To serve, in a large bowl, toss the greens with all but 2 tablespoons of the vinaigrette. Mound onto plates. Top with the vegetables and chicken. Drizzle the remaining vinaigrette over the chicken. Put two of the croûtes at the edge of each salad.

TEST-KITCHEN TIPS

■ It's easiest to grill the green beans if you set a barbecue grid over your regular grill. That way the beans won't fall through the grill. You can buy barbecue grids at stores that sell grilling accessories.

■ A great way to light a charcoal fire is with a chimney charcoal starter. You can buy one at almost any hardware store. They're inexpensive and they last for years.

PARMESAN CROUTES

MAKES 8 CROUTES

8 ½-inch slices country bread or sourdough bread

2 tablespoons olive oil

¼ cup grated Parmesan cheese

1. Light the grill or heat the broiler. Brush both sides of the bread with the oil.

2. Grill or broil the bread until just beginning to brown, about 1 minute. Turn and top with the Parmesan. Continue cooking until the cheese melts, about 2 minutes longer.

ROASTED-POTATO AND CHICKEN SALAD

Green beans, cherry tomatoes, rosemary, and black olives give interest to the already tasty roasted new potatoes and chicken here.

WINE RECOMMENDATION A German kabinett riesling (such as one from the Mosel-Saar-Ruwer region) has the fruit and acidity to work well with all the disparate elements of this salad.

SERVES 4

1¾ pounds small red new potatoes, cut in half, or larger potatoes cut in chunks

8½ tablespoons olive oil

1 tablespoon chopped fresh rosemary, or 1 teaspoon dried, crumbled

1¼ teaspoons salt

Fresh-ground black pepper

4 boneless, skinless chicken breasts (about 1⅓ pounds in all)

¾ pound green beans, cut crosswise in half

2 tablespoons red-wine vinegar

1 teaspoon Dijon mustard

1 clove garlic, minced

2 tablespoons chopped fresh chives or scallion tops

3 cups cherry tomatoes, cut in half

3 cups mixed salad greens (about 2 ounces)

¼ cup black olives, such as Niçoise or Kalamata, pitted

1. Heat the oven to 400°. In a roasting pan, toss the potatoes with 1½ tablespoons of the oil, the rosemary, ½ teaspoon of the salt, and a pinch of pepper. Turn the potatoes skin-side down so that they won't stick to the pan. Cover with aluminum foil and bake for 15 minutes. Remove the foil and stir. Cook, uncovered, stirring once, until browned and tender, about 30 minutes longer. Let cool.

2. Heat a grill pan over moderate heat. Coat the chicken with 1 tablespoon of the oil and season with ¼ teaspoon of the salt and ⅛ teaspoon pepper. Cook the chicken for 5 minutes. Turn and cook until browned and just done, about 4 minutes longer. Let cool. Cut the chicken diagonally into ¼-inch slices. Alternatively, heat the oil in a large, heavy frying pan. Season, cook, and slice the chicken in the same way.

3. In a medium saucepan of boiling, salted water, cook the beans until just done, about 5 minutes. Drain. Rinse with cold water and drain thoroughly.

4. In a large bowl, whisk the vinegar with the mustard, the remaining ½ teaspoon salt, the garlic, chives, and ¼ teaspoon pepper. Add the remaining 6 tablespoons oil slowly, whisking. Toss in the potatoes, chicken, beans, tomatoes, greens, and olives.

GREEN SALAD WITH CHICKEN LIVERS, APPLES, AND BACON

The sweetness of the apples contrasts perfectly with the slight bitterness of the livers and the tang of the warm bacon dressing in this delicious, homey salad.

WINE RECOMMENDATION
The various strong flavors of this salad will work best with always-flexible riesling, particularly a slightly off-dry version from Germany. Look for a kabinett from the Mosel-Saar-Ruwer or Rheingau region.

SERVES 4

⅓ pound bacon

   About 4 tablespoons cooking oil

1 pound chicken livers, each cut in half

½ teaspoon salt

   Fresh-ground black pepper

2½ tablespoons sherry vinegar or red-wine vinegar

1½ heads red or green leaf lettuce, torn into bite-size pieces (about 3 quarts)

2 apples, peeled, cored, and chopped

1 red onion, chopped fine

1. Fry the bacon until crisp. Reserve the fat. Drain the bacon on paper towels and then crumble. Pour the bacon fat into a measuring cup and add enough oil to make ⅓ cup. Set aside.

2. In a large nonstick frying pan, heat 1 tablespoon of the cooking oil over moderately high heat. Season the chicken livers with ¼ teaspoon of the salt and ⅛ teaspoon pepper. Add half the livers to the pan and cook 2 minutes. Turn and cook until browned but still pink inside, about 2 minutes longer. Remove. Repeat with the remaining livers and 1 tablespoon of the cooking oil. Put in a warm spot.

3. Wipe out the pan. Add the reserved bacon fat to the pan along with the vinegar, the remaining ¼ teaspoon salt, and ¼ teaspoon pepper. Bring almost to a simmer.

4. In a large bowl, combine the lettuce, apples, onion, and all but 2 tablespoons of the bacon. Add the warm dressing and toss. Put the salad on plates and top with the livers. Sprinkle with the reserved bacon.

Wild-Rice Salad with Smoked Turkey and Dried Cranberries

If you can't get good-quality smoked turkey for this autumnal salad, use the roasted turkey available at many supermarket delis. This recipe is also a great way to use up leftover turkey meat from the holiday bird.

WINE RECOMMENDATION

The light body, slight smokiness, and citrus flavors of an Oregon pinot gris will both mirror and provide counterpoint to this all-American dish.

SERVES 4

- 2 cups wild rice
- 3 cups Chicken Stock, page 303, or canned low-sodium chicken broth
- 1/2 teaspoon salt
- 1 cup dried cranberries
- 1 cup boiling water
- 1 1/2-pound piece smoked turkey, cut into 1/2-inch chunks
- 2 heads Belgian endive, cut crosswise into 1-inch pieces
- 4 scallions including green tops, chopped
- 2 tablespoons chopped flat-leaf parsley
  Citrus Vinaigrette

1. Rinse the rice in several changes of cold water. Drain. In a medium pot, combine the rice, stock, and salt. Add enough water to cover the rice by about 2 inches. Bring to a boil over moderate heat. Cover, reduce the heat, and cook at a gentle boil until the rice is tender. The cooking time can vary from 35 to 60 minutes. If necessary, drain the rice. Let cool.

2. Put the cranberries and boiling water in a small bowl. Let soak until softened, about 10 minutes. Drain and let cool.

3. In a large bowl, combine the rice, cranberries, turkey, Belgian endive, scallions, and parsley. Add the vinaigrette and toss.

Citrus Vinaigrette

MAKES ABOUT 1/2 CUP

- 2 tablespoons red-wine vinegar
- 1 tablespoon lemon juice
- 1 teaspoon Dijon mustard
- 1/2 teaspoon grated orange zest
- 3/4 teaspoon salt
- 1/2 teaspoon fresh-ground black pepper
- 6 tablespoons olive oil

In a small bowl, whisk together all the ingredients but the oil. Add the oil slowly, whisking.

Warm Potato Salad with Corned Beef and Wilted Greens

You have to make a warm vinaigrette for most wilted green salads, but not this one—the heat of the potatoes "cooks" the tender escarole perfectly. The addition of corned beef transforms potato salad from a side dish into a meal.

WINE RECOMMENDATION
While a red wine would usually be good with corned beef, in the context of this salad, it's best to go with a full-bodied white wine. Try a rich pinot gris from Alsace in France.

SERVES 4

- 2 pounds boiling potatoes (about 6), peeled and cut into 1-inch pieces
- 2 tablespoons white-wine vinegar
- ½ teaspoon Dijon mustard
- ¼ teaspoon salt
- ¼ teaspoon fresh-ground black pepper
- 6 tablespoons olive oil
- 1 small head escarole, shredded (about 3 packed cups)
- 1 ½-pound piece corned beef, cut into matchstick strips about 1 inch long
- 2 tablespoons chopped flat-leaf parsley

1. Put the potatoes in a large saucepan of salted water. Bring to a boil and simmer until just tender, about 10 minutes.

2. Meanwhile, in a large bowl, whisk together the vinegar, mustard, salt, and pepper. Add the oil slowly, whisking.

3. Drain the potatoes and add them to the dressing. Add the escarole and toss until the greens are wilted. Add the corned beef and parsley and toss again. Serve warm or at room temperature.

—Judith Sutton

Variation

Use a ¾-pound piece of kielbasa in place of the corned beef. Cut the kielbasa in half lengthwise and then into thin slices. Add to the simmering potatoes after 5 minutes. Drain the potatoes and kielbasa and add to the dressing.

STEAK SALAD WITH PARSLEY CAPER DRESSING

A bright-green dressing lends its caper and garlic piquancy to sturdy greens and rosy sliced sirloin. You can serve the steak warm or at room temperature.

WINE RECOMMENDATION
The wine should be red for the steak, light and acidic for the dressing. Try a gamay from France's Loire Valley or a Beaujolais-Villages (also made from the gamay grape).

SERVES 4

1¼ pounds sirloin steak, about 1 inch thick

¼ teaspoon salt

¼ teaspoon fresh-ground black pepper

1 head romaine lettuce, torn into bite-size pieces (about 1½ quarts)

1 head green leaf lettuce, torn into bite-size pieces (about 1½ quarts)

1 small red onion, cut into thin slices

Parsley Caper Dressing

1. Heat the broiler. Sprinkle the meat with the salt and pepper. Broil the steak for 6 minutes. Turn the meat and cook to your taste, about 6 minutes longer for medium rare. Transfer the steak to a carving board and leave to rest in a warm spot for at least 5 minutes. Cut the steak diagonally into thin slices.

2. In a large bowl, toss the romaine lettuce, green leaf lettuce, and onion with all but 2 tablespoons of the dressing.

3. Divide the greens among four plates. Top each salad with the steak and drizzle the remaining dressing over the meat.

—SUSAN SHAPIRO JASLOVE

PARSLEY CAPER DRESSING

MAKES ABOUT ²/₃ CUP

2 tablespoons red-wine vinegar

1 large clove garlic, minced

3 tablespoons capers

2 teaspoons Dijon mustard

½ cup chopped flat-leaf parsley

½ teaspoon salt

¼ teaspoon fresh-ground black pepper

½ cup olive oil

In a small bowl, whisk together all the ingredients but the oil. Add the oil slowly, whisking.

COLD-ROAST-BEEF SALAD
WITH WALNUTS AND PARMESAN CHEESE

Slices of cold roast beef encircle lettuce, green beans, cherry tomatoes, and walnuts, all tossed with a sherry-vinegar and mustard dressing and topped with Parmesan shavings. You can get excellent rare beef from the deli counter in most supermarkets, or use up leftovers from a weekend roast.

WINE RECOMMENDATION

This is a doubly tough dish to match with wine: It's a salad and an unusual combination of ingredients. A kabinett riesling from Germany's Mosel-Saar-Ruwer region has the acidity to pair with the salad and the richness to complement the cheese and nuts.

SERVES 4

½ cup chopped walnuts

¾ pound green beans, cut in half crosswise

1 pound thin-sliced roast beef

1 large head red leaf lettuce, torn into bite-size pieces (about 2 quarts)

1 cup cherry tomatoes, cut in half

   Sherry and Mustard Vinaigrette, opposite page

1 ¼-pound chunk Parmesan cheese, or ⅓ cup grated Parmesan

¼ teaspoon fresh-ground black pepper

   Thin Croûtes (optional), opposite page

1. In a medium frying pan, toast the walnuts over moderately low heat, stirring frequently, until golden brown, about 5 minutes. Or toast them in a 350° oven for about 8 minutes. Let cool.

2. In a large saucepan of boiling, salted water, cook the beans until just done, about 5 minutes. Drain. Rinse with cold water and drain thoroughly.

3. On four plates, arrange the slices of roast beef, folded into thirds, in a circle around the edge of the plates. Put the beans between the slices.

4. In a large bowl, toss the lettuce, walnuts, tomatoes, and all but 2 tablespoons of the vinaigrette. Mound the salad in the center of the plates. Drizzle the remaining vinaigrette over the beans.

5. Top the lettuce with the grated Parmesan, if using, or with strips of Parmesan shaved from the chunk of cheese with a vegetable peeler. Sprinkle the pepper over the salads. Serve with two croûtes on the side of each plate.

SHERRY AND MUSTARD VINAIGRETTE

MAKES ABOUT ²/₃ CUP

- 2 tablespoons sherry vinegar
- 2 teaspoons grainy or Dijon mustard
- 2 tablespoons chopped fresh chives or scallion tops (optional)
- 1 clove garlic, minced (optional)
- ¾ teaspoon salt
- ¼ teaspoon fresh-ground black pepper
- ½ cup olive oil

In a small bowl, whisk together all the ingredients but the oil. Add the oil slowly, whisking.

THIN CROUTES

MAKES 8 CROUTES

- 8 ¼-inch slices French baguette or sourdough baguette, or an equal quantity of halved or quartered slices from a larger loaf of country bread
- 1 tablespoon olive oil
  Pinch salt

1. Light the grill or heat the broiler. Brush both sides of the bread with the oil.

2. Grill or broil the bread on both sides until golden brown, about 3 minutes in all. Sprinkle with the salt. Serve warm or at room temperature.

Vietnamese Noodle Salad with Vegetables and Beef

Noodles, lettuce, and bean sprouts, tossed with Nuoc Cham Sauce, form the base of this popular Vietnamese salad. Topped with thin slices of garlicky stir-fried beef, peanuts, and cilantro, it makes a delicious and refreshing meal.

WINE RECOMMENDATION
Beer is often the best bet with Vietnamese food. If you prefer wine, try an Alsatian or California gewürztraminer.

SERVES 4

1½ pounds sirloin steak or top round, cut into ¼-inch slices about 2 inches long

3 cloves garlic, minced

4 teaspoons Asian fish sauce (nam pla or nuoc mam)*

2 teaspoons lime juice

⅛ teaspoon fresh-ground black pepper

2 tablespoons cooking oil

½ pound angel-hair pasta, broken into approximately 2-inch pieces

1 head Boston lettuce, torn into bite-size pieces (about 1½ quarts)

3 carrots, grated

1 large tomato, seeded and chopped

6 ounces bean sprouts (about 2 cups)

1 cup lightly packed cilantro with thick stems removed

¼ cup chopped fresh mint

   Nuoc Cham Sauce, next page

½ cup chopped peanuts

   *Available at Asian markets

1. In a shallow glass dish or stainless-steel pan, combine the beef, garlic, fish sauce, lime juice, pepper, and oil.

2. In a large pot of boiling, salted water, cook the pasta until just done, about 3 minutes. Drain. Rinse with cold water and drain thoroughly. Put in a large bowl.

3. Add the lettuce, carrots, tomato, bean sprouts, ½ cup of the cilantro, and the mint. Chill until ready to serve.

4. Drain the beef. Heat a large, heavy frying pan until very hot. Add half the beef and cook, stirring, until browned and just cooked through, about 1 minute. Remove. Wipe the pan with a paper towel. Repeat with the remaining meat. Cool to room temperature.

5. To serve, toss the salad with ¾ cup of the Nuoc Cham Sauce. Mound onto plates and top with the beef, the peanuts, and the remaining ½ cup cilantro leaves. Serve the remaining sauce alongside. ➤

VARIATIONS

■ Use about 1 pound of shelled medium shrimp in place of the beef.

■ Use pork loin or tenderloin in place of the beef.

■ Add 1 avocado, cut into chunks, to the vegetables.

■ Use about 12 cherry tomatoes, cut in half, in place of the large tomato.

NUOC CHAM SAUCE

Made with pungent Asian fish sauce, lime juice, hot pepper, garlic, and fresh mint, this condiment is widely used in Vietnamese cooking as a dressing for salads and as a dipping sauce for finger foods. If you like, add more hot pepper to taste.

MAKES ABOUT 1 1/4 CUPS

6 tablespoons Asian fish sauce (nam pla or nuoc mam)*

3 tablespoons lime juice (from about 2 limes)

2 1/4 teaspoons rice- or white-wine vinegar

3 1/2 tablespoons sugar

1 large clove garlic, minced

1 1/2 tablespoons chopped fresh mint

1/4 teaspoon dried red-pepper flakes

1/2 cup plus 1 tablespoon warm water

*Available at Asian markets

In a small bowl, combine all of the ingredients and stir until the sugar is dissolved.

ANTIPASTO CAESAR SALAD WITH PARMESAN CROUTES

Small spheres of fresh mozzarella, along with *soppressata*, bell pepper, capers, and olives, sit in a glorious nest of Caesar salad. Slices of country bread, toasted with Parmesan cheese, complete the picture.

WINE RECOMMENDATION
The Mediterranean flavors here are perfect with a light, gulpable Italian white wine, such as a pinot grigio.

SERVES 4

½   pound salted fresh mozzarella cheese, bocconcini or a larger ball

    No-Egg Caesar Dressing, page 250

⅓   pound thin-sliced *soppressata* or hard salami, cut into quarters

1   red or green bell pepper, cut lengthwise into thin slices

1   cup black olives, such as Niçoise or Kalamata, or good-quality green olives, or a mixture

1   large head romaine lettuce, torn into bite-size pieces (about 2½ quarts)

1½   tablespoons capers

    Parmesan Croûtes, page 69

1. If using bocconcini, drain them. If using a larger ball of cheese, cut it into ¾-inch cubes. In a large glass or stainless-steel bowl, combine the mozzarella with 2 tablespoons of the dressing and let marinate about 10 minutes. Add the *soppressata*, bell pepper, and olives, and toss.

2. In a large bowl, toss the lettuce with the remaining dressing and the capers. Put the salad on plates. Mound the mozzarella mixture in the center of the lettuce and set the croûtes at the edge.

VARIATIONS

Top the mozzarella mixture with anchovy fillets, pickled Italian-style vegetables, or a combination of the two.

ROQUEFORT-SANDWICH SALAD

Essentially, this is a salad topped with a crisp, golden grilled-cheese sandwich. The warm, pungent blue cheese oozes out onto the crisp greens.

WINE RECOMMENDATION
To match the salty creaminess of the Roquefort and the acidity of the dressing, try a light, fruity red wine from Italy, such as a Dolcetto from the Piedmont region.

SERVES 4

- 2 tablespoons red-wine vinegar
- 1 clove garlic, minced
- 1/2 teaspoon salt
- 1/2 teaspoon fresh-ground black pepper
- 1/3 cup olive oil
- 1/4 pound Roquefort or other blue cheese, at room temperature
- 8 slices good-quality white bread
- 2 tablespoons butter
- 1 head romaine lettuce, torn into bite-size pieces (about 1 1/2 quarts)
- 1 head green leaf lettuce, torn into bite-size pieces (about 1 1/2 quarts)
- 4 scallions including green tops, cut diagonally into 1/2-inch pieces
- 1 cup cherry tomatoes, cut in half

1. In a large bowl, whisk together the vinegar, garlic, salt, and pepper. Add the oil slowly, whisking.

2. Make four sandwiches, using 1 ounce of cheese and two pieces of bread in each.

3. In each of two frying pans, melt 1 tablespoon butter over moderate heat. Fry the sandwiches until the bread is golden brown and the cheese melts, about 3 minutes per side. Or cook the sandwiches in batches.

4. Add the lettuce, scallions, and tomatoes to the dressing and toss. Put the greens on four plates. Cut each cheese sandwich into four triangles and top each salad with a sandwich.

—SUSAN SHAPIRO JASLOVE

VARIATIONS

■ If you don't have any scallions on hand, use paper-thin slices of regular yellow onions, soaked in cold water to crisp them and mellow their flavor.

■ Nuts, such as walnuts or pecans, are a a happy addition to this combination of flavors.

Lentil Salad with Goat Cheese

In this satisfying salad, tangy goat cheese and lemon vinaigrette enliven lentils, bell peppers, and mixed greens.

WINE RECOMMENDATION
Sauvignon blanc is a classic with goat cheese. Try a bottling from New Zealand or California.

SERVES 4

1½ tablespoons olive oil

1 onion, chopped fine

2 cloves garlic, minced

1 pound lentils (about 2⅓ cups)

1 quart water

1 tablespoon chopped fresh thyme, or 1 teaspoon dried

1 bay leaf

1½ teaspoons salt

3 bell peppers, green, yellow, red, or a combination, cut into ¼-inch pieces

¼ teaspoon fresh-ground black pepper

¼ cup chopped fresh parsley

Lemon Vinaigrette

3 quarts mixed salad greens (about ½ pound)

6 ounces mild goat cheese, such as Montrachet, crumbled

1. In a large pot, heat ½ tablespoon of the oil over moderately low heat. Add the onion and garlic. Cook, stirring occasionally, until translucent, about 5 minutes. Add the lentils, water, half of the thyme, the bay leaf, and 1 teaspoon of the salt. Bring to a boil, reduce the heat, and simmer, partially covered, until the lentils are just tender but not falling apart, about 35 minutes. Discard the bay leaf. Transfer to a large bowl to cool.

2. In a large frying pan, heat the remaining tablespoon oil over moderately high heat. Add the bell peppers, the remaining thyme and ½ teaspoon salt, and the black pepper. Cook, stirring frequently, until tender, about 8 minutes. Add to the lentils with the parsley and 6 tablespoons of the vinaigrette.

3. Toss the greens with the remaining vinaigrette. Put the greens on plates and top with the lentils and the goat cheese.

Lemon Vinaigrette

MAKES ABOUT ³/₄ CUP

3½ tablespoons lemon juice

1½ teaspoons Dijon mustard

¾ teaspoon salt

¼ teaspoon fresh-ground black pepper

½ cup olive oil

In a small bowl, whisk together all of the ingredients but the oil. Add the oil slowly, whisking.

PASTA, PIZZA & CALZONI

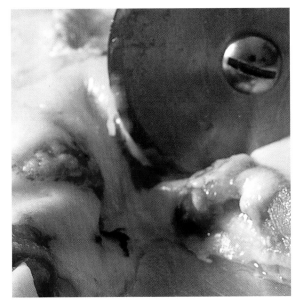

Pizza Margherita, page 109

THE WHOLE COUNTRY, IT SEEMS, NOW THINKS PASTA when it thinks quick meals. So our basic idea here—pasta tossed with either a simple sauce or individual ingredients that form a sauce—isn't new. But the combinations are original, and run from Italian-inspired to Asian to just-made-up-out-of-our-heads. They all call for readily available dried pasta, which we think is as good as if not better than most harder-to-find fresh pasta anyway. Homemade pizza and calzoni are not so obvious when you think of fast meals. We've found, though, that with fresh or frozen store-bought dough anything is possible. The pizza dough that you can buy in supermarkets is very good; fresh out of the oven with your own topping or filling, it's divine.

Spicy Whole-Wheat Spaghetti with Shrimp, Cucumber, and Radish

This Asian-inspired pasta is traditionally prepared with soba (buckwheat) noodles, but we find it's an excellent treatment for whole-wheat spaghetti, too. Adding the shrimp to the spaghetti during the last minutes of cooking, and draining the two together, makes cleanup quicker, too—there's just one pot to wash.

♦ WINE RECOMMENDATION
The shellfish and spices in this salad are best with a very acidic white wine. A Muscadet de Sèvre-et-Maine from France has the requisite acidity and is also a classic shellfish wine.

SERVES 4

¾ pound whole-wheat spaghetti

1 pound medium shrimp, shelled

2 cucumbers, peeled, halved lengthwise, seeded, and cut crosswise into 2-inch pieces, and then lengthwise into ¼-inch strips

6 radishes, cut in half and then into thin slices

2 scallions including green tops, cut into thin slices

3 tablespoons chopped cilantro or fresh mint (optional)

3 tablespoons Asian fish sauce (nam pla or nuoc mam)*

2 tablespoons white-wine vinegar

1½ tablespoons cooking oil

¾ teaspoon Asian sesame oil

1½ teaspoons lemon juice

¾ teaspoon grated lemon zest

2 teaspoons grated fresh ginger

⅛ teaspoon cayenne

⅛ teaspoon salt

*Available at Asian markets

1. In a large pot of boiling, salted water, cook the spaghetti until almost done, about 13 minutes. Add the shrimp and cook until just done, 2 minutes longer. Drain the pasta and shrimp and rinse briefly with cold water. Drain again thoroughly. Put in a large bowl with the cucumbers, radishes, scallions, and cilantro.

2. In a small bowl, combine the fish sauce, vinegar, cooking and sesame oils, lemon juice and zest, ginger, cayenne, and salt. Just before serving, add this mixture to the noodles and toss.

SUMMER PASTA WITH GRILLED SHRIMP

Linguine tossed with chunks of tomato, fresh basil, and grilled shrimp is a welcome dish in the hot summer months when tomatoes and basil are at their best. This pasta is delicious either warm or at room temperature.

 **WINE RECOMMENDATION**
Look for a refreshing but intensely flavored white wine, such as a grassy sauvignon blanc from California, to match the lively ingredients of this dish.

SERVES 4

1	pound medium shrimp, shelled
7	tablespoons olive oil
2	cloves garlic
1¼	teaspoons salt
	Fresh-ground black pepper
1½	pounds tomatoes (about 3), cut into ½-inch dice
¾	cup chopped fresh basil
2	teaspoons balsamic or red-wine vinegar
¾	pound linguine

1. In a medium bowl, combine the shrimp, 1 tablespoon of the olive oil, half of the garlic, ¼ teaspoon of the salt, and ⅛ teaspoon pepper. Light the grill. Thread the shrimp on skewers.

2. In a large bowl, combine the diced tomatoes, the remaining 6 tablespoons olive oil, the remaining garlic, the basil, vinegar, the remaining 1 teaspoon salt, and ½ teaspoon pepper.

3. In a large pot of boiling, salted water, cook the linguine until just done, about 12 minutes. Drain.

4. Grill the shrimp, turning once, until just done, about 3 minutes in all. Remove the shrimp from the skewers. Or, heat a large, heavy frying pan over moderate heat. Add half the shrimp and cook for 1 minute. Turn and cook until just done, 1 to 2 minutes. Repeat with the remaining shrimp.

5. Toss the pasta with the shrimp and the tomato mixture.

PASTA VARIATION

Some sauces are best with a certain shape of pasta, but here you can replace the linguine with virtually any pasta you like. Fettuccine, spaghetti, penne, and shells are all good choices.

Pasta with Crab, Garlic, and Fresh Herbs

Perfect for a weeknight celebration, this pasta is luxury on a time budget. Use parsley in place of the mixed herbs if that's more convenient.

WINE RECOMMENDATION
Crab is usually matched with a rich white wine, but with all the garlic in this dish, it's best to keep the selection simple. Try a full-bodied white Côtes-du-Rhône.

SERVES 4

- ¾ pound linguine
- ½ cup olive oil
- 6 cloves garlic, minced
- ¼ cup mixed, chopped fresh herbs, such as tarragon, chives, and parsley
- ⅛ teaspoon dried red-pepper flakes
- 1¼ teaspoons salt
- ⅛ teaspoon fresh-ground black pepper
- ¾ pound lump crabmeat, picked free of shell

1. In a large pot of boiling, salted water, cook the linguine until just done, about 12 minutes.

2. Meanwhile, heat the oil in a small frying pan over moderately low heat. Add the garlic, herbs, red-pepper flakes, salt, and black pepper, and cook, stirring, until the garlic softens, about 1 minute.

3. Drain the pasta and put it back into the pot. Add the garlic mixture and the crabmeat. Toss gently over moderate heat until the crab is just warmed through, about 1 minute. Avoid tossing too vigorously or the chunks of crab will fall apart.

—Alvio Renzini

White-Wine Variation

If you happen to have a bottle of dry white wine open, add about 2 tablespoons to the pasta along with the crab.

Test-Kitchen Tip

In a simple preparation such as this, the ingredients must be prime quality. Choose fresh lump crabmeat or the pasteurized crab available in refrigerated cans. Regular canned crab just won't cut it here.

FETTUCCINE WITH SCALLOPS AND PARSLEY PESTO

A delicious variation on the usual basil version, parsley pesto has the advantage that you can make it any time of year. Here it's tossed into fettuccine and then topped with golden-brown scallops. You can always replace the scallops with grilled chicken or grilled shrimp, if you prefer.

WINE RECOMMENDATION
The strong flavors of pesto pair well with an aggressive white wine, such as a sauvignon blanc from California, New Zealand, or South Africa.

SERVES 4

¾ pound fettuccine

1 pound sea scallops

¾ teaspoon salt

½ teaspoon fresh-ground black pepper

1 tablespoon olive oil

1½ teaspoons lemon juice

Parsley Pesto

1. In a large pot of boiling, salted water, cook the fettuccine until just done, about 12 minutes.

2. Meanwhile, season the scallops with ½ teaspoon of the salt and ¼ teaspoon of the pepper. In a large nonstick frying pan, heat the oil over moderately high heat. Sear the scallops, in two batches if necessary, until brown, 1 to 2 minutes per side. Sprinkle the scallops with 1 teaspoon of the lemon juice.

3. Reserve 2 tablespoons pasta water. Drain the pasta. Toss with all but 2 tablespoons of the pesto, the reserved pasta water, and the remaining ¼ teaspoon salt, ¼ teaspoon pepper, and ½ teaspoon lemon juice.

4. To serve, top the pasta with the scallops and drizzle the remaining 2 tablespoons pesto over the scallops.

PARSLEY PESTO

MAKES ABOUT ¹/₂ CUP

¾ cup lightly packed flat-leaf parsley with thick stems removed

¼ cup pine nuts

1 clove garlic, chopped

2 tablespoons grated Parmesan cheese

6 tablespoons olive oil

½ teaspoon salt

In a food processor or blender, puree the parsley, pine nuts, garlic, and Parmesan with the oil and salt.

PENNE WITH TUNA, PESTO, PINE NUTS, AND RAISINS

Make this flavorful Italian sauce in the time it takes to cook the pasta. The acidity of the capers and vinegar balances the sweetness of the raisins.

WINE RECOMMENDATION
Try this hearty pasta with an Italian white wine such as a full-bodied, full-flavored tocai or a sauvignon blanc, both from the Friuli or Veneto region.

SERVES 4

- ½ cup pine nuts or chopped walnuts
- ¼ cup olive oil
- 1 onion, chopped
- 2 6-ounce cans tuna packed in oil, drained
- ½ cup raisins
- 3 tablespoons red-wine vinegar
- 1 teaspoon salt
- ½ teaspoon fresh-ground black pepper
- ¾ pound penne
- ¾ cup store-bought pesto

1. In a small frying pan, toast the pine nuts over moderately low heat, stirring frequently, until golden brown, about 4 minutes. Or toast them in a 350° oven for 6 minutes.

2. In a medium saucepan, heat the oil over moderately low heat. Add the onion and cook, covered, stirring occasionally, until soft, about 10 minutes. Add the tuna, raisins, vinegar, salt, and pepper, and remove from the heat.

3. Meanwhile, in a large pot of boiling, salted water, cook the penne until just done, about 12 minutes. Drain. Toss the pasta with the tuna sauce, pesto, and pine nuts.

—PAUL GRIMES

PARSLEY-PESTO VARIATION

If you're tired of basil pesto, replace it with Parsley Pesto, opposite page. Use 1 cup lightly packed parsley, 6 tablespoons pine nuts, 1 chopped garlic clove, 3 tablespoons grated Parmesan cheese, ½ cup olive oil, and ¾ teaspoon salt.

SESAME-CRUSTED TUNA ON SOBA NOODLES WITH WASABI DRESSING

Soba noodles are tossed with cucumber, watercress, scallions, and a spicy dressing. Topped with seared tuna, the noodles make a simple summertime meal.

WINE RECOMMENDATION
A kabinett riesling (combining fruit and acidity) from Germany's Mosel-Saar-Ruwer region is an ideal choice with the slight spice of the wasabi and the strong soy flavor of the noodles.

SERVES 4

5 tablespoons rice-wine vinegar

3 tablespoons Asian sesame oil

1½ tablespoons soy sauce

2 tablespoons powdered wasabi*, or ¾ teaspoon Tabasco sauce

2 tablespoons sugar

1 teaspoon salt

3 tablespoons sesame seeds

1½ pounds tuna steaks, about 2 inches thick, cut into 3-by-3-inch pieces

2 teaspoons cooking oil

¼ teaspoon fresh-ground black pepper

¾ pound soba noodles or linguine

1 cucumber, peeled, seeded, and cut into ¼-inch slices

1 bunch watercress (about 5 ounces), tough stems removed

3 scallions including green tops, cut into ¼-inch slices

*Available at Asian markets

1. In a small bowl, whisk together the vinegar, sesame oil, soy sauce, wasabi, sugar, and ¾ teaspoon of the salt. In a small frying pan, toast the sesame seeds over moderate heat, stirring frequently, until light brown, about 3 minutes.

2. Heat a grill pan over moderate heat. Coat the tuna with the cooking oil and season with the remaining ¼ teaspoon salt and the pepper. Cook about 1½ minutes per side. Or heat the cooking oil in a large, heavy frying pan. Season and cook the tuna in the same way.

3. Remove the tuna. Let sit for 3 minutes. The fish will be rare. Press the tuna into the sesame seeds to coat all sides. Cut the tuna across the grain into ¼-inch slices.

4. Meanwhile, in a large pot of boiling, salted water, cook the soba noodles until just done, 2 to 4 minutes, or the linguine, if using, for about 12 minutes. Drain. Rinse with cold water and drain thoroughly.

5. To serve, toss the noodles with all but 2 tablespoons of the wasabi dressing, the cucumber, watercress, and scallions. Top with the tuna. Spoon the remaining 2 tablespoons dressing over the tuna.

COLD SESAME NOODLES WITH CHICKEN, BEAN SPROUTS, AND SCALLIONS

This uncooked sauce is simply whipped up in a blender. If the noodles soak it up before you serve them, just toss with a little more stock or some water.

WINE RECOMMENDATION
Pair these unusual textures and flavors with a full-bodied, acidic white wine, such as a riesling from Alsace in France.

SERVES 4

2½ tablespoons cooking oil

3 boneless, skinless chicken breasts (about 1 pound in all)

1 teaspoon salt

⅛ teaspoon fresh-ground black pepper

¾ pound Chinese egg noodles or spaghettini

½ cup salted peanuts, ¼ cup chopped

⅓ cup Chicken Stock, page 303, or canned low-sodium chicken broth

¼ cup tahini

½ teaspoon grated fresh ginger

1 small clove garlic, chopped

1 tablespoon lime juice

1 tablespoon rice- or red-wine vinegar

1 tablespoon soy sauce

½ teaspoon Asian sesame oil

½ teaspoon sugar

¼ teaspoon cayenne

¼ pound bean sprouts (about 1½ cups)

4 scallions including green tops, cut into ¼-inch slices

1. In a medium nonstick frying pan, heat 1 tablespoon of the oil over moderate heat. Season the chicken with ½ teaspoon of the salt and the pepper. Cook the chicken until browned on one side, about 5 minutes. Turn and cook until almost done, about 3 minutes longer. Cover the pan, remove from the heat, and let sit 5 minutes. Reserve any pan juices. Let the chicken cool to room temperature and then cut it diagonally into ¼-inch slices.

2. In a large pot of boiling, salted water, cook the noodles until just done, about 8 minutes. Drain. Rinse with cold water and drain thoroughly.

3. In a blender, puree the ¼ cup whole peanuts with the stock, tahini, ginger, garlic, lime juice, vinegar, soy sauce, sesame oil, sugar, cayenne, and the remaining 1½ tablespoons cooking oil and ½ teaspoon salt. Toss with the cold pasta.

4. To serve, put half of the noodles on plates. Scatter each serving with bean sprouts and then top with the remaining noodles. Top with the chicken slices and spoon the reserved pan juices over them. Sprinkle with the scallions and the chopped peanuts.

PENNE WITH CHICKEN, ROASTED-RED-PEPPER PESTO, AND OLIVES

Grilled chicken, olives, and an intensely flavored pesto made from roasted red peppers, garlic, walnuts, and cayenne are all tossed with penne for a robust and satisfying pasta. Because the pesto calls for bottled red peppers, you can make this dish in minutes.

WINE RECOMMENDATION
Sauvignon blanc has the acidity and intense flavor to stand up to and complement the assertive ingredients in this dish. Try a bottle from California or New Zealand.

SERVES 4

- 1 7-ounce jar roasted red peppers, drained (about ¾ cup)
- ¾ cup walnuts
- 3 cloves garlic, chopped
- 2½ tablespoons olive oil
- 1 tablespoon chopped fresh sage, or 1 teaspoon dried
- 1¾ teaspoons salt
- ¾ teaspoon lemon juice or wine vinegar
- ⅛ teaspoon cayenne
- 1 pound penne
- 4 boneless, skinless chicken breasts (about 1⅓ pounds in all)
- ⅛ teaspoon fresh-ground black pepper
- ⅓ cup black olives, such as Niçoise or Kalamata, halved and pitted
- 1 tablespoon chopped fresh chives or scallion tops
- 1 tablespoon chopped fresh parsley

1. In a food processor or blender, puree the roasted peppers, the walnuts, and the garlic with 1½ tablespoons of the oil, the sage, 1 teaspoon of the salt, the lemon juice, and the cayenne.

2. In a large pot of boiling, salted water, cook the penne until just done, about 13 minutes.

3. Meanwhile, coat the chicken with the remaining 1 tablespoon oil. Season with the black pepper and ¼ teaspoon of the salt. Heat a grill pan over moderate heat. Cook the chicken for 5 minutes. Turn and cook until browned and just done, about 4 minutes longer. Remove. Cut crosswise into ¼-inch slices. Alternatively, heat the oil in a large, heavy frying pan. Season, cook, and slice the chicken in the same way.

4. Reserve ½ cup of the pasta water. Drain the pasta. Toss the pasta with ¼ cup of the reserved pasta water, the pesto, the chicken with any accumulated juices, the remaining ½ teaspoon salt, the olives, and the chives. If the sauce seems too thick, add more of the reserved pasta water. Serve the pasta sprinkled with the parsley.

Fettuccine and Chicken with Zucchini and Sun-Dried-Tomato Sauce

An unusual sauce of grated zucchini, garlic, sun-dried tomatoes, and a little ricotta cheese is simultaneously light and creamy—the perfect dressing.

WINE RECOMMENDATION
Look for a refreshing white wine to pair with this lively Italian dish. Try a pinot grigio or a Galestro from Italy.

SERVES 4

- 4 boneless, skinless chicken breasts (about 1⅓ pounds in all)
- 3 tablespoons olive oil
- 1¼ teaspoons salt
- ¼ teaspoon fresh-ground black pepper
- 1½ pounds zucchini (about 4), grated
- 3 cloves garlic, minced
- 1 tablespoon chopped fresh thyme, or 1 teaspoon dried
- ½ cup ricotta cheese
- ½ cup sun-dried tomatoes packed in oil, drained and chopped
- ¾ pound fettuccine
- ¼ cup grated Parmesan cheese

1. Heat a grill pan over moderate heat. Coat the chicken with 1 tablespoon of the oil and season with ¼ teaspoon of the salt and ⅛ teaspoon of the pepper. Cook the chicken for 5 minutes. Turn and cook until browned and just done, about 4 minutes longer. Remove. Cut the chicken crosswise into ¼-inch slices. Alternatively, heat 1 tablespoon of the oil in a large, heavy frying pan. Season, cook, and slice the chicken in the same way.

2. In a large frying pan, heat the remaining 2 tablespoons oil over moderately high heat. Add the zucchini, garlic, the remaining 1 teaspoon salt, and the thyme, and cook, stirring, until tender, about 5 minutes. Add the ricotta, sun-dried tomatoes, and the remaining ⅛ teaspoon pepper.

3. In a large pot of boiling, salted water, cook the fettuccine until just done, about 12 minutes. Drain. Toss the pasta with the zucchini sauce and the chicken with any accumulated juices. Top with the Parmesan.

PASTA WITH BROCCOLI RABE, ITALIAN SAUSAGE, AND OLIVES

Increasingly popular and available, broccoli rabe stars in this dish. It's blanched to make it less bitter and then tossed with spaghettini, mild Italian sausage, and black olives.

WINE RECOMMENDATION

The leafy broccoli rabe is ideal with a grassy, acidic sauvignon blanc. If you can find one, try a bottle from Alto Adige, a region of northern Italy.

SERVES 4

- 6 tablespoons olive oil
- 4 mild Italian sausages (about ¾ pound)
- ½ pound broccoli rabe, tough stems removed
- ¾ pound spaghettini
- 4 cloves garlic, minced
- ⅓ cup black olives, such as Niçoise or Kalamata, halved and pitted
- ½ teaspoon salt
- ¼ cup dry white wine
- ¼ cup chopped fresh basil (optional)
- 2 tablespoons chopped flat-leaf parsley
- ¼ teaspoon fresh-ground black pepper
- ½ cup grated Parmesan cheese

1. In a medium frying pan, heat 1 tablespoon of the oil over moderate heat. Add the sausages and cook, turning, until browned and cooked through, about 8 minutes. When cool enough to handle, cut the sausages into ¼-inch slices.

2. In a large pot of boiling, salted water, cook the broccoli rabe for 1 minute. Remove with tongs and keep the pot of water. Rinse the broccoli rabe with cold water and drain thoroughly. Cut into 2-inch pieces.

3. Bring the water back to a boil, add the spaghettini to the pot, and cook until just done, about 9 minutes.

4. Meanwhile, in a large frying pan, heat the remaining 5 tablespoons oil over moderate heat. Add the garlic, broccoli rabe, olives, and salt, and cook, stirring frequently, for 4 minutes. Add the sausages and wine and cook, stirring, for 1 minute longer. Stir in the basil, parsley, and pepper. Drain the pasta and toss with the sauce. Top with the Parmesan and serve.

MOZZARELLA VARIATION

Omit the sausage. Add ½ pound fresh mozzarella, cut into ¼-inch cubes, along with the parsley. The heat of the pasta will soften the cheese.

FETTUCCINE WITH PEAS AND BACON

Don't hesitate to use frozen peas here. Unless you have your own pea patch, they're almost always the better choice over fresh. You don't even need to defrost the peas before adding them to the marjoram-scented cream sauce.

WINE RECOMMENDATION
Sauvignon blanc goes very well with the flavor of peas and also has enough body and acidity to accompany the cream sauce here. Try a bottle from California or Washington State.

SERVES 4

- ½ pound bacon, cut crosswise into thin slices
- 1 tablespoon butter
- 1 small onion, minced
- 1 teaspoon chopped fresh marjoram, or ½ teaspoon dried
- 1 cup heavy cream
- 1½ cups frozen peas
- 1¼ teaspoons salt
- ⅛ teaspoon fresh-ground black pepper
- 2 teaspoons lemon juice
- 1 pound fettuccine
- ½ cup grated Parmesan cheese, plus more for serving

1. In a large frying pan, cook the bacon until crisp. Drain on paper towels. Pour the fat from the pan.

2. Melt the butter in the pan over moderately low heat. Add the onion and the dried marjoram, if using. Cook, stirring occasionally, until the onion is translucent, about 5 minutes. Add the fresh marjoram, if using, and cook 1 minute longer. Stir in the cream, peas, salt, and pepper. Bring to a simmer, add the lemon juice, and remove from the heat.

3. In a large pot of boiling, salted water, cook the fettuccine until just done, about 12 minutes. Reserve about ½ cup of the pasta water. Drain the pasta. Toss with the sauce, bacon, Parmesan, and 2 tablespoons of the pasta water. If the sauce seems too thick, stir in a few more tablespoons water. Serve with additional Parmesan.

VARIATIONS

- **Pancetta:** Omit the bacon and cut ¼ pound sliced pancetta into thin strips. Cook the pancetta in 1 tablespoon butter until browned, about 3 minutes. Remove. Finish the pasta as directed.

- **Prosciutto:** Omit the bacon and cut ¼ pound thin-sliced prosciutto into thin strips. Add to the pasta when tossing.

LINGUINE WITH PANCETTA, CABBAGE, AND CARAMELIZED ONIONS

When onions cook slowly until they become soft and golden brown, their sugar caramelizes. They're sweet and especially delicious when combined with salty pancetta and earthy cabbage.

WINE RECOMMENDATION

The cabbage is the ingredient to match here. An excellent choice would be an acidic sauvignon blanc with lots of character from either the Loire Valley in France (such as a Sancerre) or from California.

SERVES 4

  3 tablespoons butter

  6 ounces pancetta or bacon, chopped

  2 onions, cut into thin slices

  2 teaspoons dried thyme

1¼ teaspoons salt

  ¾ cup dry white wine

1¼ pounds Savoy or green cabbage (about ⅓ head), shredded (about 5 cups)

  ¼ teaspoon fresh-ground black pepper

  ¾ pound linguine

  ½ cup grated Parmesan cheese, plus more for serving

  2 tablespoons chopped flat-leaf parsley (optional)

1. In a large frying pan, melt 1 tablespoon of the butter over moderate heat. Add the pancetta and cook until it is golden and most of the fat has rendered. Remove the pancetta with a slotted spoon. If using bacon, omit the 1 tablespoon butter. Cook the bacon until crisp and pour off all but 1 tablespoon of the fat.

2. Melt the remaining 2 tablespoons butter in the pan and add the onions, thyme, and salt. Cover the pan and cook over moderately low heat, stirring occasionally, until the onions are soft, about 8 minutes. Uncover the pan, raise the heat to moderate, and cook, stirring, until golden, about 5 minutes longer.

3. Add the wine and cabbage. Cover the pan and cook until the cabbage is wilted, about 5 minutes. Uncover and cook until golden, about 5 minutes longer. Add the pepper.

4. In a large pot of boiling, salted water, cook the linguine until just done, about 12 minutes. Reserve ¾ cup of the pasta water. Drain the pasta. Stir the reserved water into the cabbage mixture. Add the pasta, the pancetta or bacon, and the Parmesan, and toss. Top with the parsley. Serve with additional Parmesan.

BOW TIES WITH SALAMI AND ARTICHOKE HEARTS

Ingredients traditionally served as antipasto are sautéed with garlic and tossed with bow-tie pasta for a satisfying meal.

WINE RECOMMENDATION
This light-hearted pasta dish deserves a similar wine. Try a fruity red Beaujolais-Villages from France and serve the wine slightly chilled.

SERVES 4

¾   pound bow ties

¼   cup olive oil

¾   pound sliced hard salami or *soppressata*, cut into ¼-inch strips about 1½ inches long

6   cloves garlic, minced

1¼   pounds tomatoes (about 3), seeded and chopped, or 3 cups canned tomatoes, drained and chopped

1½   cups drained marinated artichoke hearts, cut in half lengthwise

⅓   cup black olives, such as Niçoise or Kalamata, halved and pitted

¼   teaspoon fresh-ground black pepper

⅓   cup chopped flat-leaf parsley

1. In a large pot of boiling, salted water, cook the bow ties until just done, about 15 minutes.

2. Meanwhile, in a large frying pan, heat the oil over moderately high heat. Add the salami and cook for 2 to 3 minutes.

Add the garlic and cook until softened, about 1 minute. Add the tomatoes and cook 1 minute longer for fresh and 2 minutes for canned. Stir in the artichoke hearts, olives, and pepper, and cook until heated through.

3. Drain the pasta. Toss with the sauce and parsley.

VEGETARIAN VARIATIONS

You can simply omit the salami. If you like, cut ½ pound salted fresh mozzarella into ½-inch cubes. Add the cheese to the pasta when tossing.

Spaghettini with Asparagus and Walnut Brown Butter

The already nutty flavor of brown butter is enhanced by the addition of walnuts. The combination is tossed with asparagus and spaghettini and topped with grated Parmesan for a deliciously simple main course.

WINE RECOMMENDATION
Asparagus dishes do best with white wines that have plenty of acidity and character. Try a dry chenin blanc from France's Loire Valley.

SERVES 4

1½ pounds asparagus

1 pound spaghettini

¼ pound butter, cut into pieces

⅔ cup walnuts, chopped

2 teaspoons salt

4 cloves garlic, minced

¼ teaspoon fresh-ground black pepper

Grated Parmesan cheese, for serving

1. Snap off the ends of the asparagus. Cut the asparagus stems into ½-inch pieces, leaving the tips intact.

2. In a large pot of boiling, salted water, cook the spaghettini until almost done, about 5 minutes. Add the asparagus and cook until both are done, about 4 minutes longer. Drain.

3. Meanwhile, in a small frying pan, melt the butter over low heat. Cook, stirring, for 2 minutes. Add the walnuts and salt and cook, stirring, until the butter is golden brown, about 3 minutes longer. Add the garlic and cook for 20 seconds. Stir in the pepper. Toss with the pasta and asparagus and serve with Parmesan.

> ### Test-Kitchen Tip
>
> Toss the pasta with the other ingredients right in the original pasta-cooking pot. The pasta will stay hot, and you'll avoid dirtying a bowl.

FETTUCCINE WITH WILD-MUSHROOM SAUCE

We call for a variety of fresh mushrooms in this recipe, but don't go out of your way if they're not all available in your market. Simply use whichever one or two types you can find.

WINE RECOMMENDATION
This earthy dish is delightful with a rustic, hearty red wine from the South of Italy. Try a Salice Salentino.

SERVES 4

- ½ ounce dried porcini, or other dried mushrooms
- 1 cup boiling water
- 1 pound mixed wild mushrooms, such as shiitake, portobello, and cremini
- 2 tablespoons olive oil
- ½ pound white mushrooms, sliced
- 1 tablespoon chopped fresh rosemary, or 1 teaspoon dried, crumbled
- 1 onion, chopped
- 4 cloves garlic, minced
- 1 cup red wine
- 1¾ teaspoons salt
- ⅛ teaspoon fresh-ground black pepper
- 1 pound fettuccine
- 1 tablespoon butter
- ¾ cup grated Parmesan cheese, plus more for serving
- 3 tablespoons chopped flat-leaf parsley

1. Put the dried mushrooms in a small bowl and pour the boiling water over them. Soak until softened, about 20 minutes. Remove the mushrooms, reserving the soaking liquid, and chop them. If the liquid is gritty, strain it through a paper-towel-lined sieve.

2. If using shiitakes or portobellos, remove the stems. Slice the wild mushrooms. In a large frying pan, heat 1 tablespoon of the oil over moderate heat. Add the sliced wild and white mushrooms and the rosemary. Cook, stirring occasionally, until all of the liquid has evaporated, about 5 minutes.

3. Stir in the remaining 1 tablespoon oil and the onion. Cook, stirring occasionally, until the onion and mushrooms are brown, about 3 minutes longer. Add the garlic and cook 1 minute longer. Stir in the wine, the dried mushrooms with the soaking liquid, and the salt. Simmer until the sauce is slightly thickened, about 5 minutes. Stir in the pepper.

4. Meanwhile, in a large pot of boiling, salted water, cook the fettuccine until just done, about 12 minutes. Drain. Toss with the mushroom sauce, butter, Parmesan, and parsley. Serve with additional Parmesan.

BAKED PENNE WITH EGGPLANT, RED PEPPER, AND THREE CHEESES

Similar to a vegetarian lasagne, this hearty dish takes a fraction of the time to prepare. Since the eggplant is broiled instead of fried, it's less oily than usual.

WINE RECOMMENDATION With its full, mellow flavors, this pasta will benefit from a vibrantly fruity red wine, such as a Chianti Classico from Italy.

SERVES 4

- 1 small eggplant (about ¾ pound), peeled and cut lengthwise into ¼-inch slices
- 3 tablespoons olive oil
- Salt and fresh-ground black pepper
- 1 onion, chopped
- 1 red bell pepper, cut into 1-inch pieces
- 2 cloves garlic, minced
- 1¾ cups canned crushed tomatoes in thick puree
- ¾ cup heavy cream
- 1 tablespoon chopped fresh rosemary, or 1 teaspoon dried, crumbled
- ½ pound penne
- 1 cup ricotta cheese
- ⅓ cup grated Parmesan cheese
- 1½ tablespoons chopped flat-leaf parsley
- 6 ounces Fontina cheese, grated (about 1½ cups)

1. Heat the broiler. Brush both sides of the eggplant slices with 1½ tablespoons of the oil and season with ½ teaspoon salt and ¼ teaspoon pepper. Put the eggplant slices on a large baking sheet and broil, 6 inches from the heat if possible, until browned, about 5 minutes. Turn and broil the eggplant until browned on the other side, about 5 minutes longer. When it is cool enough to handle, cut the eggplant into 1-inch slices.

2. Heat the oven to 450°. In a large frying pan, heat ½ tablespoon of the oil over moderately low heat. Add the onion and cook, stirring occasionally, until translucent, about 5 minutes. Raise the heat to moderate. Add the bell pepper and ¼ teaspoon salt and cook, stirring occasionally, until the onion and bell pepper are golden brown, about 5 minutes. Stir in the garlic. Add the crushed tomatoes, cream, rosemary, and ½ teaspoon salt, and bring to a simmer, stirring occasionally. Stir in ¼ teaspoon pepper.

3. Meanwhile, in a large pot of boiling, salted water, cook the penne until partially done, about 4 minutes. Drain.

4. In a small bowl, combine the ricotta, 1½ tablespoons of the Parmesan, the parsley, and a pinch each of salt and pepper.

5. Oil a 9-by-13-inch baking dish. Toss the pasta with the sauce, 2½ tablespoons of

the Parmesan, and half of the Fontina. Put the pasta in the prepared pan and spread in an even layer. Spoon a dollop of the ricotta mixture onto each quarter.

6. Sprinkle with the remaining Fontina and Parmesan. Drizzle with the remaining 1 tablespoon oil. Bake until golden brown, about 20 minutes.

TEST-KITCHEN TIP

In this recipe, we call for "crushed tomatoes in puree." Depending on the brand, this mix of crushed tomatoes and tomato puree may also be described as crushed tomatoes with puree, with added puree, in tomato puree, thick style, and in thick puree. You can use any of these here. What's important is that the can indicates that the crushed tomatoes are either thick or contain puree. Cans labeled simply "crushed tomatoes" aren't thick enough for this recipe.

PENNE WITH EGGPLANT, FENNEL, SMOKED MOZZARELLA, AND BASIL

Eggplant and fennel, roasted to a golden brown, give depth of flavor. The heat of the pasta softens the cheese, so that the smoky flavor spreads throughout the dish.

WINE RECOMMENDATION
Everything about this pasta—from the vinegar to the assertive flavors of the fennel and basil—makes it ideal with an aggressive, slightly acidic sauvignon blanc from California.

SERVES 4

- 1 eggplant (about 1¼ pounds), cut into 1-inch cubes
- 1 large fennel bulb, cut into 1-inch pieces
- 3 tablespoons olive oil
- 1 teaspoon salt
- 4 cloves garlic, minced
- 1 tablespoon balsamic vinegar (optional)
- ¾ pound penne
- ¾ pound smoked mozzarella cheese, cut into ¼-inch cubes, at room temperature
- ¼ cup fresh basil, chopped
- ¼ teaspoon fresh-ground black pepper
- ¼ cup grated Parmesan cheese

1. Heat the oven to 450°. In a large roasting pan, combine the eggplant, fennel, oil, and ½ teaspoon of the salt. Bake, stirring twice, until the vegetables are browned and tender, about 45 minutes. Stir in the garlic and the vinegar, if using, and bake for 2 more minutes.

2. Meanwhile, in a large pot of boiling, salted water, cook the penne until just done, about 13 minutes. Drain.

3. Toss the pasta with the vegetables, mozzarella, basil, the remaining ½ teaspoon salt, and the pepper. Avoid stirring too much or the mozzarella will become stringy. Serve topped with the Parmesan.

FETTUCCINE WITH GOAT CHEESE, GREEN BEANS, AND TOASTED WALNUTS

Earthy toasted walnuts and tangy goat cheese are an ideal marriage. Here the combination is made into a creamy sauce with the simple addition of some of the pasta-cooking water. What could be easier?

WINE RECOMMENDATION

Goat cheese finds an ideal accompaniment in the grassy, acidic wines made from sauvignon blanc. Look for one from the Veneto region of Italy.

SERVES 4

1	tablespoon butter
⅔	cup walnuts, chopped
3	cloves garlic, minced
1	pound fettuccine
¾	pound green beans, cut into 1-inch pieces
5	ounces mild goat cheese, such as Montrachet, cut into pieces
2	scallions including green tops, chopped
2	tablespoons chopped flat-leaf parsley
1¾	teaspoons salt
¼	teaspoon fresh-ground black pepper

1. In a small frying pan, melt the butter over moderately low heat. Add the walnuts and cook for 2 to 3 minutes. Add the garlic. Cook until softened, 1 to 2 minutes longer.

2. In a large pot of boiling, salted water, cook the fettuccine until just done, about 12 minutes. Add the green beans about 5 minutes before the pasta is done.

3. Reserve 1½ cups of the pasta water and drain the pasta. Put the goat cheese and 1 cup of the water in the pasta pot. Heat, stirring, until the cheese is melted and smooth. Stir in the walnut mixture, scallions, parsley, salt, and pepper. Add the pasta and green beans and toss. If the sauce seems too thick, add more pasta water.

RICOTTA VARIATION

We love the tangy, earthy flavor of goat cheese, but some people find the taste a bit strong. If you count yourself among them, soften the flavor by using only 3 ounces of goat cheese and replacing the rest with ½ cup of ricotta.

Pizza Margherita

Fresh tomatoes and basil make this the ultimate summertime pizza. It's surprisingly quick to put together.

WINE RECOMMENDATION
This simple pizza is perfectly matched by a light, straightforward Italian white, such as a pinot grigio or Soave, both from the Veneto region in northeastern Italy.

MAKES ONE 12-INCH PIZZA

10 ounces store-bought pizza dough*

1½ pounds tomatoes (about 3), cut into ⅛-inch slices and seeded

½ cup lightly packed basil leaves, chopped

¾ teaspoon salt

½ teaspoon fresh-ground black pepper

6 ounces unsalted fresh mozzarella cheese, cut into ¼-inch cubes

6 tablespoons grated Parmesan cheese

2 tablespoons olive oil

*Available at supermarkets

1. Heat the oven to 425°. Oil a 12-inch pizza pan or a large baking sheet. Press the pizza dough to an approximately 12-inch round on the prepared pan. Bake until the dough begins to brown, about 10 minutes.

2. Drain the tomato slices between sheets of paper towel.

3. In a large bowl, combine the tomato, basil, salt, and pepper. Arrange the tomatoes, overlapping slightly, on the partially baked crust. Scatter the mozzarella over the tomatoes. Sprinkle with the Parmesan and drizzle with the oil.

4. Bake until the cheese is bubbling and beginning to brown, 8 to 10 minutes.

Variations

Try these individually or together.

■ **Black Olive:** Top the pizza with ½ cup pitted black olives, such as Niçoise or Kalamata, before adding the oil.

■ **Anchovy:** Drain a 2-ounce tin of anchovy fillets and arrange them on the pizza before drizzling with the oil.

Test-Kitchen Tip

To avoid a soggy pizza crust, we recommend seeding the tomatoes. The fastest way to get thin, seeded slices is to slice the tomatoes first with a serrated knife (a bread knife is perfect). Stack about four slices together and poke your fingers through them to release the seeds.

CARAMELIZED-ONION PIZZA WITH ROQUEFORT AND WALNUTS

Onions, cooked until deep brown and soft, are the perfect foil for salty Roquefort and crunchy walnuts on this delectable pizza.

WINE RECOMMENDATION With its cheese and nuts, this pizza's quite rich. It will be best with a slightly chilled bottle of fruity Beaujolais-Villages or California gamay.

MAKES ONE 12-INCH PIZZA

 5 tablespoons olive oil

 4 tablespoons butter

 4 large onions (about 4 pounds in all), cut into thin slices

 2 teaspoons salt

 1 teaspoon sugar

 ½ teaspoon fresh-ground black pepper

 10 ounces store-bought pizza dough*

 ⅔ cup walnuts, chopped

 3 ounces Roquefort or other blue cheese, crumbled (about ¾ cup)

   *Available at supermarkets

1. In a large, heavy pot, heat 4 tablespoons of the oil with the butter over moderately high heat. Add the onions and salt and cook, stirring occasionally, until beginning to brown, about 20 minutes. Add the sugar and cook, stirring frequently, until well browned, about 15 minutes longer. Stir in the pepper.

2. Meanwhile, heat the oven to 425°. Oil a 12-inch pizza pan or a large baking sheet. Press the pizza dough to an approximately 12-inch round on the prepared pan. Bake until the dough begins to brown, about 10 minutes.

3. Spread the onions on the partially baked pizza crust and top with the walnuts and cheese. Drizzle with the remaining 1 tablespoon oil. Bake until the cheese is beginning to brown, 8 to 10 minutes longer.

VARIATIONS

■ Use pine nuts or pecans in place of the walnuts.

■ Add 2 teaspoons dried rosemary, crumbled, or herbes de Provence to the onions with the salt.

WHITE CLAM PIZZA

A specialty in New Haven, Connecticut, this delicious pizza is bursting with the flavor of fresh clams, garlic, mozzarella, and fresh herbs. While shucked littlenecks make this pizza sublime, the more reasonably priced fresh, chopped clams are excellent, too.

WINE RECOMMENDATION
A simple, refreshing white wine is a perfect partner for this dish. Try a pinot grigio from the Alto Adige region of Italy.

MAKES ONE 12-INCH PIZZA

- 10 ounces store-bought pizza dough*
- 1 pound chopped clams, drained well (about 2 cups), or 4 dozen littlenecks, shucked and drained well (about 2 cups)
- ½ cup mixed, chopped fresh herbs, such as basil, thyme, and parsley
- 2 cloves garlic, minced
- ¼ teaspoon fresh-ground black pepper
- 6 ounces mozzarella cheese, preferably low-moisture, grated (about 1½ cups)
- 3 tablespoons grated Parmesan cheese
- 2 tablespoons olive oil

*Available at supermarkets

1. Heat the oven to 425°. Oil a 12-inch pizza pan or a large baking sheet. Press the pizza dough to an approximately 12-inch round on the prepared baking pan. Bake until the dough begins to brown, about 10 minutes.

2. Meanwhile, line a strainer with several paper towels. Put the drained clams in the strainer and press gently to remove excess moisture. Transfer the clams to a bowl. Stir in the herbs, garlic, and pepper.

3. Spread the clam mixture on the partially baked pizza crust and top with the mozzarella. Sprinkle with the Parmesan and drizzle with the oil.

4. Bake until the cheese is bubbling and beginning to brown, 8 to 10 minutes longer. Do not overcook or the clams will toughen.

TEST-KITCHEN TIP

While Pizza Margherita, page 109, is best with fresh mozzarella, here we prefer packaged. Because fresh mozzarella and clams both contain a lot of moisture, the combination can leave you with a soggy crust. For best results, look for low-moisture mozzarella.

CHICKEN, MUSHROOM, AND GRUYERE CALZONI

Most supermarkets now sell ready-made pizza dough—a real boon that puts designer calzoni squarely among the dishes quick enough for a weeknight dinner. Many pizza places sell dough, too. It's worth asking.

WINE RECOMMENDATION
This is perfect food to eat with a simple Italian red wine, such as a Dolcetto from the Piedmont region or the more moderately priced Valpolicella from the Veneto.

SERVES 4

2 tablespoons olive oil

2 pounds mushrooms, sliced

2 teaspoons salt

4 cloves garlic, minced

4 boneless, skinless chicken breasts (about 1⅓ pounds in all), cut crosswise into ½-inch strips

1 pound store-bought pizza dough*

½ pound Gruyère cheese, cut into thin slices

*Available at supermarkets

1. In a large frying pan, heat 1 tablespoon of the oil over moderate heat. Add the mushrooms and 1 teaspoon of the salt and cook, stirring occasionally, until all the liquid evaporates, about 5 minutes. Add the garlic and cook 1 minute longer.

2. Add the chicken and the remaining 1 teaspoon salt and cook until the chicken is almost cooked through, about 3 minutes. The chicken will finish cooking while the calzoni bake.

3. Oil a baking sheet. Cut the pizza dough into four pieces. On a floured surface, roll one of the pieces into an 8-inch round. Put a quarter of the filling on one half of the dough, leaving a ¾-inch border. Top the filling with a quarter of the cheese. Brush the border with water. Fold the dough over the filling and seal the edges by folding the bottom edge of dough over the top and pinching the layers together. Transfer to the prepared baking sheet and repeat with the remaining filling, cheese, and dough.

4. Brush the calzoni with the remaining 1 tablespoon oil. Bake until golden, 15 to 20 minutes.

SAUSAGE AND PEPPER CALZONI

Whether tossed with pasta, served on pizza, or baked into calzoni, Italian sausage and bell peppers are a dependable match. We suggest half hot and half mild sausage, but use all of one or the other if you prefer.

WINE RECOMMENDATION
Try these meaty calzoni with a sauvignon blanc from the Alto Adige region of Italy or from California.

SERVES 4

- 1 fresh red bell pepper, or 1 bottled roasted red pepper
- 2 tablespoons olive oil
- 2 onions, cut into thin slices
- 2 hot Italian sausages (about 6 ounces), casing removed
- 2 mild Italian sausages (about 6 ounces), casing removed
- 4 cloves garlic, minced
- 1 teaspoon dried thyme
- 1 teaspoon salt
- ⅔ cup black olives, such as Niçoise or Kalamata, pitted and chopped
- 3 tablespoons chopped flat-leaf parsley (optional)
- 1 pound store-bought pizza dough*
- 6 ounces packaged mozzarella cheese, cut into thin slices

*Available at supermarkets

1. If using a fresh bell pepper, roast it over an open flame or broil, turning with tongs, until charred all over, about 10 minutes. When the pepper is cool enough to handle, pull off the skin. Remove the stem, seeds, and ribs. Cut into thin slices. If using a bottled roasted pepper, cut into thin slices.

2. Heat the oven to 450°. In a large frying pan, heat 1 tablespoon of the oil over moderate heat. Add the onions and cook, stirring occasionally, until golden, about 5 minutes. Add the sausage, garlic, thyme, and salt, and cook, breaking up the sausage meat with a fork, until no longer pink, about 3 minutes. Add the roasted pepper, olives, and parsley. Let cool slightly.

3. Oil a baking sheet. Cut the pizza dough into four pieces. On a floured surface, roll one of the pieces into an 8-inch round. Put a quarter of the filling on one half of the dough, leaving a ¾-inch border. Top the filling with a quarter of the cheese. Brush the border with water. Fold the dough over the filling and seal the edges by folding the bottom edge of dough over the top and pinching the layers together. Transfer to the prepared baking sheet and repeat with the remaining filling, cheese, and dough.

4. Brush the calzoni with the remaining 1 tablespoon oil. Bake until golden, 15 to 20 minutes.

RISOTTO, POLENTA & OTHER WAYS WITH GRAINS

Broiled Salmon on Couscous-and-Vegetable Salad, page 125

JUST AS PASTA BEGAN AS A FIRST COURSE in Italy and wound up a main dish here, risotto and polenta are being transformed from an appetizer and a side dish, respectively, into whole meals. Our contributions to this evolution, along with recipes for other rice dishes, grits, and couscous, make up this chapter. Couscous is a bit of an oddity, a pasta that is treated as a grain. However you categorize it, delightful flavor and texture make it a comer—and it cooks in five minutes.

SOFT POLENTA WITH MEAT RAGU

Creamy, Parmesan-flavored polenta sets off a hearty meat and tomato sauce. This is comfort food par excellence.

WINE RECOMMENDATION
A Chianti Classico would be an ideal wine match for this rustic Italian-influenced dish. Experiment with other, lesser-known Italian red wines, such as Salice Salentino.

SERVES 4

- 1 tablespoon olive oil
- 1 onion, chopped
- 1 carrot, chopped
- 3 cloves garlic, minced
- 1 teaspoon dried thyme
- ¾ teaspoon dried rosemary, crumbled
- ¾ pound ground beef
- 2 mild Italian sausages (about 6 ounces in all), casing removed
- 1½ cups canned crushed tomatoes
- ¾ cup red wine
- 8¼ cups water
- 1 tablespoon tomato paste
- 2¼ teaspoons salt
- 4 tablespoons chopped flat-leaf parsley
- ¼ teaspoon fresh-ground black pepper
- 2 cups coarse or medium cornmeal
- 5 tablespoons grated Parmesan cheese, plus more for serving

1. In a deep frying pan, heat the oil over moderately low heat. Add the onion, carrot, garlic, thyme, and rosemary. Cover and cook, stirring occasionally, until the vegetables are soft, about 5 minutes. Add the beef and sausages and cook, breaking up the meat with a fork, until no longer pink, about 3 minutes.

2. Stir in the tomatoes, wine, ¾ cup of the water, the tomato paste, and 1¼ teaspoons of the salt. Cover and simmer for 10 minutes. Uncover and simmer for 15 to 20 minutes longer. Stir in 3 tablespoons of the parsley and the pepper.

3. Meanwhile, in a large saucepan, bring the remaining 7½ cups water to a boil with the remaining 1 teaspoon salt. Add the cornmeal in a slow stream, whisking constantly. Reduce the heat and simmer, stirring frequently with a wooden spoon, until the polenta is very thick, about 20 minutes. Stir in 4 tablespoons of the Parmesan.

4. Serve the polenta topped with the meat ragù. Sprinkle with the remaining 1 tablespoon each of parsley and Parmesan. Pass additional Parmesan.

POLENTA WITH GRILLED VEGETABLES AND TWO CHEESES

Smoked mozzarella and Parmesan flavor this creamy polenta. Topped with grilled eggplant, zucchini, and red peppers, the dish makes a hearty vegetarian meal.

WINE RECOMMENDATION
A simple Italian white wine will be just fine with the mozzarella and vegetables here. Try a pinot grigio from the Alto Adige region or elsewhere in the North.

SERVES 4

- 1 small eggplant (about 1 pound), cut into ¼-inch rounds
- 2 small zucchini, cut lengthwise into ¼-inch slices
- 1 red bell pepper, cut into quarters
- ½ pound large shiitake mushrooms, stems removed
- ¼ cup olive oil
- 1½ teaspoons chopped fresh thyme, or ½ teaspoon dried
- 2 teaspoons salt
- ¼ teaspoon fresh-ground black pepper
- 1½ teaspoons balsamic vinegar (optional)
- 3¾ cups water
- 1 cup coarse or medium cornmeal
- 2 tablespoons butter
- ¼ pound smoked mozzarella, grated (about 1 cup)
- 6 tablespoons grated Parmesan cheese

1. Light the grill or heat the broiler. In a large bowl, toss the eggplant, zucchini, bell pepper, mushroom caps, oil, thyme, 1 teaspoon of the salt, and the black pepper. If using the broiler, arrange the vegetables in a single layer on two baking sheets, and cook in batches. Grill or broil the vegetables, turning once, until lightly browned and tender, 10 to 12 minutes. Cut the eggplant into 1½-inch strips and the bell pepper into 2-inch pieces. Toss all the vegetables with the vinegar.

2. Heat the oven to 400°. Oil a 7-by-11-inch baking dish. In a medium saucepan, bring the water and the remaining 1 teaspoon salt to a boil. Add the cornmeal in a slow stream, whisking constantly. Reduce the heat and simmer, stirring frequently with a wooden spoon, until the polenta is very thick, about 20 minutes. Stir in the butter, mozzarella, and 4 tablespoons of the Parmesan. Spread the polenta in the prepared dish.

3. Top the polenta with the vegetables and sprinkle with the remaining 2 tablespoons Parmesan. Bake until hot, 5 to 10 minutes.

SHRIMP AND CHEESE GRITS

Grits are not just breakfast food. Here they're topped with a shrimp sauté accented by bell pepper, tomatoes, and onions. Crisp bacon and chopped scallions top this appealing combination.

WINE RECOMMENDATION
Creamy grits, rich shrimp, and cheese—this is a dish for as ripe and weighty a chardonnay as you can find. Try one from either California or Australia.

SERVES 4

- 3 strips bacon, cut crosswise into ¼-inch slices
- 2 onions, chopped
- 1 green bell pepper, chopped
- 1 teaspoon dried oregano
- 2¼ teaspoons salt
- 1½ cups canned tomatoes, drained and chopped
- 1 tablespoon tomato paste
- ½ cup dry white wine
- 1½ pounds medium shrimp, shelled
- 5½ cups water
- ¼ cup heavy cream
- ⅛ teaspoon Tabasco sauce, more to taste
- 1¼ cups old-fashioned grits
- 6 ounces Gruyère cheese, grated (about 1½ cups)
- 2 scallions including green tops, chopped

1. In a large frying pan, cook the bacon until crisp. Remove with a slotted spoon and drain on paper towels. Add the onions, bell pepper, oregano, and 1½ teaspoons of the salt to the pan. Cover and cook over moderate heat, stirring occasionally, until soft, about 5 minutes. Uncover and cook until golden, about 5 minutes longer.

2. Add the tomatoes and tomato paste and cook, stirring, until dry, about 4 minutes. Stir in the wine and cook until almost evaporated. Add the shrimp and cook, stirring, until just done, 1 to 2 minutes. Stir in ½ cup of the water, the cream, and the Tabasco. Remove from the heat.

3. In a medium saucepan, bring the remaining 5 cups water and ¾ teaspoon salt to a boil. Add the grits in a slow stream, whisking constantly. Reduce the heat, cover, and simmer, stirring frequently with a wooden spoon, until the grits are very thick, about 20 minutes. Stir the cheese into the grits.

4. Bring the shrimp mixture back to a simmer. Spoon the grits onto plates and top with the shrimp. Sprinkle with the bacon and scallions.

CHICKEN THIGHS WITH MUSTARD SAUCE AND COUSCOUS

A simple sauté with a piquant deglazing sauce proves a perfect partner to couscous cooked with spinach and chicken stock.

WINE RECOMMENDATION The tang of the mustard sauce works wonderfully with the grassy flavors and high acidity of a sauvignon blanc, such as a Sancerre from France or a California bottling of the varietal.

SERVES 4

- 1 tablespoon cooking oil
- 8 boneless chicken thighs
- 1 teaspoon salt
- ¼ teaspoon fresh-ground black pepper
- 2¼ cups Chicken Stock, page 303, or canned low-sodium chicken broth
- 1⅓ cups couscous
- ½ pound spinach, stems removed, leaves washed and cut into thin slices (about 5 cups)
- 2 cloves garlic, minced
- 1 teaspoon Dijon mustard

1. In a large, deep frying pan, heat the oil over moderately high heat. Sprinkle the chicken with ¼ teaspoon of the salt and ⅛ teaspoon of the pepper. Add half the chicken to the pan, skin-side down. Cook until brown, 5 to 7 minutes. Turn the chicken and continue cooking until brown and cooked through, about 7 minutes longer. Remove and put in a warm spot. Repeat with the remaining chicken. Pour off all but 1 tablespoon of the fat and set the pan aside.

2. In a large saucepan, bring 2 cups of the stock and the remaining ¾ teaspoon salt and ⅛ teaspoon pepper to a boil. Remove from the heat. Add the couscous and spinach. Cover. Let stand for 5 minutes. Fluff with a fork.

3. Heat the frying pan over low heat. Add the garlic and cook, stirring, until softened, about 1 minute. Add the remaining ¼ cup stock and bring to a simmer, scraping the bottom of the pan to dislodge any brown bits. Stir in the mustard. Return the chicken to the pan with any accumulated juices. Cook, turning the chicken to coat with the sauce, until heated through, about 1 minute. Mound the couscous on plates and top with the chicken and sauce.

MUSTARD-GREEN VARIATION

If mustard greens are in season, use them instead of spinach. In that case, use slightly less, about ⅓ pound, and add the greens to the stock before you bring it to a boil.

One-Pot Chicken Couscous with Bell Peppers and Chickpeas

Couscous is traditionally steamed and served with a brothy North African stew of fish, chicken, meat, or vegetables. In this one-dish recipe, the couscous cooks right in the stew.

WINE RECOMMENDATION

Look for a refreshing white wine from Provence or the Coteaux du Languedoc region in southern France to pair with the Mediterranean flavors of this dish.

SERVES 4

- 1 tablespoon butter
- 1 tablespoon cooking oil
- 1 chicken (3 to 3½ pounds), cut into 8 pieces
- 1½ teaspoons salt
- ½ teaspoon fresh-ground black pepper
- 2 onions, sliced
- 3 bell peppers, red, yellow, green, or a combination, cut into thin slices
- 6 cloves garlic, minced
- ½ teaspoon ground coriander
- ½ teaspoon ground ginger
- 1 cup water
- ¼ cup chopped fresh parsley
- 1 15-ounce can chickpeas, drained and rinsed (about 1⅔ cups)
- 1 cup couscous

1. Heat the oven to 400°. In a large ovenproof pot, melt the butter with the oil over moderately high heat. Sprinkle the chicken with ½ teaspoon of the salt and ¼ teaspoon of the black pepper. Add half the chicken to the pot and brown well on both sides, about 8 minutes in all. Remove. Brown the remaining chicken and remove.

2. Pour off all but 1 tablespoon of the fat. Reduce the heat to moderate. Add the onions, bell peppers, and the remaining 1 teaspoon salt and cook, stirring occasionally, until the vegetables are golden, about 10 minutes. Stir in the garlic, coriander, and ginger, and cook 1 minute longer. Stir in the chicken, water, and parsley, and bring to a simmer.

3. Cover and bake for 20 minutes. Stir in the chickpeas and bake until the chicken is just done, about 10 minutes longer.

4. Remove from the oven. Stir in the couscous and the remaining ¼ teaspoon black pepper. Cover and let stand 5 minutes.

—Stephanie Lyness

LAMB STEW WITH COUSCOUS

Lamb meatballs flavored with cumin seeds, allspice, and cayenne simmer with cauliflower florets and chickpeas in a savory broth. The stew is served on a mound of fluffy couscous.

WINE RECOMMENDATION
This lightly spiced dish has a Mediterranean feel that will work well with a rosé from the Provence region of France.

SERVES 4

1½ pounds ground lamb

5 tablespoons chopped flat-leaf parsley

2 onions, chopped

2 teaspoons salt

1¼ teaspoons cumin seeds or ground cumin

Ground allspice

¼ teaspoon turmeric

Cayenne

2 tablespoons butter

3 cups water

1 cup canned crushed tomatoes

1 cup Chicken Stock, page 303, or canned low-sodium chicken broth

1 small head cauliflower (about 1½ pounds), cut into florets

1 15-ounce can chickpeas, drained and rinsed (about 1⅔ cups)

1⅓ cups couscous

1. In a medium bowl, combine the lamb, 3 tablespoons of the parsley, 2 tablespoons of the chopped onion, ¾ teaspoon of the salt, ¼ teaspoon of the cumin, ⅛ teaspoon allspice, the turmeric, and a pinch of cayenne. Stir together until thoroughly mixed. Shape the lamb mixture into twelve meatballs.

2. In a large pot, heat the butter over moderately low heat. Add the remaining onions and cook, stirring occasionally, until translucent, about 5 minutes. Add the remaining 1 teaspoon cumin, ¼ teaspoon allspice, ¼ teaspoon cayenne, and 1 teaspoon of the salt. Cook, stirring, for 1 minute. Add 1 cup of the water, the tomatoes, and the stock. Bring to a boil. Add the cauliflower, reduce the heat, and simmer, covered, for 10 minutes.

3. Stir in the chickpeas. Gently stir in the meatballs. Bring back to a simmer, cover, and cook until the meatballs are done, 10 to 12 minutes longer.

4. In a medium saucepan, bring the remaining 2 cups water to a boil. Add the remaining ¼ teaspoon salt and the couscous. Cover. Remove the pot from the heat and let the couscous stand for 5 minutes. Fluff with a fork. Stir the remaining 2 tablespoons parsley into the stew. Serve the stew over the couscous.

CURRIED TUNA CAKES WITH VEGETABLE COUSCOUS

Salmon cakes, crab cakes—and now tuna cakes. Couscous spiced with cumin complements the curry-scented tuna nicely. You can use other vegetables in the couscous, such as broccoli florets, carrots, or green beans.

WINE RECOMMENDATION
Gewürztraminer from France's Alsace region is a fine accompaniment to most curries, and its acidity (often not found in California versions) helps cut through the richness of the tuna.

SERVES 4

2   6-ounce cans tuna packed in oil, drained well

3½ tablespoons dry bread crumbs

¼   cup mayonnaise

½   teaspoon curry powder

Salt and fresh-ground black pepper

2   tablespoons cooking oil, plus more for frying

1   onion, chopped fine

1   red bell pepper, diced

3   zucchini (about 1¼ pounds), quartered lengthwise and cut crosswise into ½-inch slices

2½ cups Chicken Stock, page 303, or canned low-sodium chicken broth

¼   teaspoon ground cumin

1⅓ cups couscous

½   cup flour

3   scallions including green tops, chopped

1. In a medium bowl, flake the tuna. Add the bread crumbs, mayonnaise, curry powder, ⅛ teaspoon salt, and ⅛ teaspoon black pepper, and mix well. Shape into twelve oval cakes.

2. In a large frying pan, heat the 2 tablespoons oil over moderately high heat. Add the onion and bell pepper and cook, stirring occasionally, until softened, about 5 minutes. Add the zucchini, 1½ teaspoons salt, and ¼ teaspoon black pepper. Cover, reduce the heat to moderate, and cook, stirring occasionally, until the zucchini is soft, about 10 minutes.

3. Add the stock and the cumin. Bring to a boil. Stir in the couscous, cover, remove from the heat, and let sit for 5 minutes.

4. Meanwhile, in a large nonstick frying pan, heat about ¼ inch of oil over moderate heat. Dust the tuna cakes with the flour and pat off the excess. Fry the cakes until golden brown and crisp, about 2 minutes a side. Drain on paper towels.

5. Stir the scallions into the couscous and serve with the tuna cakes.

BROILED SALMON ON COUSCOUS-AND-VEGETABLE SALAD

Golden-brown salmon fillets sit atop a flavorful couscous salad flecked with zucchini, carrots, and tomatoes. Serve the salmon hot or at room temperature.

WINE RECOMMENDATION
Salmon usually works well with a full-bodied white wine, while vegetables and cilantro do best paired with an acidic white. A sauvignon blanc from New Zealand or South Africa combines both qualities.

SERVES 4

 1 cup Chicken Stock, page 303, or canned low-sodium chicken broth

2¾ teaspoons salt

 ¾ cup couscous

 3 carrots, grated

 ½ pound plum tomatoes (about 3), cut into ¼-inch dice

 1 small zucchini, grated

 ⅓ cup chopped cilantro (optional)

 3 tablespoons cooking oil

 2 tablespoons tarragon vinegar or white-wine vinegar

 ½ teaspoon fresh-ground black pepper

1½ pounds skinless salmon fillet, cut into 4 pieces

1. In a medium saucepan, bring the stock and ¾ teaspoon of the salt to a boil. Stir in the couscous. Cover, remove from the heat, and let sit 5 minutes. Transfer to a large bowl and let cool.

2. Add the carrots, tomatoes, zucchini, cilantro, 2 tablespoons of the oil, the vinegar, 1½ teaspoons of the salt, and ¼ teaspoon of the pepper to the couscous and toss. Let sit at room temperature until ready to serve.

3. Heat the broiler. Oil a broiler pan or baking sheet. Coat the salmon with the remaining 1 tablespoon oil and sprinkle with the remaining ½ teaspoon salt and ¼ teaspoon pepper. Put it on the pan. Broil until just barely done (the fish should still be translucent in the center), about 4 minutes depending on the thickness of the fillets. Mound the couscous mixture on plates and top with the salmon.

TEST-KITCHEN TIP

For easy cleanup when broiling, line the pan with aluminum foil. When you finish broiling, carefully lift up the foil. If no juices have leaked over the edges of the foil, you won't even have to rinse off the pan.

BLACK-EYED-PEA RISOTTO WITH RED WINE AND BACON

Italian risotto meets the Old South with the addition of black-eyed peas and smoky bacon.

WINE RECOMMENDATION
Look for a rustic red to pair with the earthy flavors here. Try a Côtes-du-Rhône from France or a zinfandel from California.

SERVES 4

- 5 cups Chicken Stock, page 303, or canned low-sodium chicken broth
- 5 strips bacon, cut crosswise into thin slices
- 1 onion, cut into thin slices
- 3 cloves garlic, minced
- 1½ cups arborio rice
- 1¼ cups red wine
- 1 teaspoon salt
- 1 10-ounce package frozen black-eyed peas
- ½ cup grated Parmesan cheese, plus more for serving
- 3 tablespoons minced fresh parsley
- ½ teaspoon fresh-ground black pepper

1. In a medium saucepan, bring the stock to a simmer.

2. In a large pot, cook the bacon until almost crisp. Pour off all but 2 tablespoons of the fat. Add the onion and garlic. Cook over moderate heat, stirring, for 2 minutes.

3. Add the rice to the pot. Stir until the rice begins to turn opaque, about 2 minutes. Add the wine and the salt and cook, stirring frequently, until all the wine has been absorbed. Stir in the black-eyed peas.

4. Add about ½ cup of the simmering stock to the rice and cook, stirring frequently, until the stock has been completely absorbed. The rice and stock should bubble gently; adjust the heat as needed. Continue cooking the rice, adding the stock ½ cup at a time and allowing the rice to absorb the stock before adding the next ½ cup. Cook the rice in this way until tender, 25 to 30 minutes in all. The stock that hasn't been absorbed should be thickened by the starch from the rice. You may not need to use all of the liquid, or you may need more stock or some water.

5. Stir in the Parmesan, parsley, and pepper. Serve with additional Parmesan.

RISOTTO WITH BLUE CHEESE AND WALNUTS

Mildly flavored with blue cheese and topped with toasted walnuts, this risotto is creamy and crunchy and comforting. Round out the meal with a tossed green salad.

WINE RECOMMENDATION
Try a lush, fruity merlot from California or a Rioja from Spain with the unusual flavors of this dish.

SERVES 4

½ cup walnuts, chopped

1½ quarts Chicken Stock, page 303, or canned low-sodium chicken broth

3 tablespoons olive oil

1 onion, chopped

2 cups arborio rice

⅔ cup dry white wine

1¾ teaspoons salt

¼ pound blue cheese, crumbled (about 1 cup)

1½ tablespoons butter

¼ teaspoon fresh-ground black pepper

1. In a small frying pan, toast the walnuts over moderately low heat, stirring frequently, until golden brown, about 5 minutes. Or toast them in a 350° oven for about 8 minutes.

2. In a medium saucepan, bring the stock to a simmer. In a large pot, heat the oil over moderately low heat. Add the onion and cook, stirring occasionally, until translucent, about 5 minutes.

3. Add the rice to the pot and stir until it begins to turn opaque, about 2 minutes. Add the wine and salt and cook, stirring frequently, until all the wine has been absorbed.

4. Add about ½ cup of the simmering stock to the rice and cook, stirring frequently, until the stock has been completely absorbed. The rice and stock should bubble gently; adjust the heat as needed. Continue cooking the rice, adding the stock ½ cup at a time and allowing the rice to absorb the stock before adding the next ½ cup. Cook the rice in this way until tender, 25 to 30 minutes in all. The stock that hasn't been absorbed should be thickened by the starch from the rice. You may not need to use all of the liquid, or you may need to add more stock or some water.

5. Stir in half the blue cheese, the butter, and the pepper. Mound the risotto onto plates. Top with the remaining cheese and the toasted walnuts.

SUN-DRIED-TOMATO AND THYME RISOTTO WITH LAMB CHOPS

The star here is the risotto. It's cooked with sun-dried tomatoes, which give it a lovely red-gold color and robust flavor. A small lamb chop on the side completes this delicious dish.

WINE RECOMMENDATION
A full-bodied, off-dry white wine, such as a pinot gris from the region of Alsace in France, is a good choice for this salty, meaty dish.

SERVES 4

1½   quarts Chicken Stock, page 303, or canned low-sodium chicken broth

4   tablespoons olive oil

1   onion, chopped

1   clove garlic, minced

2   cups arborio rice

⅔   cup dry white wine

2¾   teaspoons salt

8   sun-dried tomatoes, chopped fine

1   teaspoon dried thyme

4   lamb rib chops, about 1¼ inches thick

Fresh-ground black pepper

¼   cup grated Parmesan cheese, plus more for serving

2   tablespoons butter

2   tablespoons chopped flat-leaf parsley

1. In a medium saucepan, bring the stock to a simmer.

2. In a large pot, heat 3 tablespoons of the oil over moderately low heat. Add the onion and cook, stirring occasionally, until translucent, about 5 minutes. Add the garlic and rice and stir until the rice begins to turn opaque, about 2 minutes.

3. Add the wine and 2½ teaspoons of the salt to the rice and cook, stirring frequently, until all the wine has been absorbed.

4. Stir in the tomatoes and thyme. Add about ½ cup of the simmering stock and cook, stirring frequently, until the stock has been completely absorbed. The rice and stock should bubble gently; adjust the heat as needed. Continue cooking the rice, adding the stock ½ cup at a time and allowing the rice to absorb the stock before adding the next ½ cup. Cook the rice in this way until tender, 25 to 30 minutes in all. The stock that hasn't been absorbed should be thickened by the starch from the rice. You may not need to use all of the liquid, or you may need to add more stock or some water.

5. Meanwhile, heat the broiler. Coat the chops with the remaining 1 tablespoon oil and season with ⅛ teaspoon pepper and

the remaining ¼ teaspoon salt. Broil the chops for 5 minutes. Turn and broil until cooked to your taste, about 4 minutes longer for medium rare.

6. Stir the Parmesan, butter, and ¼ teaspoon pepper into the risotto. Mound the risotto onto plates. Top with the parsley and put the chops alongside. Pass extra Parmesan.

PINE-NUT VARIATION

In a small frying pan, toast ¼ cup pine nuts over moderately low heat, stirring frequently, until golden brown, about 4 minutes. Or toast them in a 350° oven for about 6 minutes. Sprinkle the pine nuts on the finished risotto along with the parsley.

TEST-KITCHEN TIP

Sun-dried tomatoes come either completely dried out or packed in oil. The oil-packed type is more expensive, but is convenient because the dried ones usually need to be softened in hot water for about 15 minutes. In this recipe, however, you can use the dried type without losing time; the tomatoes soften with the slow cooking of the risotto, so there's no need to rehydrate them first.

LEMON RISOTTO WITH ASPARAGUS AND SHIITAKE MUSHROOMS

Delicately flavored with lemon and Parmesan cheese, studded with asparagus, and topped with golden-brown shiitake mushrooms, this risotto is a natural for springtime, when asparagus is at its best.

WINE RECOMMENDATION
Match the asparagus and cheese with an acidic white, such as a sauvignon blanc or chenin blanc from France's Loire Valley.

SERVES 4

- 1 pound asparagus
- 4 tablespoons olive oil
- 2 tablespoons butter
- 1 pound shiitake mushrooms, stems removed and caps cut into 1½-inch pieces
- 1¾ teaspoons salt
  Fresh-ground black pepper
- 2 cloves garlic, minced
- 2 teaspoons chopped fresh thyme, or ¾ teaspoon dried
- 5 cups Chicken Stock, page 303, or canned low-sodium chicken broth
- 1 small onion, chopped
- 1½ cups arborio rice
- ½ cup dry white wine
- ½ teaspoon grated lemon zest
- ⅓ cup grated Parmesan cheese, plus more for serving

1. Snap the tough ends off the asparagus and discard them. Cut the spears into 1-inch lengths. In a large pot of boiling, salted water, cook the asparagus until just done, about 5 minutes. Drain. Rinse with cold water and drain thoroughly.

2. In a large frying pan, heat 2 tablespoons of the oil and 1 tablespoon of the butter over moderately high heat. Add the mushroom caps, ½ teaspoon of the salt, and ¼ teaspoon pepper. Cook, stirring frequently, until browned, about 5 minutes. Add the garlic and thyme and cook, stirring, for 30 seconds longer. Remove from the heat and leave in the pan.

3. In a medium saucepan, bring the stock to a simmer.

4. In the large pot, heat the remaining 2 tablespoons oil over moderately low heat. Add the onion and cook, stirring occasionally, until translucent, about 5 minutes. Add the rice and stir until it begins to turn opaque, about 2 minutes.

5. Add the wine and the remaining 1¼ teaspoons salt to the rice and cook, stirring frequently, until all the wine has been absorbed. Add about ½ cup of the simmering stock and cook, stirring frequently, until the

stock has been absorbed. The rice and stock should bubble gently; adjust the heat as needed. Continue cooking the rice, adding the stock ½ cup at a time and allowing the rice to absorb the stock before adding the next ½ cup. Cook the rice in this way until tender, 25 to 30 minutes in all. Before adding the last ½ cup of stock, stir in the lemon zest. The stock that hasn't been absorbed should be thickened by the starch from the rice. You may not need to use all of the liquid, or you may need more stock or some water.

6. Stir in the asparagus, half of the mushrooms, the remaining 1 tablespoon butter, the Parmesan, and ⅛ teaspoon pepper and cook, stirring, until the vegetables are heated through. Reheat the remaining mushrooms. Mound the risotto onto plates. Top with the remaining mushrooms. Pass extra Parmesan.

CHICKEN VARIATION

Omit the mushrooms. Coat 1 pound boneless, skinless chicken breasts with 2 teaspoons olive oil. Season with ¼ teaspoon salt and ⅛ teaspoon pepper. Heat a grill pan or large, heavy frying pan over moderate heat. Add the chicken and cook for 5 minutes. Turn and cook until browned and just done, about 5 minutes longer. Let rest for about 4 minutes. Cut the chicken diagonally into ¼-inch slices and stir into the risotto just before serving.

TEST-KITCHEN TIP

Parmesan curls look dramatic, and making them is actually faster than grating the cheese. Just use a vegetable peeler to shave thin strips from a chunk of Parmesan right onto the risotto.

SHRIMP JAMBALAYA

In Louisiana you'll find jambalaya made with *andouille*, but this hot smoked sausage can be hard to find in the rest of the country. If it's not available in your area, use whatever you can get—spicy, garlicky, smoked, or mild sausage. If you have any leftover cooked pork or chicken on hand, toss it in when you add the shrimp.

WINE RECOMMENDATION

Could there be a better match than an ice-cold beer with spicy jambalaya? If you must drink wine, make it white, cold, and simple, such as a Muscadet de Sèvre-et-Maine from France or a vinho verde from Portugal.

SERVES 4

1	tablespoon cooking oil
1	onion, chopped
1	rib celery, chopped
1	green bell pepper, chopped
3	cloves garlic, minced
¾	pound sausage, such as *andouille*, kielbasa, Italian, or chorizo, casing removed and sausage chopped
1¾	cups canned crushed tomatoes
2	cups Chicken Stock, page 303, or canned low-sodium chicken broth
¾	teaspoon dried oregano
¾	teaspoon dried thyme
1	teaspoon paprika
1½	teaspoons salt
¼	teaspoon cayenne
1¼	cups rice
1	pound medium shrimp, shelled

1. In a large saucepan, heat the oil over moderately low heat. Add the onion, celery, bell pepper, and garlic. Cover and cook, stirring occasionally, until the vegetables are soft, about 5 minutes.

2. Add the sausage and cook for 5 minutes. Add the tomatoes, stock, oregano, thyme, paprika, salt, and cayenne. Bring to a boil. Add the rice. Reduce the heat and simmer, covered, for 20 minutes.

3. Raise the heat to moderate and stir in the shrimp. Cover and cook, stirring occasionally, until the rice and shrimp are done, about 6 minutes longer.

Arroz con Pollo

Pieces of chicken simmer gently with rice in a garlic-and-oregano-flavored broth. The effect is similar to that of an all-chicken paella.

WINE RECOMMENDATION This mild and comforting dish deserves a pleasant and unassuming white wine, such as a Rueda or white Rioja, both from Spain.

SERVES 4

- 2 tablespoons cooking oil
- 2 onions, chopped
- 1 green bell pepper, diced
- 3 cloves garlic, minced
- 1¼ cups rice, preferably medium-grain
- ¾ cup canned tomatoes, drained and chopped
- ½ cup bottled roasted red peppers, drained and diced
- ½ cup dry white wine
- 1¾ cups Chicken Stock, page 303, or canned low-sodium chicken broth
- ½ teaspoon dried oregano
- ¼ teaspoon saffron (optional)
- 1¾ teaspoons salt
- ⅛ teaspoon fresh-ground black pepper
- 4 skinless chicken drumsticks
- 4 skinless chicken thighs

1. In a large, deep frying pan, heat the oil over moderate heat. Add the onions, bell pepper, and garlic. Cover and cook, stirring occasionally, until the vegetables are soft, about 5 minutes. Add the rice and cook, stirring, for 1 minute longer.

2. Stir in the tomatoes, roasted red peppers, wine, stock, oregano, saffron, salt, and black pepper. Add the chicken pieces and bring to a simmer. Cover and cook, stirring the mixture two or three times, until the rice and the chicken pieces are done, about 25 minutes.

TEST-KITCHEN TIP

For this recipe, we prefer medium-grain rice, which the Spanish use. It holds its shape better than regular long-grain rice and has a firmer bite. Of course, long-grain will work here, too.

INDIAN-SPICED RICE WITH CHICKEN

Sweetened with currants and seasoned with cinnamon, cardamom, and coriander, this savory rice cooks with the chicken so that one flavors the other. Remove the cinnamon stick and cardamom pods before serving, or leave them in the rice as is done in India (but don't eat them).

WINE RECOMMENDATION
You'll need to look for a wine that's rich and acidic enough to stand up to the spices in this dish. A good choice would be a kabinett riesling from Germany's Mosel-Saar-Ruwer region.

SERVES 4

1   tablespoon cooking oil
1   chicken (3 to 3½ pounds), cut into 8 pieces
1½ teaspoons salt
    Fresh-ground black pepper
2   onions, chopped
2   cloves garlic, minced
1¼ cups rice
¼   cup currants or raisins
½   cinnamon stick
½   teaspoon ground coriander
4   cardamom pods (optional)
2¼ cups water

1. In a large, deep frying pan, heat the oil over moderately high heat. Sprinkle the chicken with ½ teaspoon of the salt and ⅛ teaspoon pepper. Put the chicken in the pan and brown well on both sides, about 8 minutes in all. Remove. Pour off all but 1 tablespoon of the fat. Reduce the heat to moderately low.

2. Add the onions and cook, stirring occasionally, until translucent, about 5 minutes. Add the garlic and cook 1 minute longer. Stir in the rice, currants, cinnamon, coriander, cardamom, the remaining 1 teaspoon salt, and ¼ teaspoon pepper. Cook, stirring, for 1 minute.

3. Stir in the water. Add the chicken pieces and bring to a simmer. Cover and cook, stirring the mixture two or three times, until the rice and chicken are done, about 25 minutes.

TEST-KITCHEN TIP

When it comes to flavor and texture in rice, basmati from India is tops in the long-grain department. Texmati, an American-grown rice that's similar, is a good substitute, as is jasmine rice from Thailand.

KEDGEREE

A curried rice dish with hard-cooked eggs and smoked fish, kedgeree comes from the colonial cuisine developed by British expatriates in India. If you'd like to add some crunch to this surprisingly homey dish, top it with chopped red onion.

WINE RECOMMENDATION
Look for an acidic white wine with lots of character to work with the various ingredients in this dish. Try a sauvignon blanc from the Loire Valley in France (such as a Sancerre). Alternatively, try an English ale.

SERVES 4

- 1 cup rice
- 4 fillets smoked trout, or 2 whole smoked trout
- 5 tablespoons butter
- 1 onion, cut into thin slices
- ½ teaspoon dried thyme
- ½ teaspoon salt
- 1 clove garlic, minced
- 1¾ teaspoons curry powder
- 5 hard-cooked eggs, chopped coarse
- ¾ cup heavy cream
- 2 tablespoons chopped fresh parsley
- ¼ teaspoon fresh-ground black pepper

1. In a medium pot of boiling, salted water, cook the rice until tender, about 15 minutes. Drain.

2. If using whole trout, remove the skin and lift each fillet off the bone. Flake the fillets. Melt the butter in a large pot over moderately low heat. Add the onion, thyme, and salt. Cover and cook, stirring occasionally, until the onion is soft, about 10 minutes. Add the garlic and curry powder and cook for 1 minute.

3. Fold the rice, trout, eggs, cream, parsley, and pepper into the onions and cook just until hot.

—PAUL GRIMES

TEST-KITCHEN TIP

Depending on the variety and the age of the grain, and even on the weather, the amount of water and time needed to steam rice to perfection vary dramatically. Rather than try to guess the needs of your particular grain, you can simplify matters by boiling the rice. Pour it into boiling, salted water, test a bite occasionally, and when it is done, drain it—just like cooking pasta. Boiling rice as we direct in this recipe is quicker than steaming and is foolproof. You can use the technique in any recipe that calls for plain cooked rice, though we don't recommend it for fragrant rice, such as basmati or jasmine.

RICE AND BLACK BEANS

The combination of rice and beans is a favorite in most Latin American countries. This version, spiced with chorizo and flavored with tomato and cilantro, is substantial enough to serve as a main dish.

WINE RECOMMENDATION
Stick with the Latin feel of this spicy dish and experiment with one of the reasonably priced cabernet sauvignons or merlots from Chile.

SERVES 4

1½ tablespoons olive oil

2 ounces chorizo or other dried, hot sausage, cut into ¼-inch pieces

1 onion, minced

2 cloves garlic, minced

½ cup bottled pimientos, drained and chopped

1 15-ounce can black beans, drained and rinsed (about 1⅔ cups)

1½ cups canned crushed tomatoes

3 tablespoons chopped cilantro or parsley

3 cups water

1½ cups rice, preferably medium-grain

2 teaspoons salt

⅛ teaspoon fresh-ground black pepper

1. In a large, deep frying pan, heat the oil over moderately low heat. Add the chorizo and cook, stirring occasionally, until golden, about 5 minutes. Add the onion and garlic and cook, stirring occasionally, until the onion is translucent, about 5 minutes. Add the pimientos, beans, tomatoes, and cilantro. Bring to a simmer and cook, stirring frequently, for 5 minutes.

2. Add the water, rice, salt, and pepper. Raise the heat to moderately high and bring to a low boil. Cook until all the water is absorbed, about 12 minutes. Reduce the heat to very low, cover, and cook until just done, about 15 minutes.

VEGETARIAN VARIATION

Omit the chorizo and increase the oil to 2 tablespoons. Add an extra ¼ teaspoon salt.

TEST-KITCHEN TIP

For firm canned black beans that won't fall apart during simmering, we prefer Goya brand.

STIR-FRIES

Beef, Green-Bean, and Cherry-Tomato Stir-Fry, page 151

STIR-FRYING QUICKLY COMBINES ASIAN INGREDIENTS to make tasty, endlessly varied dishes. But there's no reason to stop there. In this chapter we treat Western ingredients in the same way and come up with some remarkable stir-fries—Creole chicken, sausage and artichoke, even pastrami and cabbage. You can use the recipes in this chapter as models and substitute your favorite ingredients to produce innovations of your own. Use a wok or a large frying pan; we find they work equally well.

SHRIMP AND WATERCRESS STIR-FRY WITH LEMON GARLIC SAUCE

Don't be alarmed by all the garlic in this stir-fry; it flavors the sauce without overpowering the shrimp. Serve with steamed rice or vermicelli.

WINE RECOMMENDATION
The quantity of garlic in this dish makes a high-acid white wine a perfect match. Try the classic shellfish white from France, Muscadet de Sèvre-et-Maine.

SERVES 4

½ cup Chicken Stock, page 303, or canned low-sodium chicken broth

2 tablespoons soy sauce

1 teaspoon sugar

2 teaspoons cornstarch

2 tablespoons water

4 tablespoons cooking oil

1 pound medium shrimp, shelled

½ teaspoon salt

12 cloves garlic, minced

2 small shallots, cut into thin slices

3 to 4 tablespoons lemon juice

1 quart packed watercress with large stems removed (about 3 bunches), or 1 quart arugula leaves (about 6 bunches)

½ teaspoon fresh-ground black pepper

1. In a small bowl, combine the stock, soy sauce, and sugar. In another small bowl, combine the cornstarch and water.

2. In a wok or large frying pan, heat 2 tablespoons of the oil over moderately high heat until very hot. Add the shrimp and salt. Stir-fry until just pink, about 1½ minutes. Remove the shrimp and add the remaining 2 tablespoons oil. Reduce the heat to moderate and add the garlic. Cook, stirring, until soft, about 3 minutes. Add the shallots and stir-fry until translucent, about 2 minutes.

3. Increase the heat to high. Add the stock mixture and boil for 2 minutes. Add 3 tablespoons of the lemon juice. Stir the cornstarch mixture and add it to the pan. Stir well and bring to a simmer. Add the watercress and cook just until wilted, 30 to 60 seconds. Add the shrimp and pepper and heat through. Taste and add more lemon juice if you like.

—MARCIA KIESEL

SPICY STIR-FRY WITH SQUID AND GARLIC

The coconut milk tempers the flavor of the curry powder in this creamy seafood stir-fry. If you can't find unsweetened coconut milk, you can use heavy cream instead.

WINE RECOMMENDATION
The sweetness of the coconut milk and the heat of the spices call for a cold beer. As an alternative, try a high-acid white wine, such as a chenin blanc from France's Loire Valley.

SERVES 4

- 5   tablespoons cooking oil
- 1   pound cleaned squid, bodies cut into $\frac{1}{2}$-inch rings, tentacles cut in half
- $\frac{1}{2}$ teaspoon salt
- 4   cloves garlic, minced
- 2   tablespoons grated fresh ginger
- 1   onion, cut into thin slices
- 4   teaspoons curry powder
- $\frac{1}{4}$ teaspoon dried red-pepper flakes, plus more to taste
- 2   teaspoons tomato paste
- $\frac{1}{2}$ cup Chicken Stock, page 303, or canned low-sodium chicken broth
- $\frac{1}{4}$ cup dry white wine
- 2   tablespoons soy sauce
- 4   small zucchini (about $1\frac{1}{2}$ pounds), cut into $\frac{1}{4}$-inch slices
- 1   cup canned unsweetened coconut milk or heavy cream
- 2   tablespoons lemon or lime juice

1. In a wok or large frying pan, heat 1 tablespoon of the oil over high heat. Add half of the squid and $\frac{1}{8}$ teaspoon of the salt and stir-fry until just cooked through, 2 to 3 minutes. Remove. Add another 1 tablespoon oil to the pan. Add the remaining squid and $\frac{1}{8}$ teaspoon of the salt and stir-fry. Remove.

2. Add the remaining 3 tablespoons oil to the pan and reduce the heat to moderate. Add the garlic, ginger, onion, and the remaining $\frac{1}{4}$ teaspoon salt, and stir-fry until the onion has softened, about 3 minutes. Add the curry powder, red-pepper flakes, and tomato paste, and stir-fry for 2 minutes.

3. Stir in the stock, wine, soy sauce, and zucchini. Simmer until the zucchini is almost done, about 5 minutes. Add the coconut milk and simmer for 2 minutes. Stir in the squid with any accumulated juices and heat through. Add the lemon juice.

—MARCIA KIESEL

GLAZED CHICKEN WITH SCALLIONS

Cubes of chicken and pieces of scallion are stir-fried and then coated in a sweet, pungent glaze including brown sugar, soy sauce, ginger, and hot pepper.

WINE RECOMMENDATION

It takes a forceful wine to stand up to the strong flavors of the glaze in this recipe. A solid choice would be an extremely dry and acidic chenin blanc from the Loire Valley in France, such as an Anjou or the more expensive Vouvray.

SERVES 4

- 2 tablespoons brown sugar
- 4 teaspoons soy sauce
- 3 tablespoons Asian fish sauce (nam pla or nuoc mam)*
- 1 tablespoon dry sherry
- 1½ teaspoons grated fresh ginger
  Pinch dried red-pepper flakes
- 3 tablespoons cooking oil
- 10 scallions including green tops, cut into 1-inch pieces
- 6 boneless, skinless chicken breasts (about 2 pounds in all), cut into 1-inch cubes

*Available at Asian markets

1. In a small bowl, combine the brown sugar, soy sauce, fish sauce, sherry, ginger, and red-pepper flakes.

2. In a wok or large frying pan, heat 1 tablespoon of the oil over moderately high heat until very hot. Add the scallions and stir-fry just until golden, 30 to 60 seconds. Remove.

3. Add another 1 tablespoon oil to the pan. Add half of the chicken and stir-fry until it is almost done and beginning to brown, 2 to 3 minutes. Remove. Repeat with the remaining 1 tablespoon oil and chicken. Remove.

4. Add the brown-sugar mixture to the pan and boil until syrupy, 3 to 4 minutes. Add the chicken with any accumulated juices and cook, stirring, until the chicken is done and the liquid is reduced to a glaze, about 1 minute longer. Stir in the scallions.

VARIATIONS

In place of the chicken, use turkey breast or pork tenderloin.

STIR-FRIED CHICKEN WITH BOK CHOY AND CARROTS

Quick and full of flavor, this stir-fry, typical of those served in Asian restaurants, is just as tasty and practical for a fast meal at home.

WINE RECOMMENDATION
The aggressive flavors of the fish sauce, ginger, and garlic limit the range of wine choices to bold whites. Look for a grassy, assertive sauvignon blanc, preferably from New Zealand or South Africa.

SERVES 4

- 4 boneless, skinless chicken breasts (about 1⅓ pounds in all), cut crosswise into ¼-inch slices
- 3 tablespoons Asian fish sauce (nam pla or nuoc mam)*
- 2 teaspoons grated fresh ginger
- 2 teaspoons sugar
- ¼ teaspoon dried red-pepper flakes
- 4½ teaspoons cooking oil
- 3 carrots, cut into 2-inch-long slices about ½ inch wide and ⅛ inch thick
- 1 onion, chopped
- 1 pound bok choy (about ½ head), cut into 1-inch pieces (about 1½ quarts)
- 3 scallions including green tops, cut into 1-inch pieces
- 2 cloves garlic, minced
- ¼ cup Chicken Stock, page 303, or canned low-sodium chicken broth

*Available at Asian markets

1. In a medium bowl, toss the chicken with the fish sauce, ginger, sugar, and red-pepper flakes. If possible, let marinate at room temperature for 20 to 30 minutes.

2. In a wok or large frying pan, heat 1½ teaspoons of the oil over moderately high heat. Add half of the chicken and marinade and cook, stirring, until the chicken is lightly browned and almost cooked through, 1 to 2 minutes. Remove. Repeat with 1½ teaspoons of the oil and the remaining chicken and marinade. Remove.

3. Add the remaining 1½ teaspoons oil to the pan. Add the carrots and cook, stirring, for 2 minutes. Add the onion and cook 3 minutes longer. Stir in the bok choy, scallions, and garlic, and cook the vegetables, stirring, until just tender, 3 to 4 minutes. Add the chicken with any accumulated juices and the stock. Cook until the chicken is done, 1 to 2 minutes.

STIR-FRIED PORK WITH PEANUT SAUCE

With plenty of coconut milk and some stock, the Thai peanut sauce in this dish has a milder peanut flavor than those served with satays—just enough to complement the pork and vegetables without overpowering them.

WINE RECOMMENDATION
The mild, sweet flavors in this dish go well with a wine that's high in acidity and has a bit of sweetness itself. An ideal choice would be a kabinett riesling from the Mosel-Saar-Ruwer region of Germany.

SERVES 4

3 tablespoons cooking oil

1½ pounds pork loin, cut into ⅛-inch-thick slices about ½ inch wide and 2 inches long

1 onion, chopped

1½ teaspoons grated fresh ginger

Pinch dried red-pepper flakes

½ pound snow peas

¾ cup canned unsweetened coconut milk

⅓ cup Chicken Stock, page 303, or canned low-sodium chicken broth

3 tablespoons peanut butter

4 teaspoons soy sauce

1 teaspoon sugar

¼ pound bean sprouts (about 1¼ cups)

3 scallions including green tops, sliced

2½ tablespoons lime or lemon juice

1. In a wok or large frying pan, heat 1 tablespoon of the oil over high heat until very hot. Add half of the pork and stir-fry until brown, 2 to 3 minutes. Remove. Add another 1 tablespoon oil to the pan and cook the remaining pork in the same way. Remove.

2. Reduce the heat to moderately high. Add the remaining 1 tablespoon oil to the pan. Add the onion, ginger, and red-pepper flakes, and stir-fry until the onions have softened, about 3 minutes. Add the snow peas and stir-fry until tender, about 4 minutes longer.

3. Stir in the coconut milk, stock, peanut butter, soy sauce, and sugar. Stir until the peanut butter has melted.

4. Return the pork with any accumulated juices to the pan. Add the bean sprouts and scallions and cook until heated through. Stir in the lime juice.

VARIATION

The snow peas and bean sprouts can be replaced with whatever vegetables you prefer. Broccoli or sugar snap peas would work well.

TOFU WITH SPICY PORK AND SNOW PEAS

Large cubes of tofu are the perfect addition to this gingery pork and snow-pea stir-fry. The bland soybean curd takes on the spicy character of the dish. Serve with steamed rice.

WINE RECOMMENDATION
A gewürztraminer from Alsace in France is a popular choice for many Asian dishes, and it works perfectly with this stir-fry. You might also try one from California.

SERVES 4

- 1 cup plus 2 tablespoons Chicken Stock, page 303, or canned low-sodium chicken broth
- 1/3 cup soy sauce
- 3/4 teaspoon sugar
- 1 tablespoon cornstarch
- 1 1/2 tablespoons water
- 3 tablespoons cooking oil
- 5 cloves garlic, minced
- 1 1/2 tablespoons grated fresh ginger
- 1 small onion, minced
- 1/2 teaspoon dried red-pepper flakes, plus more to taste
- 3/4 pound ground pork
- 1/4 teaspoon salt
- 6 ounces snow peas, cut into 1/2-inch pieces
- 1 1/2 pounds firm tofu, cut into 2-inch cubes
- 3/4 teaspoon Asian sesame oil

1. In a small bowl, combine the stock, soy sauce, and sugar. In another small bowl, combine the cornstarch and water.

2. In a wok or large frying pan, heat the oil over moderately high heat. Add the garlic and ginger and stir-fry until fragrant, about 30 seconds. Add the onion and red-pepper flakes and stir-fry for 1 minute. Increase the heat to high and add the pork and salt. Stir-fry, breaking the meat into small bits with a metal spatula or spoon, until the meat is no longer pink, about 3 minutes.

3. Add the stock mixture and bring to a boil. Reduce the heat to moderately high and add the snow peas and tofu. Simmer, stirring gently, until the tofu is heated through, about 3 minutes. Stir the cornstarch mixture and add it to the pan. Simmer until thickened. Stir in the sesame oil.

—MARCIA KIESEL

Beef with Eggplant, Garlic, and Scallions

Strips of sirloin and cubes of tender stir-fried eggplant simmer in a simple sauce of soy, vinegar, and ginger. The final addition of uncooked scallions and a spoonful of vinegar is just the right touch to balance the rich flavors of this dish.

WINE RECOMMENDATION

The vinegar in this dish really comes through and should be matched with a fairly acidic red wine. Look for a Chianti Classico from Italy.

SERVES 4

1½	pounds sirloin steak or top round, cut into ⅛-inch slices about 1 inch wide and 2 inches long
5	tablespoons plus 2 teaspoons cooking oil
2	tablespoons plus 4 teaspoons soy sauce
1	tablespoon grated fresh ginger
1½	teaspoons cornstarch
1	tablespoon water
1	large eggplant (about 2 pounds), cut into 1-inch cubes
¾	teaspoon salt
3	cloves garlic, minced
¼	teaspoon dried red-pepper flakes
¾	cup Chicken Stock, page 303, or canned low-sodium chicken broth
4	scallions including green tops, sliced
3	tablespoons chopped cilantro (optional)
1	tablespoon red-wine vinegar

1. In a shallow glass dish, toss the beef with 2 tablespoons of the oil, the 2 tablespoons soy sauce, and 1 teaspoon of the ginger. In a small bowl, combine the cornstarch and water.

2. In a wok or large frying pan, heat 1 tablespoon of the oil over high heat. Add half of the beef and stir-fry until browned, 2 to 3 minutes. Remove. Add another 1 tablespoon oil to the pan and cook the remaining beef. Remove.

3. Add 1 tablespoon of the oil to the pan. Add the eggplant, sprinkle with the salt, and stir-fry for 2 minutes. Reduce the heat to moderate, cover, and cook, stirring occasionally, until tender, about 10 minutes. Remove.

4. Add the remaining 2 teaspoons oil to the pan. Add the remaining 2 teaspoons ginger, the garlic, and the red-pepper flakes. Stir-fry for 30 seconds. Add the stock and the remaining 4 teaspoons soy sauce. Bring to a simmer. Stir the cornstarch mixture, add it to the pan, and simmer until thickened.

5. Return the eggplant and beef with any accumulated juices to the pan. Cook 1 minute. Add the scallions, cilantro, and vinegar.

STIR-FRY INGREDIENT EXCHANGE

Stir-frying is an invitation to innovation. Although you'll want to avoid the wastebasket school of cooking, according to which you fling in any old thing that's around, you can do a lot of mixing and matching of ingredients when making a stir-fry and still keep it within the realm of good taste. If you don't like a certain ingredient, or don't have it on hand, or just feel like trying a new combination, you certainly needn't hold fast to our choices. Each of the columns below is a list of ingredients that, because of their flavor, texture, or cooking time, can often be used interchangeably.

MEAT / FISH		VEGETABLES		
		FIRM	MEDIUM	LEAFY
pork	shrimp	broccoli	bok choy	watercress
beef	squid	bell peppers	napa cabbage	spinach
duck	lobster	green beans	green cabbage	Belgian endive
turkey	scallops	asparagus	Savoy cabbage	various lettuces
chicken	chicken	carrots	mushrooms	
tofu	tofu	cauliflower	snow peas	
		eggplant	sugar snap peas	
			zucchini	
			escarole	
			Swiss chard	

BEEF, GREEN-BEAN, AND CHERRY-TOMATO STIR-FRY

Shake up your sirloin steak and green beans by stir-frying them with Asian flavoring. This would be good with anything from rice to mashed potatoes.

WINE RECOMMENDATION
Match the acidic tomatoes with a light, acidic red wine, such as a Chianti from Italy or a gamay from the Loire Valley in France.

SERVES 4

1½ pounds sirloin steak or top round, cut into ⅛-inch slices about 1 inch wide and 2 inches long

¼ cup plus 2 tablespoons dry white wine

2½ tablespoons Asian fish sauce (nam pla or nuoc mam)*

¾ teaspoon sugar

2 teaspoons grated fresh ginger

¾ cup Chicken Stock, page 303, or canned low-sodium chicken broth

2 teaspoons soy sauce

2 teaspoons cornstarch

1 tablespoon water

¾ pound thin or regular green beans

4 tablespoons cooking oil

6 cloves garlic, cut into thin slivers

3 cups cherry tomatoes, cut in half

*Available at Asian markets

1. In a shallow glass dish or stainless-steel pan, toss the beef with the 2 tablespoons wine, 1 tablespoon of the fish sauce, ¼ teaspoon of the sugar, and ½ teaspoon of the ginger.

2. In a small bowl, combine the stock and soy sauce with the remaining ¼ cup wine, 1½ tablespoons fish sauce, and ½ teaspoon sugar. In another small bowl, combine the cornstarch and water. In a pot of boiling, salted water, cook the green beans until almost tender, about 3 minutes for thin ones and 4 minutes for regular. Drain.

3. In a wok or large frying pan, heat 1 tablespoon of the oil over high heat. Add half of the beef and stir-fry until browned, about 2 minutes. Remove. Add another 1 tablespoon oil to the pan and cook the remaining beef. Remove.

4. Reduce the heat to moderately high. Put the remaining 2 tablespoons oil in the pan. Add the remaining 1½ teaspoons ginger and the garlic and stir-fry until fragrant, about 30 seconds. Add the green beans and stir-fry for 1 minute. Add the stock mixture and simmer for 2 minutes. Stir the cornstarch mixture, add it to the sauce, and cook until thickened. Return the beef to the pan with any accumulated juices. Simmer for 1 minute. Stir in the tomatoes and cook just until they're warm.

BEEF WITH CABBAGE

During the winter months, when the price of red peppers can be prohibitively high, you can substitute sliced carrots to get that touch of sweetness.

WINE RECOMMENDATION
A fruity, acidic red wine, such as a Beaujolais-Villages from France, will be a pleasant accompaniment to both the mellow beef and the strong cabbage flavors found in this dish.

SERVES 4

- 1 pound sirloin steak or top round, cut into 1/8-inch slices about 1 inch wide and 2 inches long
- 3 cloves garlic, minced
- 2 1/2 teaspoons grated fresh ginger
- 1 1/2 teaspoons Asian sesame oil
- 1/2 teaspoon salt
- 1/2 teaspoon fresh-ground black pepper
- 2 tablespoons oyster sauce
- 1/4 cup dry white wine
- 1 1/2 tablespoons soy sauce
- 3/4 teaspoon cornstarch
- 1 1/2 tablespoons water
- 2 tablespoons cooking oil
- 1 onion, cut into thin slices
- 3/4 pound green cabbage (about 1/4 head), shredded (about 3 cups)
- 1 red bell pepper, cut into 1-inch squares
- 2 teaspoons red-wine vinegar

1. In a medium bowl, toss the slices of beef with the garlic, ginger, sesame oil, 1/4 teaspoon of the salt, and 1/4 teaspoon of the black pepper.

2. In a small bowl, combine the oyster sauce, wine, and soy sauce. In another small bowl, combine the cornstarch and water.

3. In a wok or large frying pan, heat 1 tablespoon of the oil over high heat. Add half of the beef and cook undisturbed to brown on one side, about 2 minutes. Remove. Add the remaining 1 tablespoon oil to the pan. Add the remaining beef and brown in the same way. Return all of the meat to the pan with any accumulated juices and stir a few times, allowing the juices to caramelize.

4. Add the onion, cabbage, bell pepper, and the remaining 1/4 teaspoon salt and reduce the heat to moderate. Cook, stirring, until the vegetables are just beginning to soften, 3 to 4 minutes. Add the oyster-sauce mixture. Increase the heat to high. Simmer for 1 to 2 minutes. Stir the cornstarch mixture, add it to the pan, and simmer, stirring, until thickened. Stir in the vinegar and the remaining 1/4 teaspoon black pepper.

—MARCIA KIESEL

Stir-Fried Tofu, Shiitakes, and Asparagus

Firm tofu keeps its shape during cooking, and so it's the best choice for stir-fries. On its own, it's rather mild, but once added to the dish, tofu acts as a sponge, absorbing the savory flavors of the sauce.

WINE RECOMMENDATION
Try a California or New Zealand sauvignon blanc. It has the acidity and character to deal with asparagus's strong flavor, and works well with the Asian ingredients here.

SERVES 4

1½ pounds asparagus

2 teaspoons cornstarch

1 tablespoon water

2 tablespoons cooking oil

4 cloves garlic, minced

1 large onion, chopped

1 pound shiitake mushrooms, stems removed and caps sliced, or white mushrooms, sliced

¾ cup Chicken Stock, page 303, or canned low-sodium chicken broth

3 tablespoons soy sauce

5 teaspoons white-wine vinegar

¾ teaspoon Asian sesame oil

¾ teaspoon salt

2 pounds firm tofu, cut into 1½-inch cubes

1 tablespoon toasted sesame seeds (optional)

1. Snap off the tough ends of the asparagus and discard them. Cut the asparagus into 1-inch lengths. In a large pot of boiling, salted water, cook the asparagus for 3 minutes. Drain. In a small bowl, combine the cornstarch and water.

2. In a wok or large frying pan, heat the oil over moderately high heat. Add the garlic. Stir-fry until fragrant, about 30 seconds. Add the onion and stir-fry until softened, about 3 minutes. Add the sliced mushrooms and stir-fry until brown, about 5 minutes.

3. Stir in the stock, soy sauce, 3 teaspoons of the vinegar, the sesame oil, and the salt. Simmer for 2 minutes. Stir the cornstarch mixture, add it to the pan, and simmer until the sauce has thickened. Add the tofu and simmer for 3 minutes. Add the asparagus and simmer until hot, about 2 minutes longer. Stir in the remaining 2 teaspoons vinegar. Serve topped with the sesame seeds.

Green-Bean Variation

During the winter, you may want to replace the asparagus with 1½ pounds green beans. Cut them in half crosswise and boil for 4 minutes.

STIR-FRIED SWORDFISH WITH CUCUMBER, BELL PEPPER, AND CAPERS

Swordfish is not one of your typical stir-fry ingredients, but this firm, moist fish is well suited to wok cooking. Here it's teamed with cucumber and red-bell-pepper strips and finished with a tangy caper and lemon sauce.

WINE RECOMMENDATION

Meaty swordfish lends itself to a full-bodied white wine. Try a ripe, but preferably not very oaky, California chardonnay.

SERVES 4

½ cup Chicken Stock, page 303, or canned low-sodium chicken broth

1½ teaspoons cornstarch

4 tablespoons cooking oil

1¾ pounds swordfish steaks, skinned and cut into 1-inch chunks

¾ teaspoon salt

1 cucumber, peeled, halved lengthwise, seeded, cut crosswise into 2-inch pieces and then lengthwise into ½-inch strips

1 red bell pepper, cut into thin slices

1 onion, cut into thin slices

1 teaspoon dried oregano

1 tablespoon capers

2 tablespoons butter, cut into pieces

2 scallions including green tops, cut into 1-inch pieces

2 tablespoons lemon juice

¼ teaspoon fresh-ground black pepper

1. In a small bowl, combine the stock and cornstarch.

2. In a wok or large frying pan, heat 1 tablespoon of the oil over moderately high heat. Add half of the swordfish and ¼ teaspoon of the salt. Cook until the fish is browned and almost done, about 3 minutes. Remove. Repeat with another 1 tablespoon oil, the remaining swordfish, and ¼ teaspoon of the salt. Remove.

3. Add another 1 tablespoon oil to the pan. Add the cucumber and stir-fry until slightly softened, about 2 minutes. Remove.

4. Add the remaining 1 tablespoon oil. Add the bell pepper and stir-fry for 5 minutes. Add the onion and the remaining ¼ teaspoon salt and cook until the vegetables are soft, about 5 minutes longer.

5. Stir the cornstarch mixture and add it to the pan. Bring to a simmer. Stir in the oregano, capers, and butter. Add the fish, cucumbers, and scallions to the pan and cook until the fish is just done, about 2 minutes. Stir in the lemon juice and black pepper.

CREOLE CHICKEN STIR-FRY

An Asian technique with Creole ingredients? Why not? Green bell pepper, Tabasco sauce, and cubes of ham give this spicy chicken stir-fry its New Orleans flavor. Serve the chicken and its sauce over rice.

WINE RECOMMENDATION
A very acidic white wine with plenty of body is a good bet with the sweet-and-sour flavor of the tomatoes. Try a sauvignon blanc from South Africa or New Zealand.

SERVES 4

1 cup Chicken Stock, page 303, or canned low-sodium chicken broth

2 tablespoons flour

4 tablespoons olive oil

4 boneless, skinless chicken breasts (about 1⅓ pounds in all), cut crosswise into 1-inch strips

¾ teaspoon salt

Fresh-ground black pepper

1 ½-pound piece of ham, cut into ¼-inch dice

2 onions, chopped

2 ribs celery, cut into ¼-inch dice

1 small green bell pepper, cut into ¼-inch dice

1 28-ounce can tomatoes (about 3½ cups), drained and chopped

1 bay leaf

1 teaspoon dried marjoram or thyme

½ teaspoon Tabasco sauce, more to taste

1. In a small bowl, stir together ¼ cup of the stock and the flour until smooth.

2. In a wok or large frying pan, heat 2 tablespoons of the oil over moderately high heat. Sprinkle the chicken with ¼ teaspoon of the salt and ⅛ teaspoon black pepper. Put half of the chicken in the pan and stir-fry until lightly browned on both sides, about 3 minutes. Remove. Add the remaining chicken and brown in the same way. Remove.

3. Add 1 tablespoon of the oil to the pan. Add the ham and onions and cook, stirring, until lightly browned, about 4 minutes. Remove. Heat the remaining 1 tablespoon oil in the pan and add the celery and bell pepper. Cook, stirring, until softened, about 5 minutes.

4. Return the ham and onions to the pan. Add the tomatoes, bay leaf, marjoram, and the remaining ¾ cup stock and ½ teaspoon salt. Bring to a boil. Continue boiling for 2 minutes. Add the chicken and simmer until almost done, about 3 minutes. Push the chicken and vegetables to the side of the pan. Stir the flour mixture and add it to the sauce, stirring constantly. Simmer until the chicken is done and the sauce is thickened, about 2 minutes longer. Remove the bay leaf. Add the Tabasco sauce and ¼ teaspoon black pepper.

—PAUL GRIMES

SAUSAGE, ARTICHOKE, AND MUSHROOM STIR-FRY

This Mediterranean stir-fry tastes great served over fettuccine or orzo. If you like spicy food, replace half of the mild Italian sausage with hot. The canned artichokes called for here fall into the don't-knock-'em-'til-you've-tried-'em category. We were pleasantly surprised by how good they are.

WINE RECOMMENDATION

Slightly sweet-tasting due to the artichokes, this dish will work nicely with a fairly bland, slightly acidic white wine, such as a pinot blanc from Alsace in France.

SERVES 4

1 tablespoon cornstarch

1 cup Chicken Stock, page 303, or canned low-sodium chicken broth

2 tablespoons olive oil

1½ pounds mild Italian sausage, casing removed and meat cut into ½-inch pieces

2 onions, cut into thin slices

3 cloves garlic, minced

1 14-ounce can artichoke hearts packed in water, drained and halved

5 plum tomatoes (about 1 pound), chopped

¼ pound mushrooms, sliced

1 teaspoon dried thyme

1 teaspoon fennel seeds, crushed

1 bay leaf

¾ teaspoon salt

2 tablespoons chopped flat-leaf parsley

½ teaspoon fresh-ground black pepper

1. In a small bowl, combine the cornstarch and ¼ cup of the stock.

2. In a wok or large frying pan, heat 1 tablespoon of the oil over moderately high heat. Add the sausage and cook, stirring, until browned, about 5 minutes. Remove the sausage. Reduce the heat to moderately low and add the remaining 1 tablespoon oil. Add the onions and stir-fry until golden, about 5 minutes. Add the garlic and cook 1 minute longer.

3. Add the sausage, artichoke hearts, tomatoes, mushrooms, the remaining ¾ cup stock, the thyme, fennel seeds, bay leaf, and salt. Bring to a boil. Reduce the heat and simmer, uncovered, until the sausage is just done, about 5 minutes.

4. Remove the bay leaf. Stir the cornstarch mixture and add it to the simmering liquid. Simmer, stirring, until thickened. Add the parsley and pepper.

—PAUL GRIMES

157

PASTRAMI AND CABBAGE STIR-FRY

The searing heat of stir-frying is perfect for the classic Western combination of pastrami, potatoes, and cabbage. Here, the hot pastrami and crisp cabbage get a kick from a generous jolt of Dijon mustard.

WINE RECOMMENDATION
What's a good match for pastrami? Beer. If you would prefer wine, look for an acidic white with a forceful personality. A California or New Zealand sauvignon blanc would be fine.

SERVES 4

¾ pound boiling potatoes (about 2), peeled, halved lengthwise, and sliced about ¼-inch thick

4 tablespoons cooking oil

1 onion, cut into thin slices

3 carrots, cut into thin slices

1 1-pound piece of pastrami, diced

1 pound green cabbage (about ⅓ head), cut into thin slices (about 1 quart)

¾ teaspoon salt

¼ teaspoon fresh-ground black pepper

2 tablespoons Dijon mustard

½ cup Chicken Stock, page 303, or canned low-sodium chicken broth

1. Put the potatoes in a medium saucepan of salted water. Bring to a boil. Reduce the heat and simmer until tender, about 5 minutes. Drain.

2. In a wok or large frying pan, heat 1 tablespoon of the oil over high heat. Add the onion and carrots and stir-fry until lightly browned, 1 to 2 minutes. Remove. Add another 1 tablespoon of the oil to the pan and stir-fry the potatoes until lightly browned, 1 to 2 minutes. Remove. Add another 1 tablespoon of the oil to the pan and stir-fry the pastrami until browned, 1 to 2 minutes. Remove. Add the remaining 1 tablespoon oil to the pan and stir-fry the cabbage until wilted, 3 to 4 minutes.

3. Return all the cooked ingredients to the pan. Stir in the salt and pepper. In a small bowl, whisk together the mustard and stock. Add to the stir-fry. Bring the liquid to a simmer and cook for 1 minute.

CABBAGE VARIATION

Use napa cabbage or bok choy in place of the green cabbage.

LIVER AND ONION STIR-FRY

Liver-and-onion fans, rejoice. This one-pan meal includes potatoes, plenty of golden-brown onions, and two unusual additions—sage and sour cream. Rather than making the stir-fry seem overly rich, the sour cream adds a complementary touch of acidity.

WINE RECOMMENDATION

A rich, velvety merlot will match the richness of the liver and the cream sauce. A bottle from California will be fine, but if you can find a St.-Emilion from Bordeaux (made principally from merlot), its higher acidity will make it an even better choice.

SERVES 4

4½ tablespoons cooking oil

1 pound calf's liver, cut into 2-inch strips about ½ inch wide and ¼ inch thick

1¼ teaspoons salt

¾ teaspoon fresh-ground black pepper

¼ cup flour

¾ pound boiling potatoes (about 2), cut into ⅛-inch-thick slices

2 onions, cut into thin slices

1 clove garlic, minced

1 cup Chicken Stock, page 303, or canned low-sodium chicken broth

1 cup sour cream

1½ teaspoons dried sage

2 tablespoons cider vinegar

2 tablespoons chopped flat-leaf parsley

1. In a large frying pan, heat 1 tablespoon of the oil over high heat. Season the liver with ¼ teaspoon of the salt and ¼ teaspoon of the pepper. Dust the liver with the flour and shake off the excess. Add half of the liver to the pan and brown well on both sides, about 1 minute. Remove and add 1 more tablespoon of the oil to the pan. Brown the remaining liver. Remove.

2. Wipe out the frying pan. Heat 1½ tablespoons of the oil in the pan over moderately high heat. Add the potatoes and cook, stirring, until tender, 10 to 12 minutes. Remove. Heat the remaining 1 tablespoon oil over moderate heat. Add the onions and cook, stirring, until browned, about 5 minutes. Add the garlic and cook for 1 minute.

3. Return the potatoes to the pan. Add the stock, sour cream, sage, and the remaining 1 teaspoon salt and ½ teaspoon pepper. Bring just to a simmer. Do not boil or the sour cream may curdle. Add the liver and cook until heated through. Stir in the vinegar and parsley.

—PAUL GRIMES

FROM THE SAUTÉ PAN

Chicken Breasts with Peppers, Onion, and Olives, page 169

NEARLY ALL OF US HAVE HAD SOME PERIOD IN OUR LIVES when we've cooked with only one pan—in school, on a stint abroad, in a first apartment, when just married, or just divorced. Although one cook of our acquaintance claims to have made dinner every night for a year on a waffle iron (with the grids removed), the one-pan experience is virtually always with a frying (or sauté) pan. And with good reason: You can use it to prepare a great variety of ingredients and types of dishes quickly and well. In this chapter, you will find eighteen main dishes, many with built-in side dishes. Ninety percent of the recipes use only that single practical pan (one uses an extra saucepan, and one uses *two* frying pans).

COD CAKES WITH SCALLIONS AND HERBS

Scallions, basil, parsley, and lemon juice enliven the flavor of cod in these tasty cakes. Sweet red bell pepper is an attractive addition but can be omitted if you prefer. Serve the cakes right from the pan with lemon-flavored mayonnaise, or use them to make terrific sandwiches.

WINE RECOMMENDATION
Chardonnay is a good match for mild cod, and its lemony taste will echo the lemon juice in this recipe.

SERVES 4

- ¾ teaspoon salt
- 2 pounds cod fillet
- 1½ cups dry bread crumbs
- ¼ cup mayonnaise
- ¼ cup lemon juice
- 1 egg, beaten to mix
- ½ red bell pepper, chopped fine (optional)
- 4 scallions including green tops, minced
- 2 tablespoons chopped fresh basil (optional)
- 2 tablespoons chopped flat-leaf parsley
  Pinch cayenne
- ⅛ teaspoon fresh-ground black pepper
  Cooking oil, for frying
  Lemon Mayonnaise

1. Put 1 inch of water in a large frying pan. Add ¼ teaspoon of the salt and bring to a simmer. Put the cod in the pan. Cook, covered, until just done, about 6 minutes. Remove the cod from the water and let cool. Pour out the water and wipe the pan.

2. With your fingers, flake the fish into a large bowl, removing any bones as you go. Add ¾ cup of the bread crumbs, the mayonnaise, lemon juice, egg, bell pepper, scallions, basil, parsley, cayenne, the remaining ½ teaspoon salt, and the black pepper. Stir until well combined.

3. Divide the cod mixture into 12 portions and shape into patties. Coat the patties with the remaining ¾ cup bread crumbs and pat off the excess.

4. In the frying pan, heat about ¼ inch of oil over moderate heat. Working in batches if necessary, fry the cakes until golden brown and crisp, about 2 minutes. Turn and fry until golden brown on the other side, about 2 minutes longer. Drain on paper towels. Serve with the Lemon Mayonnaise.

LEMON MAYONNAISE

- ½ cup mayonnaise
- 2 teaspoons lemon juice
- ⅛ teaspoon fresh-ground black pepper

In a small bowl, stir all the ingredients together.

Cornmeal-Coated Fish with Corn Relish

Virtually any lean fish will work here; choose your favorite. The cornmeal-coated fish is nicely complemented by the tangy corn relish. Lemon Mayonnaise, preceding page, is an even easier alternative.

WINE RECOMMENDATION
This down-home dish is perfect with a simple white wine that has good body but not too much personality. Ideal candidates are a pinot blanc from Alsace in France or your favorite California chardonnay.

SERVES 4

¼   cup olive oil

1   red bell pepper, chopped

1   clove garlic, minced

2   cups fresh (cut from about 3 ears) or frozen corn kernels

2   tablespoons red-wine vinegar

1   teaspoon sugar

1¾ teaspoons salt

½   teaspoon fresh-ground black pepper

2   scallions including green tops, chopped

¾   cup cornmeal

2   eggs, beaten to mix

2   pounds lean fish fillets, such as flounder, cod, or catfish, cut across into 3-inch pieces

Cooking oil, for frying

1. Heat the oven to 250°. Line a baking sheet with paper towels.

2. In a medium frying pan, heat the olive oil over moderate heat. Add the bell pepper and cook, stirring occasionally, until soft, about 4 minutes. Add the garlic and cook 1 minute longer. Stir in the corn, vinegar, sugar, ½ teaspoon of the salt, and ¼ teaspoon of the pepper. Cook, stirring occasionally, until the corn is done, about 5 minutes longer. Let cool. Add the scallions.

3. Combine the cornmeal and the remaining 1¼ teaspoons salt and ¼ teaspoon pepper. Dip a few pieces of fish into the beaten eggs and then into the cornmeal. Shake off the excess cornmeal.

4. In a large nonstick frying pan, heat about ¼ inch of cooking oil over moderate heat. Add the cornmeal-coated fish and fry, turning once, until golden on the outside and just done in the center, about 5 minutes in all. The cooking time will vary depending on the type and thickness of the fish you use. Transfer to the prepared baking sheet and keep warm in the oven while coating and frying the remaining fish. Serve with the corn relish.

SAUTEED SPICED CATFISH

A blend of black pepper, oregano, cumin, coriander, cloves, and garlic lends a piquant flavor to sautéed catfish fillets, and the crisp, brown crust contrasts nicely with the moist fish. Mashed Potatoes, page 260, and Zucchini and Summer Squash with Fresh Oregano, page 245, go well with the fish.

WINE RECOMMENDATION
The full flavor of the catfish and the liveliness of the spices are best with a cold beer or a gutsy white wine, such as one from the Côtes-du-Rhône in France.

SERVES 4

- 2 cloves garlic, chopped
- 1½ teaspoons fresh-ground black pepper
- 1½ teaspoons dried oregano
- 1½ teaspoons ground cumin
- 1½ teaspoons ground coriander
- 1¼ teaspoons salt
- ⅛ teaspoon ground cloves
- 2 tablespoons flour
- 1 tablespoon cooking oil
- 1 tablespoon butter
- 4 catfish fillets (about 2 pounds in all)

1. Put the garlic, pepper, oregano, cumin, coriander, salt, and cloves into a spice grinder and pulverize. Transfer to a small bowl and stir in the flour. Alternatively, mince the garlic and combine with the spices, herbs, salt, and flour in a small bowl.

2. In a large frying pan, heat the oil and butter over moderate heat. Dust the fish with the spice mixture and shake off any excess. Put in the pan and cook for 4 minutes. Turn and cook until browned and just done, about 3 minutes longer.

VARIATION

Use flounder or scrod in place of the catfish. Reduce the total cooking time to about 4 minutes for flounder and 5 minutes, depending on the thickness, for scrod.

Sauteed Scallops with Shiitake Mushrooms and Garlic

Sea scallops, sautéed with shiitakes, herbs, and a touch of vermouth, make a weekday dinner a special one. Nestled on a bed of greens dressed with olive oil, the scallops are both elegant and satisfying. All you need to add is bread.

WINE RECOMMENDATION
Scallops find a perfect partner in a full-bodied white wine. Try an oaky chardonnay from either Australia or California.

SERVES 4

3½ tablespoons olive oil

¾ pound shiitake mushrooms, stems removed and caps cut into ¼-inch slices

Salt

¼ teaspoon fresh-ground black pepper

2 pounds sea scallops

3 tablespoons butter

2 cloves garlic, minced

2 tablespoons dry vermouth or dry white wine

3 tablespoons mixed, chopped fresh herbs, such as tarragon, chives, and parsley

2 teaspoons lemon juice

1 quart mixed salad greens (about 3 ounces)

1. In a large nonstick frying pan, heat 2 tablespoons of the oil over moderately high heat. Add the sliced mushrooms, ¼ teaspoon salt, and ⅛ teaspoon of the pepper and cook, stirring frequently, until browned, about 5 minutes. Remove.

2. Season the scallops with ½ teaspoon salt and the remaining ⅛ teaspoon pepper. In the same pan, heat ½ tablespoon of the oil over moderately high heat. Add half the scallops and cook until browned, about 1 minute. Turn and cook until browned on the second side and just done, about 2 minutes longer. Add to the mushrooms. Add another ½ tablespoon oil to the pan and repeat with the remaining scallops. Add to the mushrooms and wipe out the pan.

3. In the same pan, melt the butter over moderate heat. Add the garlic and cook, stirring, for 30 seconds. Add the vermouth and herbs. Cook until the sauce thickens slightly, about 1 minute. Add the scallops, mushrooms, and lemon juice, and cook, stirring, until just heated through.

4. Toss the salad greens with the remaining ½ tablespoon oil and a pinch of salt. Put the greens on plates and top with the scallops.

SAUTEED CHICKEN BREASTS WITH GARLIC AND HERBS

Flavorful with garlic and fresh herbs, these boneless, skinless chicken breasts are moist, tender, and golden brown. A quick sauté followed by a brief steaming in their own juices is the key; cooked for more than a few minutes, boneless breasts get stringy. Polenta with Parmesan, page 272, makes a comforting accompaniment.

WINE RECOMMENDATION
The mild flavors of this straightforward dish should be ideal with your favorite chardonnay from California or white Burgundy from France.

SERVES 4

1 tablespoon olive oil

4 boneless, skinless chicken breasts (about 1⅓ pounds in all)

½ teaspoon salt

⅛ teaspoon fresh-ground black pepper

1 clove garlic, minced

2 tablespoons mixed, chopped fresh herbs, such as tarragon, chives, and parsley

1. In a medium nonstick frying pan, heat the oil over moderate heat. Season the chicken with the salt and pepper and add to the pan. Cook until brown, about 5 minutes. Turn and cook until almost done, about 3 minutes longer.

2. Add the garlic and herbs. Cook, stirring, for 30 seconds. Cover the pan, remove from the heat, and let steam 5 minutes.

3. Serve the chicken with the pan juices. If you like, cut the breasts diagonally into slices, arrange on plates, and pour the pan juices over the chicken.

VARIATIONS

■ Add 1 to 2 teaspoons lemon juice to the pan juices after you remove the chicken. Or serve the chicken with lemon wedges. Either way, the tang of the lemon goes well with the dish.

■ Virtually any herb could be used here, either alone or in combination with others. Even plain parsley on its own is excellent.

CHICKEN BREASTS WITH PEPPERS, ONION, AND OLIVES

Chunks of chicken blend with bell pepper, onion, garlic, and olives. A squeeze of fresh lemon juice at the end balances the sweetness of the peppers and onions. Buttered noodles, plain steamed rice, or good bread completes the meal admirably.

WINE RECOMMENDATION
This is as versatile a dish as there is when it comes to matching with wine. It will be a pleasure with a fruity red or a favorite white, perhaps a California chardonnay.

SERVES 4

4 boneless, skinless chicken breasts (about 1⅓ pounds in all)

¾ teaspoon salt

¼ teaspoon fresh-ground black pepper

2 tablespoons olive oil

1 tablespoon butter

1 small onion, chopped

2 red bell peppers, or 1 red and 1 yellow, cut lengthwise into ¼-inch slices

2 cloves garlic, minced

2 tablespoons dry vermouth or dry white wine

⅓ cup Kalamata olives, pitted

1½ tablespoons chopped flat-leaf parsley

½ teaspoon lemon juice

1. Pull off the fillets from the underside of the chicken breasts. Cut the breasts diagonally into three equal pieces, making four pieces from each of the breasts. Season the chicken with ¼ teaspoon of the salt and ⅛ teaspoon of the pepper.

2. In a large frying pan, heat 1 tablespoon of the oil and the butter over moderately low heat. Add the onion, bell peppers, and ¼ teaspoon of the salt. Cook, covered, until tender, about 7 minutes. Uncover and cook, stirring, until the liquid evaporates, about 2 minutes. Add the garlic and cook, stirring, for 30 seconds. Remove.

3. In the same frying pan, heat the remaining 1 tablespoon oil over moderately high heat. Add the chicken and cook, stirring, until browned, about 4 minutes. Add the vermouth and stir to dislodge any brown bits that cling to the bottom of the pan. Return the bell-pepper mixture to the pan and add the remaining ¼ teaspoon salt and ⅛ teaspoon pepper. Reduce the heat to low. Cover and cook until the chicken is just done, about 2 minutes.

4. Add the olives, parsley, and lemon juice, and cook, stirring, until warmed through, about 30 seconds.

CHICKEN BREASTS WITH ISRAELI SALAD AND TAHINI SAUCE

A cucumber, tomato, and red-onion salad complements these sautéed chicken breasts served with tahini sauce. When good tomatoes are only a summer memory, you can just omit them from the salad.

WINE RECOMMENDATION
Select a simple and refreshing white wine, such as one from the Coteaux du Languedoc or Côtes de Gascogne in France.

SERVES 4

- 1 cucumber, peeled, seeded, and cut into ½-inch pieces
- 2 tomatoes, seeded and cut into ½-inch pieces
- ½ cup diced red onion
- 3 tablespoons chopped flat-leaf parsley
- 6 tablespoons olive oil
- 3 tablespoons plus 2 teaspoons lemon juice
  Fresh-ground black pepper
- 6 tablespoons tahini
- 6 tablespoons water
- ¾ teaspoon salt
- 4 boneless, skinless chicken breasts (about 1⅓ pounds in all)

1. In a large bowl, combine the cucumber, tomatoes, onion, parsley, 2 tablespoons of the oil, 1 tablespoon plus 1 teaspoon of the lemon juice, and ⅛ teaspoon pepper.

2. In a small bowl, stir together the tahini, water, and 3 tablespoons of the oil until smooth. Stir in the remaining 2 tablespoons plus 1 teaspoon lemon juice, ¼ teaspoon of the salt, and ⅛ teaspoon pepper.

3. In a medium frying pan, heat the remaining 1 tablespoon oil over moderate heat. Season the chicken breasts with ¼ teaspoon of the salt and ⅛ teaspoon pepper and add them to the pan. Cook the chicken until brown, about 5 minutes. Turn and cook until almost done, about 3 minutes longer. Cover the pan, remove from the heat, and let steam 5 minutes.

4. Add the remaining ¼ teaspoon salt to the salad. Serve the chicken with the salad and tahini sauce.

TEST-KITCHEN TIP

The cooking method used here—sautéing to brown and then setting aside, covered, to steam until done—can be applied to fish fillets as well as to chicken. Experiment with the technique. You'll find the gentle heat gives juicy results every time.

SAUTEED CHICKEN WITH VINEGAR SAUCE

The vinegar in this traditional French bistro dish mellows as it cooks, resulting in a just slightly tangy sauce.

WINE RECOMMENDATION
Match this dish with a slightly acidic wine, such as a favorite sauvignon blanc from California, or experiment with a bottle of the same varietal from South Africa.

SERVES 4

- 2 tablespoons cooking oil
- 4 unboned chicken breasts (about 2¼ pounds in all)
- ¼ teaspoon fresh-ground black pepper
- 1½ teaspoons salt
- 1 large onion, chopped
- 4 cloves garlic, minced
- ¼ cup red-wine vinegar
- 1 cup Chicken Stock, page 303, or canned low-sodium chicken broth
- 1 cup canned tomatoes, drained and chopped
- 1 bay leaf
- 1 tablespoon chopped flat-leaf parsley (optional)

1. In a large, deep frying pan, heat the cooking oil over moderately high heat. Season the chicken breasts with the pepper and ½ teaspoon of the salt. Put the chicken breasts in the frying pan and brown well on both sides, about 8 minutes in all. Remove. Pour off all but 1 tablespoon of the fat.

2. Reduce the heat to moderately low. Add the onion and garlic. Cover and cook, stirring occasionally, until soft, about 5 minutes. Add the vinegar and simmer, uncovered, for 30 seconds. Add the stock, tomatoes, bay leaf, and the remaining 1 teaspoon salt, and bring to a boil, scraping the bottom of the pan to dislodge any brown bits.

3. Return the chicken breasts to the pan and cook, covered, until the chicken is just done, about 25 minutes. Remove the bay leaf and stir in the parsley.

VINEGAR VARIATIONS

Experiment with different vinegars. Sherry vinegar and raspberry vinegar would each lend its own characteristic flavor to the dish.

SPICY CHICKEN WITH CHORIZO

Chorizo gives this stew its distinctive flavor, but don't hesitate to try a different sausage. Andouille, the spicy smoked sausage of Cajun cooking, is one alternative, and the more familiar hot Italian is another.

WINE RECOMMENDATION
Try a very cold bottle of gewürztraminer, the white wine produced in the Alsace region of France and elsewhere. Its strong flavor and off-dry taste are a great contrast to the spiciness of this dish.

SERVES 4

- 1 tablespoon cooking oil
- ½ pound chorizo sausage or other hot sausage, casing removed and sausage cut into ½-inch pieces
- 2 onions, quartered and cut into thin slices
- 1 red or green bell pepper, quartered and cut into thin slices
- 3 cloves garlic, minced
- 1 teaspoon dried oregano
- ½ teaspoon dried thyme
- ¼ teaspoon dried red-pepper flakes
- 2 bay leaves
- ¾ teaspoon salt
- 1½ cups Chicken Stock, page 303, or canned low-sodium chicken broth
- 2 tablespoons tomato paste
- 8 skinless chicken thighs (about 2½ pounds in all)
- 2 teaspoons red-wine vinegar

1. In a large frying pan, heat the oil over moderately high heat. Add the chorizo and cook until brown, about 5 minutes. Remove the chorizo with a slotted spoon. Discard all but 1 tablespoon of the fat from the pan.

2. Add the onions and bell pepper and cook over moderate heat, stirring occasionally, until golden, about 7 minutes. Add the garlic, oregano, thyme, red-pepper flakes, bay leaves, and salt, and cook, stirring, for 2 minutes longer.

3. Stir in the stock and tomato paste. Add the chorizo and chicken thighs and bring to a simmer. Cover, reduce the heat, and simmer the chicken for 25 minutes, turning the thighs once while they cook. Uncover the pan and cook 10 minutes longer. Discard the bay leaves and stir in the vinegar.

CHICKEN SAUTE WITH APPLE CIDER AND THYME

Perfect as the weather turns colder, this traditional French dish features chicken that is sautéed and then gently simmered in apple cider with sliced onions and apples. Serve it with buttered noodles, rice, or couscous.

WINE RECOMMENDATION

Look for a full-bodied, acidic white wine to play against the acidity and sweetness of the dish. A good choice would be a riesling from the Alsace region of France.

SERVES 4

- 1 tablespoon cooking oil
- 1 tablespoon butter
- 1 chicken (3 to 3½ pounds), cut into 8 pieces
- ¼ teaspoon fresh-ground black pepper
- 1 teaspoon salt
- 1 large onion, cut into thin slices
- ½ cup apple cider
- ½ cup Chicken Stock, page 303, or canned low-sodium chicken broth
- 2 teaspoons chopped fresh thyme, or ¾ teaspoon dried
- 1 apple, such as Golden Delicious, peeled, cored, and cut into thin slices

1. In a large, deep frying pan, heat the oil and butter over moderately high heat. Season the chicken pieces with the pepper and ½ teaspoon of the salt. Add the chicken to the pan and brown well on both sides, about 8 minutes in all. Remove. Pour off all but 1 tablespoon of the fat. Reduce the heat to moderately low.

2. Add the onion and cook, stirring occasionally, until brown, about 6 minutes. Add the cider, stock, thyme, and the remaining ½ teaspoon salt, and bring to a boil, scraping the bottom of the pan to dislodge any brown bits.

3. Add the chicken. Cover and simmer for 5 minutes. Stir in the apple slices. Cover and continue cooking, turning the chicken once, until just done, about 20 minutes longer.

Turkey Cutlets with a Parmesan Crust

Prepared in the same fashion as veal scaloppine, these turkey cutlets are dipped in a bread-crumb and Parmesan-cheese mixture, fried until golden, and served with lemon wedges. The crisp cutlets are shown on page 244 with Zucchini and Summer Squash with Fresh Oregano.

WINE RECOMMENDATION
Try this spin on an Italian classic with a traditional Italian white wine, such as a pinot grigio from the Alto Adige region or a Vernaccia de San Gimignano.

SERVES 4

  1   cup dry bread crumbs

  6   tablespoons grated Parmesan cheese

1½ teaspoons dried sage (optional)

 ¾   teaspoon salt

 ¼   teaspoon fresh-ground black pepper

  8   turkey cutlets (about 1½ pounds in all)

  2   eggs, beaten to mix
      Cooking oil, for frying

  1   lemon, cut into wedges, for serving

1. Heat the oven to 250°. Line a baking sheet with paper towels.

2. Combine the bread crumbs, Parmesan, sage, salt, and pepper. Dip each cutlet into the eggs and then into the bread-crumb mixture. Shake off any excess bread crumbs.

3. In a large nonstick frying pan, heat about ¼ inch of oil over moderately high heat. Add as many of the cutlets as will fit in the pan and cook until just done, 1 to 2 minutes in all. Transfer to the prepared baking sheet and keep warm in the oven while cooking the rest. Add more oil to the pan as needed. Serve with the lemon wedges.

Variations

■ Use chicken or veal cutlets in place of the turkey.

■ Try different herbs, such as dried oregano or thyme, in place of the sage.

PORK CHOPS WITH MUSTARD-HERB SAUCE

Pour stock into the frying pan after cooking the chops to deglaze the tasty bits on the bottom of the pan. All you need is a tablespoon of mustard and a sprinkling of fresh herbs to make a flavorful brown sauce.

 WINE RECOMMENDATION This straightforward presentation will be delightful with a fine red wine that has plenty of flavor complexity, such as a California pinot noir or a red Burgundy from France.

SERVES 4

1 tablespoon butter

4 pork chops, about 1 inch thick (about 2 pounds in all)

½ teaspoon salt

Fresh-ground black pepper

3 tablespoons chopped onion

¾ cup Chicken Stock, page 303, or canned low-sodium chicken broth

1 tablespoon Dijon mustard

1½ tablespoons mixed, chopped fresh herbs, such as parsley, tarragon, and chives

1. In a large frying pan, heat the butter over moderately low heat. Season the pork chops with the salt and ¼ teaspoon pepper. Add the chops to the pan and sauté for 7 minutes. Turn and cook until the chops are browned and done to medium, about 7 minutes longer. Remove the chops and put in a warm spot.

2. Add the onion to the pan and cook, stirring, until soft, about 3 minutes. Add the stock and boil until reduced to ½ cup, about 3 minutes. Stir in the mustard, herbs, and ⅛ teaspoon pepper. Put the chops on individual plates and pour the sauce over the meat.

VARIATION

If you have grainy mustard on hand, use it instead of the Dijon.

TEST-KITCHEN TIP

Today's lean pork requires a shorter cooking time than the nice, rich pork of old. With no fat to keep it juicy and tender, the meat will become dry and stringy when cooked in traditional ways. Don't worry if the pork is a bit pink in the center. We now know that trichinosis is killed at the relatively low temperature of 150°.

PORK CHOPS WITH RED CABBAGE, APPLES, AND CURRANTS

Pork chops sautéed to a golden brown are moist, tender, and delicious. Red cabbage, made sweet and sour with apple, currants, and a spoonful of vinegar, is a perfect accompaniment. To complete the meal, serve Mashed Potatoes, page 260.

WINE RECOMMENDATION

Cabbage, apples, and currants need a forceful, acidic wine, such as a kabinett riesling from the Mosel-Saar-Ruwer in Germany.

SERVES 4

- 5 tablespoons cooking oil
- 1 onion, chopped
- 1½ pounds red cabbage (about ½ head), shredded (about 1½ quarts)
- 2 tart apples, such as Granny Smith, peeled, cored, and cut into thin slices
- ⅓ cup currants or raisins
- ⅓ cup plus 2 tablespoons red wine
- 1½ tablespoons red-wine vinegar
- 2½ teaspoons dried thyme
- 2 teaspoons sugar
- Pinch grated nutmeg
- Salt
- ⅔ cup water
- ½ teaspoon fresh-ground black pepper
- 1½ tablespoons butter
- 4 pork chops, about 1 inch thick (about 2 pounds in all)

1. In a large pot, heat 3 tablespoons of the oil over moderately low heat. Add the onion and cook, stirring occasionally, until translucent, about 5 minutes. Add the cabbage, apples, currants, the ⅓ cup wine, the vinegar, 2 teaspoons of the thyme, the sugar, nutmeg, and 1 teaspoon salt. Bring to a simmer. Cook, covered, for 10 minutes. Add ⅓ cup of the water. Cook, partially covered, until the cabbage is tender, about 30 minutes longer. Add ¼ teaspoon of the pepper.

2. In a large frying pan, heat the remaining 2 tablespoons oil with 1 tablespoon of the butter over moderately low heat. Season the chops with ½ teaspoon salt and the remaining ¼ teaspoon pepper. Add the chops to the pan. Sauté for 7 minutes. Turn and cook until browned and done to medium, about 7 minutes longer. Remove and put in a warm place.

3. Pour off the fat from the pan and add the remaining ⅓ cup water, the 2 tablespoons wine, and ½ teaspoon thyme. Bring to a boil, scraping the bottom of the pan to dislodge any brown bits. Boil until reduced to ¼ cup, about 3 minutes. Stir in the remaining ½ tablespoon butter and a pinch of salt. Spoon the sauce over the chops and serve them with the cabbage.

VEAL SCALOPPINE WITH SHIITAKES, TOMATOES, GARLIC, AND HERBS

Sautéed vegetables top thin slices of tender veal, briefly cooked to a golden brown. Cook the whole dish in one pan in about 15 minutes. Roasted New Potatoes with Rosemary, page 262, are great on the side.

WINE RECOMMENDATION
A Chianti Classico from Italy, with plenty of fresh fruit to complement the garlic and ample acidity for the tomatoes, is a perfect choice.

SERVES 4

- 4 tablespoons olive oil
- 3 tablespoons butter
- 1½ pounds shiitake mushrooms, stems removed and caps cut into ¼-inch slices
- 1¼ teaspoons salt
- 2 cloves garlic, minced
- ¾ pound tomatoes (about 2 medium), seeded and cut into ½-inch pieces
- 2 tablespoons mixed, chopped fresh herbs, such as rosemary, basil, chives, and parsley
- 8 veal scaloppine (about 1½ pounds in all)
- ½ teaspoon fresh-ground black pepper
- ⅓ cup water
- ¼ cup dry vermouth or dry white wine
- ½ teaspoon lemon juice

1. In a large frying pan, heat 2 tablespoons of the oil and 1 tablespoon of the butter over moderate heat. Add the sliced mushrooms and ¼ teaspoon of the salt and cook, stirring frequently, until browned, about 5 minutes. Add the garlic and cook, stirring, for 30 seconds. Add the tomatoes and herbs and cook, stirring, until heated through, about 2 minutes longer. Remove from the pan.

2. In the same pan, heat 1 tablespoon of the oil and 1 tablespoon of the butter over moderately high heat. Season the veal with ½ teaspoon of the salt and ¼ teaspoon of the pepper. Cook half the meat, in a single layer, until browned, about 30 seconds. Turn and cook until browned and just done, about 30 seconds longer. Remove. Add the remaining 1 tablespoon oil and 1 tablespoon butter to the pan and repeat with the rest of the meat. Remove. Pour off all the fat.

3. Add the water and vermouth to the pan and cook, stirring to dislodge any brown bits that cling to the bottom of the pan. Add the mushroom mixture, any accumulated veal juices, the lemon juice, and the remaining ½ teaspoon salt and ¼ teaspoon pepper. Spoon the sauce over the scaloppine.

HAMBURGER STEAKS WITH SAUTEED PORTOBELLO MUSHROOMS AND HERBS

Topped with portobellos, scallions, herbs, and a quick sauce of sherry and pan juices, these hamburgers are as good as steak.

WINE RECOMMENDATION
Hamburgers somehow become more serious when paired with portobellos. Try these with a good California cabernet sauvignon rather than just another fruity burger wine.

SERVES 4

- 3 tablespoons olive oil
- 3 tablespoons butter
- ¾ pound portobello mushrooms, stems removed and caps cut into ¼-inch slices
- 4 scallions including green tops, cut diagonally into 1½-inch lengths
     Salt and fresh-ground black pepper
- 2 cloves garlic, minced
- 2 tablespoons mixed, chopped fresh herbs, such as basil, tarragon, and parsley
- 1⅓ pounds ground beef chuck
- ¼ cup dry sherry
- 6 tablespoons water

1. In a large frying pan, heat 2 tablespoons of the oil and 2 tablespoons of the butter over moderately high heat. Add the sliced mushrooms, scallions, ½ teaspoon salt, and ¼ teaspoon pepper. Cook, stirring, until the mushrooms and scallions brown, about 5 minutes. Add the garlic and herbs and cook, stirring, 30 seconds longer. Remove.

2. Form the ground beef into four patties about 1 inch thick. Season with ½ teaspoon salt and ¼ teaspoon pepper.

3. Heat the remaining 1 tablespoon oil and 1 tablespoon butter in the frying pan over moderately high heat. Add the hamburgers and cook 4 minutes. Turn and cook to your taste, about 5 minutes longer for medium rare. Remove. Pour off all the fat.

4. Add the sherry and water to the pan. Cook over moderate heat, scraping the bottom of the pan to dislodge any brown bits. Add the mushroom mixture, ⅛ teaspoon salt, and ⅛ teaspoon pepper, and cook until warmed through. Serve the hamburgers topped with the mushrooms and sauce.

TEST-KITCHEN TIP

The best hamburgers are those that are handled the least. Don't press the meat into patties; shape it gently to keep it as loose as possible.

LAMB SHOULDER CHOPS WITH SUN-DRIED TOMATOES, GARLIC, AND PARSLEY

Topped with sautéed onion, sun-dried tomatoes, garlic, and parsley, these flavorful lamb shoulder chops are clearly Italian in inspiration. If you prefer, substitute the more pricey rib or loin chops. They're thicker, though, so cook them a few minutes longer.

WINE RECOMMENDATION
The richness of the lamb and the acidity of the tomatoes work well with a fruity but acidic Chianti Classico from Italy.

SERVES 4

4 lamb shoulder-blade chops, 1 inch thick (about 2 pounds in all)
Salt and fresh-ground black pepper
1 tablespoon olive oil
1 tablespoon butter
1 onion, chopped
½ cup sun-dried tomatoes packed in oil, drained and cut into ¼-inch strips
3 cloves garlic, minced
6 tablespoons dry vermouth or dry white wine
2 tablespoons chopped flat-leaf parsley
½ cup water

1. Season the chops with ½ teaspoon salt and ¼ teaspoon pepper. In a large frying pan, heat the oil and butter over moderately high heat. Add the chops and cook until browned, about 2 minutes. Turn and cook 2 minutes longer. Reduce the heat to low and cook the chops until done to your taste, about 3 minutes longer for medium rare. Transfer to a plate and put in a warm place.

2. Pour off all but 1 teaspoon of the fat. Raise the heat to moderately low. Add the onion and cook, stirring occasionally, until translucent, about 5 minutes. Add the sun-dried tomatoes and garlic and cook, stirring, 30 seconds longer. Add the vermouth and cook about 1 minute, stirring to dislodge any brown bits that cling to the bottom of the pan.

3. Return the meat to the pan with any accumulated juices. Add the parsley, water, and ⅛ teaspoon salt. Bring to a simmer and cook until the sauce thickens slightly, about 1 minute. Add ⅛ teaspoon pepper. Serve the chops topped with the tomato mixture.

VARIATION

When fresh basil is plentiful, use it in place of the parsley.

CALF'S LIVER WITH LEMON CAPER BUTTER

Sautéed calf's liver is meltingly delicious topped with a tangy sauce flavored with lemon juice and capers. Serve it the way the Venetians do, with Polenta with Parmesan, page 272. The combination is superb and can be on the table in half an hour.

WINE RECOMMENDATION

Try a white with lots of body to buffer the tang of this dish as well as acidity to cut through the richness of the liver, such as a kabinett riesling from Germany's Mosel-Saar-Ruwer region.

SERVES 4

- ¼ cup flour
- ¾ teaspoon salt
  Fresh-ground black pepper
- 2 tablespoons cooking oil
- 5½ tablespoons butter
- 4 slices calf's liver (about 1½ pounds in all)
- 3 tablespoons capers
- 1½ tablespoons lemon juice

1. Combine the flour with ½ teaspoon of the salt and ¼ teaspoon pepper.

2. In a large frying pan, heat the oil with 1 tablespoon of the butter over moderate heat.

3. Meanwhile, dust the liver with the flour mixture and shake off the excess. Put the liver in the pan and cook until browned, about 3 minutes. Turn and cook until browned on the other side, 3 to 4 minutes longer. It should still be pink in the center. Remove and put in a warm place.

4. Wipe out the pan. Melt the remaining 4½ tablespoons butter over moderate heat. Add the capers, lemon juice, the remaining ¼ teaspoon salt, and ⅛ teaspoon pepper, and bring just to a simmer. Pour over the liver and serve.

VARIATIONS

■ **Fresh Herb:** Add chopped fresh herbs such as tarragon, basil, or parsley to the sauce with the capers.

■ **Balsamic Vinegar:** Use balsamic vinegar in place of the lemon juice. It adds a hint of sweetness and produces a lovely, dark-brown sauce.

CHEESE AND HERB FRITTATA

Made with cream, Parmesan, and fresh herbs, this exceptional frittata is airy and tender with a golden surface of melting mozzarella. Add a green salad and bread for a fine fast dinner.

WINE RECOMMENDATION

There are any number of basic, fruity wines that would be nice alongside this frittata. Try a Beaujolais-Villages or a bottle of mourvedre or grenache from a smaller California producer.

SERVES 4

- 8 large eggs
- 1/3 cup heavy cream, light cream, or half-and-half
- 1 cup grated Parmesan cheese
- 3 tablespoons mixed, chopped fresh herbs, such as basil, tarragon, chives, and parsley
- 1/8 teaspoon salt
- 1/8 teaspoon fresh-ground black pepper
- 2 tablespoons butter
- 1/2 cup grated salted fresh mozzarella

1. In a large bowl, beat the eggs with the cream, Parmesan, herbs, salt, and pepper until smooth.

2. In a 10-inch nonstick frying pan, melt the butter over moderately high heat. Pour in the egg mixture and reduce the heat to low. Cook, covered, until the bottom is golden brown and the top is almost set, 12 to 14 minutes.

3. Heat the broiler. Sprinkle the top of the frittata with the mozzarella. Broil the frittata 6 inches from the heat, if possible, until the eggs are set and the cheese is bubbling, about 3 minutes.

4. Lift up the edge of the frittata with a spatula and slide the frittata onto a plate. Cut into wedges and serve.

TEST-KITCHEN TIP

If the handle of your frying pan isn't ovenproof, protect it from the heat of the broiler by wrapping it with about four layers of aluminum foil.

GRILLING & BROILING

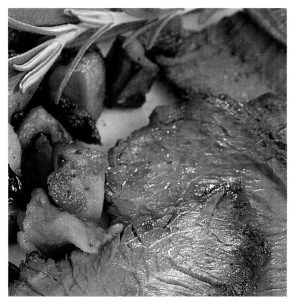

Spice-Marinated Sirloin, page 201

MANY PEOPLE COOK EVERYTHING ON THE GRILL during the summer. They'll find lots of ideas here, but nearly all the recipes can also be made in the broiler. Neither grilling nor broiling is an exact science. Both depend on the strength of the fire and how far from the heat the food can be placed. Keep in mind that our cooking times are necessarily estimates, and keep an eye on the food. Be sure to take it out of the refrigerator about thirty minutes before cooking so that it can come close to room temperature. Otherwise, not only will the times be wildly off but you're likely to wind up with charred outsides and raw insides.

GRILLED-SHRIMP TOSTADAS

Crisp flour tortillas topped with lettuce, refried black beans, guacamole, cheese, and grilled shrimp make a familiar yet festive dinner.

WINE RECOMMENDATION
One of the lighter Mexican beers is probably the best choice here, though a California chenin blanc, which is generally off-dry, would be an interesting possibility.

SERVES 4

 1 clove garlic, chopped

1½ tablespoons cooking oil, plus more for frying

 8 6-inch flour tortillas

 Refried Black Beans, page 274, without the scallion, cheese, and salsa

24 large shrimp (about 1½ pounds), shelled

¼ teaspoon salt

 Pinch fresh-ground black pepper

½ head romaine lettuce, shredded

 2 ounces queso fresco* or feta cheese, crumbled (about ½ cup)

 Guacamole

 *Available at Spanish markets

1. In a small bowl, combine the garlic with the oil.

2. In a large frying pan, heat about ¼ inch of oil over moderate heat. Fry the tortillas, one at a time, until crisp and golden brown, about 30 seconds a side. Drain on paper towels.

3. Light the grill or heat the broiler. Reheat the beans. Thread the shrimp on eight skewers. Brush the shrimp with the garlic oil and sprinkle with the salt and pepper. Grill or broil the shrimp, turning once, until just done, about 4 minutes in all.

4. Put the tortillas on plates. Top with a layer each of lettuce, cheese, beans, and guacamole. Put the shrimp skewers on top.

GUACAMOLE

MAKES ABOUT 2½ CUPS

 1 small red onion, chopped

 1 large tomato, seeded and chopped

½ jalapeño pepper, seeds and ribs removed, minced

 1 avocado, preferably Hass, cut into ½-inch chunks

 6 tablespoons chopped cilantro (optional)

 2 tablespoons lime juice

½ teaspoon salt

⅛ teaspoon fresh-ground black pepper

In a medium glass or stainless-steel bowl, combine all the ingredients.

SWORDFISH-AND-ZUCCHINI KABOBS WITH LEMON AND OREGANO

Ten minutes in the lemon-oregano marinade is all it takes to give these fish-and-zucchini kabobs their zesty flavor. Grilled Corn with Extra-Virgin Olive Oil, page 242, rice, orzo, couscous, or boiled new potatoes tossed with a little butter and parsley are all good accompaniments.

WINE RECOMMENDATION
A full-bodied California chardonnay with little or no oak will complement the robust flavor of the fish, and the typical citrusy quality of chardonnay will also mirror the zesty marinade.

SERVES 4

3   tablespoons lemon juice

2   cloves garlic, minced

2   tablespoons dried oregano

6   tablespoons olive oil

2   pounds swordfish steaks, about 1 inch thick, skinned and cut into 1-inch chunks

1   zucchini, cut in half lengthwise and cut crosswise into ⅛-inch slices

1   teaspoon salt

½   teaspoon fresh-ground black pepper

1. Light the grill or heat the broiler. In a medium glass or stainless-steel bowl, combine the lemon juice, garlic, oregano, and oil. Add the swordfish and zucchini, toss to coat, and marinate for 10 minutes.

2. Thread the chunks of swordfish alternating with the zucchini slices onto eight skewers. Sprinkle with the salt and pepper. Grill or broil, turning, until just done, about 7 minutes in all.

VARIATIONS

■ **Scallop:** Large, sweet sea scallops are a delicious alternative to the swordfish. Grill or broil for the same length of time.

■ **Halibut:** Firm halibut also holds up well on skewers. Prepare it as for the swordfish.

■ **Cherry Tomato:** Replace the zucchini with cherry tomatoes. You'll need about 2 cups. Of course, you can also use both zucchini and cherry tomatoes.

GRILLED SWORDFISH WITH ORANGE AND AVOCADO SALSA

Served with a colorful salsa of oranges, avocado, onion, tomato, jalapeño, and cilantro, grilled swordfish takes on the fruity flavors and mild heat of the Yucatán. A side of Refried Black Beans with Scallions, Queso Fresco, and Salsa, page 274, would be perfect.

WINE RECOMMENDATION

A meaty fish like swordfish usually works best with a full-bodied white, although here the salsa makes the choice a bit more difficult. Try a pinot gris from Oregon.

SERVES 4

- 2 navel oranges
- 1 small red onion, chopped
- 1 tomato, seeded and cut into ¼-inch pieces
- 1 avocado, preferably Hass, cut into ½-inch chunks
- ½ jalapeño pepper, seeds and ribs removed, minced
- 2 tablespoons chopped cilantro (optional)
- 3 tablespoons orange juice
- 2 tablespoons lime juice
- ¾ teaspoon salt
- ¼ teaspoon fresh-ground black pepper
- 4 swordfish steaks, about 1 inch thick (about 1½ pounds in all)
- 1 tablespoon cooking oil

1. Using a stainless-steel knife, peel the oranges down to the flesh, removing all of the white pith. Cut the sections away from the membranes. Put the orange sections in a medium glass or stainless-steel bowl. Add the onion, tomato, avocado, jalapeño, cilantro, orange juice, lime juice, ½ teaspoon of the salt, and ⅛ teaspoon of the pepper, and stir to combine.

2. Light the grill or heat the broiler. Coat the swordfish steaks with the oil and sprinkle with the remaining ¼ teaspoon salt and ⅛ teaspoon pepper. Grill or broil the fish for 4 minutes. Turn and cook until golden brown and just done, 4 to 5 minutes longer. Serve with the salsa.

VARIATION

You can use another firm, full-flavored fish in place of the swordfish, such as tuna or salmon. Reduce the cooking time so that the tuna is medium rare and the salmon, medium.

GRILLED TUNA STEAKS WITH LENTILS AND FENNEL

You can serve this tuna either warm or at room temperature. You'll find that the lentil and fennel salad is so good that you'll want to use it in other ways as well. Try it for lunch with dressed mixed greens.

WINE RECOMMENDATION
Sauvignon blanc will work nicely with the fennel here. Try one from California or Washington State, or look for a blend of sauvignon blanc and semillon from the Entre-Deux-Mers region of Bordeaux.

SERVES 4

2½ tablespoons olive oil

1 onion, chopped fine

1 carrot, chopped fine

2 cloves garlic, minced

1 pound lentils (about 2⅓ cups)

1 quart water

1¾ teaspoons salt

¼ teaspoon dried thyme

1 bay leaf

1 fennel bulb, cut into thin slices

2 tablespoons balsamic vinegar

½ teaspoon fresh-ground black pepper

4 tuna steaks, about 1 inch thick (about 1½ pounds in all)

Basil Vinaigrette, opposite page (optional)

1. In a large saucepan, heat ½ tablespoon of the oil over moderately low heat. Add the onion, carrot, and garlic. Cook, stirring occasionally, until the onion is translucent, about 5 minutes.

2. Add the lentils, water, 1 teaspoon of the salt, the thyme, and the bay leaf. Bring to a boil, reduce the heat, and simmer, partially covered, until the lentils are just tender but not falling apart, about 35 minutes. Discard the bay leaf. Stir in 1 tablespoon of the oil, the fennel, vinegar, ¼ teaspoon of the salt, and ¼ teaspoon of the pepper.

3. Light the grill. Coat the tuna with the remaining 1 tablespoon oil. Season with the remaining ½ teaspoon salt and ¼ teaspoon pepper. Cook the tuna for 4 minutes. Turn and cook until done to your taste, 3 to 4 minutes longer for medium rare. Divide the lentils among four plates and top with the grilled tuna. Drizzle the dressing, if using, over the fish.

BASIL VINAIGRETTE

The addition of a basil vinaigrette drizzled over the grilled tuna increases the work only slightly and is a refreshing touch that's especially welcome in the summer, when basil is at its prime.

MAKES ABOUT ¼ CUP

1 tablespoon balsamic vinegar

3 tablespoons chopped fresh basil

¼ teaspoon salt

¼ teaspoon fresh-ground black pepper

3 tablespoons olive oil

Whisk together the vinegar, basil, salt, and pepper. Add the oil slowly, whisking.

VARIATIONS

■**Grilled Swordfish:** Try swordfish in place of the tuna if you prefer. Cook until just done, about 4 to 5 minutes a side.

■**Grilled Chicken:** If you're not a fish-eater, grill 4 boneless, skinless chicken breasts in place of the tuna. You'll need to grill them about 5 minutes per side.

■**Bell Pepper:** When bell peppers are at their peak, use them in place of the fennel. Cut either a red or a yellow pepper into very thin strips. Add them to the lentils with the oil and vinegar.

TEST-KITCHEN TIP

If you want grilled flavor but don't want to light an outdoor grill, use a grill pan. It looks like a heavy frying pan with ridges; some pans are cast iron, others nonstick. They mimic the effect of grill-cooking well. Get one good and hot and follow grilling times.

GRILLED TUNA WITH TOMATO-BASIL-SALAD SAUCE

This unusual sauce contains lettuce; the effect is like eating chopped salad with your fish. We like plenty of black pepper sprinkled on the tuna before grilling, but if you're not a big fan of pepper, reduce it by half.

WINE RECOMMENDATION
Meaty grilled tuna steaks will pair up nicely with a full-bodied white wine. Try them with your favorite chardonnay from California.

SERVES 4

1½ tablespoons balsamic vinegar

2 teaspoons salt

1 teaspoon fresh-ground black pepper

7 tablespoons olive oil

1½ pounds tomatoes (about 3), seeded and cut into ½-inch chunks

1 small onion, chopped fine

⅓ cup thin-sliced basil leaves

4 tuna steaks, about 1 inch thick (about 1½ pounds in all)

2 cups chopped romaine lettuce (about 4 medium leaves)

1. In a medium bowl, whisk the balsamic vinegar with 1½ teaspoons of the salt and ½ teaspoon of the pepper. Add 6 tablespoons of the oil slowly, whisking. Stir in the tomatoes, onion, and basil leaves.

2. Light the grill. Coat the tuna steaks with the remaining 1 tablespoon oil and sprinkle with the remaining ½ teaspoon salt and ½ teaspoon pepper.

3. Grill the tuna for 4 minutes. Turn and cook until done to your taste, 3 to 4 minutes longer for medium rare.

4. To serve, put the tuna on plates. Add the lettuce to the sauce and spoon it over the fish.

VARIATION

You can use any fish steak, such as salmon, swordfish, halibut, or cod, in this recipe, but cook them a bit longer so that salmon is done to medium and the other fish are cooked through.

Broiled Red Snapper with Walnut Romesco Sauce

Red-snapper fillets taste especially delicious topped with Spanish romesco sauce—a thick, zesty puree of red peppers, garlic, walnuts, olive oil, and cayenne. The sauce keeps well in the refrigerator and is superb on chicken, pork, beef, or even spread on bread, and so if you like, make a double batch.

WINE RECOMMENDATION

This dish, with its intensely nutty sauce, is wonderful with a brisk, refreshing Spanish white wine such as an alvariño from the Galicia region. A more reasonable alternative would be a Rueda, also from Spain.

SERVES 4

- 4 red-snapper fillets, about 6 ounces each
- 1 tablespoon olive oil
- ¼ teaspoon salt
- ⅛ teaspoon fresh-ground black pepper
  Large pinch paprika
- 1 tablespoon butter
  Walnut Romesco Sauce

1. Heat the broiler. Put the fish on an oiled broiler pan or baking sheet. Coat with the 1 tablespoon oil and sprinkle with the salt, pepper, and paprika. Dot with the butter.

2. Broil the fish until golden brown and just done, about 5 minutes depending on the thickness of the fish. Spoon the sauce over the fish and serve.

Walnut Romesco Sauce

MAKES ABOUT 1 CUP

- 1 cup bottled roasted red peppers, drained
- 1 cup walnuts
- 1 large clove garlic, chopped
- ¼ cup olive oil
- 1½ teaspoons lemon juice
- ½ teaspoon salt
- ¼ teaspoon cayenne

In a food processor or blender, puree the red peppers, walnuts, and garlic with the oil, lemon juice, salt, and cayenne.

MUSTARD, LEMON, AND ROSEMARY-MARINATED BLUEFISH WITH ONION PARSLEY SALAD

Bluefish is irresistible when marinated with grainy mustard, lemon juice, and fresh rosemary and then broiled to a golden brown. It's an Atlantic fish that may be unavailable in your area. If so, mahimahi is an excellent substitute.

WINE RECOMMENDATION
Pair a bottle of bracingly crisp Muscadet de Sèvre-et-Maine with the incisive lemon and mustard flavors here; it will also cut through the richness of the fish.

SERVES 4

- 2 large Spanish or Bermuda onions (about 2 pounds), cut into thin slices
  Salt
- ¼ cup chopped flat-leaf parsley
- ¼ cup olive oil
- 2 teaspoons lemon juice
- 2 teaspoons grainy mustard
- 2½ teaspoons chopped fresh rosemary, or ¾ teaspoon dried, crumbled
  Fresh-ground black pepper
- 2 pounds bluefish fillets
- 2 tablespoons white-wine vinegar, or 2 tablespoons plus 2 teaspoons lemon juice
- ½ teaspoon sugar
- 1 lemon, cut into wedges, for serving

1. In a large glass or stainless-steel bowl, combine the onions and 2 tablespoons salt. Let sit for 10 minutes. Rinse with cold water. Put back into the bowl and cover with ice water. Let sit for 10 minutes. Drain. Dry the onions on paper towels or in a salad spinner. Put the onions back into the bowl and add the parsley.

2. In a small bowl, combine the oil, lemon juice, mustard, rosemary, and ¼ teaspoon pepper.

3. Put the fish, skin-side down, in a shallow glass dish or stainless-steel pan. Pour the mustard mixture over the fish and let marinate at least 15 minutes.

4. Heat the broiler. Put the fish, skin-side down, on a broiler pan or baking sheet. Sprinkle with ½ teaspoon salt and broil, 6 inches from the heat if possible, until just done, about 5 minutes depending on the thickness of the fish.

5. Meanwhile, stir the vinegar, sugar, ⅛ teaspoon salt, and a pinch of pepper into the onions. Serve the fish with the lemon wedges and onion salad alongside.

GRILLED TANDOORI-STYLE CHICKEN

Marinating chicken with yogurt, garlic, cumin, and coriander gives the meat, and particularly the skin, a delicious Indian flavor. Traditionally the chicken is cooked in a coal- or wood-burning tandoor oven, but you can get a similar effect by grilling it. Bottled chutney is a fine accompaniment. Rice Pilaf with Carrots and Ginger, page 271, would also be good alongside.

WINE RECOMMENDATION

Because the spices in this dish are relatively mild, there are a number of good wine alternatives. Try a red wine from southern France, such as a Coteaux du Languedoc.

SERVES 4

1	cup plain yogurt
5	cloves garlic, minced
1	tablespoon lemon juice
1	tablespoon ground coriander
1½	teaspoons ground cumin
1	teaspoon ground ginger
½	teaspoon cayenne
⅛	teaspoon turmeric
	Pinch ground cloves
1½	teaspoons salt
¼	teaspoon fresh-ground black pepper
1	chicken (3 to 3½ pounds), quartered

1. In a large, shallow glass dish or stainless-steel pan, combine the yogurt, garlic, lemon juice, coriander, cumin, ginger, cayenne, turmeric, cloves, salt, and pepper. Add the chicken and turn to coat. Let marinate for 30 minutes.

2. Light the grill. Cook the chicken over moderately high heat for 10 minutes. Turn and cook until just done, about 10 minutes longer.

BAKED VARIATION

Marinate the chicken as directed. Heat the oven to 425°. Put the chicken, skin-side up, in a roasting pan and bake until just done, about 35 minutes.

CHINESE CORNISH HENS

Soy sauce, garlic, ginger, and five-spice powder lend these tender birds an exotic flavor. Because they're butterflied, which you can have done by the butcher if you prefer, the hens cook evenly in less than half an hour.

 WINE RECOMMENDATION
Wines made from the gewürztraminer grape pair wonderfully with Asian dishes such as this. Look for a bottle from the Alsace region of France.

SERVES 4

½   cup soy sauce

¼   cup cooking oil

4   cloves garlic, chopped

1   teaspoon grated fresh ginger

2   teaspoons sugar

1½   teaspoons five-spice powder*

1½   teaspoons salt

½   teaspoon fresh-ground black pepper

4   Cornish hens, backbones removed and birds flattened

   *Available at Asian markets and some supermarkets

1. In a small bowl, combine everything but the hens. Put the hens into two large glass dishes or stainless-steel pans. Pour the marinade over the hens and turn to coat. Let marinate, skin-side down, for 30 minutes.

2. Light the grill. Cook the hens over moderate heat for 12 minutes. Turn and cook until just done, about 12 minutes longer.

HOMEMADE FIVE-SPICE POWDER

Both fennel seeds and aniseed go into traditional five-spice powder. Since their flavors are so similar, we've simplified matters by calling only for aniseed. You can use either, or half as much of each. For a perfectly smooth powder like the commercial product, pulverize the spices in a spice or coffee grinder.

MAKES 1 TABLESPOON

1½   teaspoons aniseed, crushed

½   teaspoon ground cinnamon

½   teaspoon ground ginger

¼   teaspoon ground cloves

   Combine all the ingredients.

TEST-KITCHEN TIP

If you use your coffee grinder to grind spices, a great way to clean it is to put a few tablespoons of sugar in the grinder. Cover and grind for about 10 seconds. Unplug the grinder, discard the sugar, and wipe the inside with a paper towel.

GRILLED TURKEY WITH CORN, THYME, AND BLACK-BEAN SALSA

Turkey cutlets flavored with chili powder get just a quick sear on the grill so that they stay tender and moist. The salsa served alongside makes this a colorful Southwestern meal. If you like, serve the dish with warm flour tortillas.

WINE RECOMMENDATION
This Mexican-influenced dish will be at its best with a cold beer or a light, refreshing rosé from California, such as those made from the Rhône Valley varietals grenache and mourvedre.

SERVES 4

- 3 ears corn, in their husks
- 1 15-ounce can black beans, drained and rinsed (about 1⅔ cups)
- 1 medium tomato, seeded and chopped
- ½ jalapeño pepper, seeds and ribs removed, minced
- ¼ cup chopped cilantro
- 2½ tablespoons lime juice
- 1 teaspoon chopped fresh thyme, or ¼ teaspoon dried
- 1 teaspoon salt
- ⅛ teaspoon fresh-ground black pepper
- 8 turkey cutlets (about 1½ pounds in all)
- 2 tablespoons olive oil
- 1 tablespoon chili powder
- 1 lime, cut into wedges, for serving

1. Light the grill. Peel the corn husks about a third of the way down. Pull off the tassels with as much of the silk as possible. Press the husks back in place, enclosing the corn. Soak the corn in a large bowl of water for 5 minutes.

2. Drain the corn and grill, turning occasionally, until tender, 20 to 25 minutes. The husks will blacken. Peel the husks off the corn and remove any remaining silk. Cut the kernels off the cobs. You should have about 2 cups.

3. In a medium glass or stainless-steel bowl, combine the corn, beans, tomato, jalapeño, cilantro, lime juice, thyme, ¾ teaspoon of the salt, and the black pepper.

4. Coat the turkey cutlets with the oil. Season with the remaining ¼ teaspoon salt and the chili powder.

5. Grill the turkey until browned and just done, 1 to 2 minutes a side. Serve with the corn-and-bean salsa and the lime wedges.

TIME-SAVER

Rather than grilling fresh corn, use 2 cups frozen or canned kernels

GRILLED HAMBURGER STEAKS WITH HERB BUTTER

Rediscover how delicious a great grilled burger can be. Here it's topped simply with herb-flavored butter. The heat of the burger melts the butter, forming a delicious sauce.

WINE RECOMMENDATION
Classic hamburgers are great with a silky-textured, full-bodied red wine, such as a merlot from California or a cabernet sauvignon-shiraz blend from Australia.

SERVES 4

4 tablespoons butter, at room temperature

1 tablespoon minced shallot or onion

2 tablespoons mixed, chopped fresh herbs, such as tarragon, chives, and parsley

$\frac{1}{2}$ teaspoon lemon juice

Salt and fresh-ground black pepper

$1\frac{1}{3}$ pounds ground beef chuck

1. In a small bowl, combine the butter, shallot, herbs, lemon juice, $\frac{1}{8}$ teaspoon salt, and a pinch of pepper.

2. Light the grill or heat a grill pan until hot. Form the meat into four patties, about 1 inch thick. Season the patties with $\frac{1}{2}$ teaspoon salt and $\frac{1}{4}$ teaspoon pepper.

3. Cook the hamburgers for 4 minutes. Turn and cook to your taste, about 4 minutes longer for medium rare. Put on plates and top with the herb butter.

VARIATIONS

■ **Garlic Butter:** In a small bowl, combine 4 tablespoons room-temperature butter, 1 minced garlic clove, 2 tablespoons chopped fresh parsley, $\frac{1}{8}$ teaspoon salt, and a pinch of pepper.

■ **Olive Butter:** In a small bowl, combine 4 tablespoons room-temperature butter, 2 tablespoons pitted and chopped black olives, $1\frac{1}{2}$ teaspoons chopped fresh parsley, $\frac{1}{2}$ teaspoon lemon juice, $\frac{1}{8}$ teaspoon salt, and a pinch of pepper.

TEST-KITCHEN TIP

Because flavored butters go well with so many meats and fish, they're great to have on hand. When making them, prepare a double batch. Roll the extra into a cylinder, wrap well, and store in the freezer. Cut off what you need and let it thaw before serving.

SPICE-MARINATED SIRLOIN

A mixture of paprika, chili powder, oregano, rosemary, thyme, and garlic—short on heat but long on flavor—gives this sirloin steak its sizzle. Serve the steak with grilled bread so that you can soak up all the delicious juices.

WINE RECOMMENDATION

Steak means red wine, but the slight spiciness of this dish makes it best to choose a fairly fruity red that can be served very slightly chilled. Try a grenache or a not-very-expensive pinot noir from California.

SERVES 4

- 1 clove garlic, minced
- 1 tablespoon paprika
- 2 teaspoons fresh-ground black pepper
- ½ teaspoon chili powder
- 2 teaspoons chopped fresh rosemary, or ½ teaspoon dried, crumbled
- 1 teaspoon dried oregano
- 1 teaspoon dried thyme
- ¾ teaspoon salt
- ½ teaspoon sugar
- 2 pounds sirloin steak, about 1 inch thick
- 2 tablespoons cooking oil

1. In a small bowl, combine the garlic, paprika, pepper, chili powder, rosemary, oregano, thyme, salt, and sugar.

2. Coat the steak with the cooking oil. Spread the spice mixture on both sides of the meat and let marinate for about 30 minutes.

3. Light the grill or heat the broiler. Grill the steak over moderate heat for 6 minutes. Turn and cook to your taste, about 6 minutes longer for medium rare. Don't cook the steak too close to the heat or the spices will burn and taste bitter. Alternatively, broil the steak, 6 inches from the heat if possible, for the same amount of time.

4. Transfer the steak to a carving board and leave to rest in a warm spot for about 5 minutes before slicing and serving.

VARIATIONS

■**Pork Chop:** In place of the steak, use 4 pork chops, about 1 inch thick. Grill or broil them to your taste, about 8 minutes a side for medium.

■**Fish:** This spice rub is also delicious on bluefish fillets, or on other full-flavored fish such as mackerel. Let the fish marinate for about 15 minutes instead of 30.

SIRLOIN WITH ROASTED SWEET POTATOES, PEPPERS, AND SHIITAKES

Sirloin steak is always a favorite. Tender and juicy, and served with a colorful mixture of roasted red onions, whole garlic cloves, sweet potatoes, bell peppers, and shiitakes, it makes even a weeknight meal an occasion. Try pressing a clove of garlic out of its skin and eating it with a bite of beef.

WINE RECOMMENDATION
Pair this hearty meat with as deep and flavorful a red wine as you can find. A good choice would be a cabernet sauvignon from California or Chile.

SERVES 4

1 red onion, cut into 1-inch pieces

1 head garlic, cloves separated

2 bell peppers, red, yellow, green, or a combination of two, cut into 1½-inch squares

1 sweet potato, peeled and cut into 1½-inch chunks

½ pound shiitake mushrooms, stems removed

6 tablespoons cooking oil

1¼ teaspoons salt

½ teaspoon fresh-ground black pepper

¼ cup dry vermouth or dry white wine

3 tablespoons grated Parmesan cheese

2 tablespoons mixed, chopped fresh herbs, such as marjoram, thyme, rosemary, and parsley, or 2 teaspoons mixed dried herbs

2 pounds sirloin steak, about 1 inch thick

1 tablespoon butter

1. Heat the oven to 450°. In a large roasting pan, combine the vegetables and 4 tablespoons of the oil. Add ¾ teaspoon of the salt and ¼ teaspoon of the pepper and mix well. Spread the vegetables in an even layer. Sprinkle with the vermouth.

2. Roast the vegetables in the oven for 35 minutes. Add the Parmesan and herbs and mix well. Continue roasting until the vegetables are well browned, about 10 minutes longer. Put in a warm spot and cover loosely with aluminum foil.

3. Heat the broiler. Coat the steak with the remaining 2 tablespoons oil. Sprinkle the steak with the remaining ½ teaspoon salt and ¼ teaspoon pepper and dot with the butter.

4. Broil the steak for 5 minutes. Turn the meat and cook to your taste, about 5 minutes longer for medium-rare. Transfer to a carving board and leave to rest in a warm spot for about 5 minutes. Cut into thin diagonal slices and serve with the roasted vegetables.

SKIRT STEAK WITH ROSEMARY AND GARLIC

Marinated with rosemary, garlic, and olive oil, this tender and juicy skirt steak has great Mediterranean flavor. Any one of the Mashed Potatoes, page 260, would enhance the steak. Or serve it with Roasted Vegetables, page 249, or simply a baked potato.

WINE RECOMMENDATION
Try matching this steak with a fresh, fruity red from the Coteaux du Languedoc appellation in the South of France.

SERVES 4

¼ cup olive oil

1 large clove garlic, minced

2 teaspoons chopped fresh rosemary, or ¾ teaspoon dried, crumbled

2 pounds skirt steak, cut into 3 pieces

¾ teaspoon salt

¼ teaspoon fresh-ground black pepper

1 tablespoon butter

1. In a large, shallow glass dish or stainless-steel pan, combine the oil, garlic, and rosemary. Add the steak and turn to coat. Marinate for at least 20 minutes.

2. Light the grill or heat the broiler. Sprinkle the steak with the salt and pepper and dot with the butter. Grill or broil for 3 minutes. Turn the meat and cook to your taste, 3 to 4 minutes for medium rare depending on the thickness. Transfer to a carving board and leave to rest in a warm spot for about 5 minutes. Slice the steak across the grain and on the diagonal. The slices should be about ¼ inch thick.

VARIATIONS

■ If you're lucky enough to have a butcher who carries hanger steak, also known as "butcher's cut," by all means use that in place of the skirt steak. The flavor is exceptional. Because it's thicker than skirt steak, cook hanger steak about 6 minutes a side. You can also substitute flank steak if neither skirt nor hanger is available, and cook it for the same amount of time as skirt steak.

■ Use another herb, such as thyme, marjoram, oregano, or a combination, in place of the rosemary.

MARINATED PORK TENDERLOIN WITH NAPA CABBAGE

Balsamic vinegar, ginger, garlic, and herbs give pork tenderloin scintillating flavor. Grilled napa cabbage is the perfect sidekick.

WINE RECOMMENDATION
The unusual flavors of the marinated pork go nicely with a slightly fruity, somewhat acidic red wine such as a moderately priced pinot noir from California.

SERVES 4

1½ pounds pork tenderloin

6 tablespoons olive oil

3 tablespoons balsamic vinegar

3 cloves garlic, minced

3 tablespoons chopped fresh ginger

⅓ cup mixed, chopped fresh herbs, such as thyme, tarragon, and parsley

1½ teaspoons brown sugar

1¾ teaspoons salt

½ teaspoon fresh-ground black pepper

1 napa cabbage (about 2 pounds), cut lengthwise into 8 wedges

1. Light the grill. Using a sharp knife, cut shallow incisions in the pork tenderloin at about ½-inch intervals. In a large, shallow glass dish or stainless-steel pan, combine 3 tablespoons of the olive oil with the balsamic vinegar, garlic, ginger, herbs, brown sugar, 1 teaspoon of the salt, and ¼ teaspoon of the pepper. Reserve 3 tablespoons of the marinade. Add the meat to the dish and turn to coat. Let marinate 30 minutes.

2. Grill the pork over moderate heat, turning once, until done to medium, about 12 minutes in all. Transfer the pork to a carving board and leave to rest in a warm spot.

3. Meanwhile, coat the cabbage with the remaining 3 tablespoons oil. Sprinkle with the remaining ¾ teaspoon salt and ¼ teaspoon pepper. Grill the cabbage, turning once, until it is tender, about 10 minutes.

4. Cut the pork diagonally into ½-inch slices. Put the pork and cabbage on plates and drizzle the 3 tablespoons reserved marinade over the pork.

BARBECUED PORK RIBS

Finger-lickin'-good pork ribs, grilled and served with a quick barbecue sauce, are perfect for summer evenings. This version cuts the usual hours over a low fire to a single hour of cooking, most of it unattended. Grilled Corn with Extra-Virgin Olive Oil, page 242, is an ideal accompaniment.

WINE RECOMMENDATION
The spicy sweetness of these ribs is best with an easygoing, fruity red wine such as a Corbières from the South of France or a French Beaujolais-Villages.

SERVES 4

4 pounds pork spare ribs, cut into individual ribs

1½ cups ketchup

¾ cup water

3 tablespoons dark-brown sugar

3 tablespoons lemon juice

3 tablespoons Worcestershire sauce

¼ teaspoon ground ginger

1 clove garlic, chopped

¼ cup white vinegar

¼ cup liquid smoke*

*Available at supermarkets

1. Put the ribs in a large pot and fill the pot with enough water to cover. Bring to a boil, reduce the heat, and simmer until the meat is tender, 30 to 40 minutes. Drain.

2. Meanwhile, in a small saucepan, combine the ketchup, water, brown sugar, lemon juice, Worcestershire sauce, ginger, and garlic. Bring to a simmer over low heat, stirring until the sugar dissolves. Set aside.

3. In a shallow glass dish or stainless-steel pan, combine the vinegar and liquid smoke. Add the ribs and turn to coat.

4. Light the grill. Brush the ribs with the barbecue sauce and grill for 5 minutes. Turn and continue grilling, basting with the sauce, until browned, about 5 minutes longer. Alternatively, heat the oven to 450°. Put the ribs in a large roasting pan and pour half the barbecue sauce over the ribs. Cover with aluminum foil and bake for 10 minutes. Baste the ribs and cook, uncovered, until they're browned, about 5 minutes longer.

5. Reheat the remaining sauce, if necessary, and serve with the ribs.

—JUNE GREENWALD

205

MIXED GRILL WITH A
SPICED-AND-CHARRED-TOMATO SAUCE

Because the sauce is made with charbroiled tomatoes, this mixed grill has an authentic smoky taste even though it's cooked in the broiler.

WINE RECOMMENDATION
The smokiness of the meats and spiciness of the sauce will be best with a lively red wine that is full of fresh fruit. Look for a Beaujolais-Villages from France.

SERVES 4

2 tomatoes (about 1 pound)

$\frac{1}{3}$ cup plus 1 tablespoon olive oil

1 teaspoon ground coriander

$\frac{1}{2}$ teaspoon dry mustard

$\frac{1}{8}$ teaspoon ground cumin

2 scallions including green tops, cut into thin slices

2 cloves garlic, minced

2 tablespoons chopped fresh mint (optional)

$1\frac{1}{4}$ teaspoons salt

$\frac{1}{2}$ teaspoon fresh-ground black pepper

4 chicken thighs or drumsticks

4 lamb rib chops, about $1\frac{1}{4}$ inches thick

4 mild Italian or chicken sausages (about $\frac{3}{4}$ pound in all)

1. Heat the broiler. Line a small broiling pan with aluminum foil. Broil the tomatoes 5 to 6 inches from the heat if possible, turning to cook all sides, until the skin blackens, about 15 minutes. When the tomatoes are cool, chop them with their charred skins into a bowl, collecting all the juices.

2. In a small frying pan, heat the $\frac{1}{3}$ cup oil over moderate heat with the coriander, mustard, and cumin. Cook just until the spices turn light brown, about 1 minute. Take care not to burn the spices. Stir the seasoned oil into the tomatoes and let cool. Add the scallions, garlic, mint, $\frac{3}{4}$ teaspoon of the salt, and $\frac{1}{4}$ teaspoon of the pepper.

3. Heat the broiler. Coat the chicken and chops with the remaining 1 tablespoon oil. Season with the remaining $\frac{1}{2}$ teaspoon salt and $\frac{1}{4}$ teaspoon pepper. Broil the chicken and the sausages for 6 minutes. Turn the chicken and sausages and add the lamb chops to the pan. Continue to cook the meat, turning the chops once, until the chops are done to your taste, about 9 minutes longer for medium rare. Serve the meat with the sauce.

—KATHERINE ALFORD

LAMB KABOBS WITH LEMON, PORT, AND OREGANO

Served on a bed of Orzo with Grape-Leaf Pesto, page 267, these kabobs have the look and flavor of the Greek Islands. They are also good with the rice pilaf variation with thyme and parsley on page 271, or with plain rice.

WINE RECOMMENDATION
The best wine for this dish is a simple red. Try a bottle of fruity Minervois or Corbières, both from the South of France, and serve it slightly chilled.

SERVES 4

- 2 pounds boneless leg of lamb, cut into 1½-inch cubes
- 6 tablespoons olive oil
- 3 tablespoons port
- 2 tablespoons lemon juice
- 1 clove garlic, minced
- 1 tablespoon dried oregano
- 1 teaspoon ground cumin
- ¼ teaspoon fresh-ground black pepper
- 1 lemon, cut in half lengthwise and then cut crosswise into ⅛-inch slices
- ¾ teaspoon salt

1. In a glass dish or stainless-steel pan, combine the lamb, oil, port, lemon juice, garlic, oregano, cumin, and pepper, and let marinate 20 minutes.

2. Light the grill or heat the broiler. Drain the lamb, reserving the marinade. Thread the lamb onto four skewers, putting 1 lemon slice between every two pieces of meat. Sprinkle the kabobs with the salt.

3. Grill or broil the kabobs, turning and basting with the reserved marinade, until the meat is cooked to your taste, 6 to 8 minutes for medium rare.

TEST-KITCHEN TIP

If you don't have metal skewers for the lamb, you can always use the small wooden ones that are available at most supermarkets. Soak the skewers in water for about 20 minutes so that the tips don't burn on the grill.

LAMB CHOPS WITH CARAMELIZED ONIONS AND ROSEMARY

Broiled to a golden brown and smothered with rosemary-flavored caramelized onions, these succulent lamb rib chops are bound to become a reliable, year-round favorite. If you want to be especially generous with the lamb, add another chop per person.

WINE RECOMMENDATION

A red Bordeaux (primarily cabernet sauvignon and merlot) will tame the gamey flavor of the lamb.

SERVES 4

2½ tablespoons butter

3 onions, cut into thin slices

1 tablespoon chopped fresh rosemary, or 1 teaspoon dried, crumbled

1¼ teaspoons salt

Pinch sugar

¼ cup water

2 tablespoons dry vermouth or dry white wine

Fresh-ground black pepper

8 lamb rib chops, 1¼ inches thick

1 tablespoon olive oil

1. In a large frying pan, melt 2 tablespoons of the butter over moderately low heat. Add the onions, rosemary, ¾ teaspoon of the salt, and the sugar, and cook, stirring occasionally, until well browned, about 15 minutes. Add the water, vermouth, and ⅛ teaspoon pepper. Simmer, stirring, for 1 minute. Keep warm.

2. Heat the broiler. Coat the chops with the oil and season with ¼ teaspoon pepper and the remaining ½ teaspoon salt. Dot the chops with the remaining ½ tablespoon butter. Broil the chops for 5 minutes. Turn and broil until cooked to your taste, about 4 minutes longer for medium rare. Spoon the onions over the chops.

BUTTERFLIED LAMB

Paprika, garlic, lemon, and thyme accentuate the flavor of the lamb. The piece used here is the meaty top half of the leg. Since it's butterflied, it cooks in just 20 minutes.

WINE RECOMMENDATION Meaty lamb is at its best alongside a full-bodied, hearty red, especially a Côtes-du-Rhône or Châteauneuf-du-Pape from the Rhône Valley in France.

SERVES 4

- 3 tablespoons olive oil
- 3 cloves garlic, minced
- 2 teaspoons lemon juice
- 1 tablespoon paprika
- 1 teaspoon dried thyme
- 1 teaspoon salt
- ¾ teaspoon fresh-ground black pepper
- 1 butterflied lamb butt (2½ to 3 pounds)

1. In a small bowl, combine the oil, garlic, lemon juice, paprika, thyme, salt, and pepper. Put the lamb in a large, shallow glass dish or stainless-steel pan and brush both sides of the meat with the paprika mixture. Let marinate for 30 minutes.

2. Light the grill or heat the broiler. Grill the meat over moderate heat for 10 minutes. Turn and cook until done to your taste, about 10 minutes longer, depending on the thickness, for medium rare. Don't cook the lamb too close to the heat or the paprika will burn and taste bitter. Alternatively, broil the meat, 6 inches from the heat if possible, for the same amount of time.

3. Transfer the grilled lamb to a carving board and leave to rest in a warm spot for 5 minutes. Cut thin slices against the grain.

RACLETTE

We love this Swiss dish, which is something like fondue but even easier. Traditionally, the cooking consisted of setting a half-wheel of cheese on the hearth in front of the fire. A few simple but wildly popular restaurants in Switzerland still prepare it this way, scraping off the front of the cheese as it melts and serving it with new potatoes, thin slices of air-dried beef, and cornichons. More often you'll find raclette machines in use; they're essentially tabletop grills. We find the broiler works just as well.

WINE RECOMMENDATION
Many red wines will work well with this dish, but an especially delightful match would be a light, vibrantly fruity red, such as a Dôle from Switzerland or a reasonably priced pinot noir from California.

SERVES 4

- 2 pounds new potatoes
- 1 1⅓-pound wedge Swiss raclette or other flavorful cheese that melts well, rind removed, cheese cut into ¼-inch slices
- ⅓ pound Bundnerfleisch or other cured meat
- 1 cup cornichons

1. Put the potatoes in a large saucepan of salted water. Bring to a boil and cook until tender, about 15 minutes. Drain and cut in half.

2. Heat the broiler. Put the cheese in a large baking dish in one layer. Put the cooked potatoes, the Bundnerfleisch, and the cornichons on each plate, leaving a space for the cheese.

3. Broil the cheese, 6 inches from the heat if possible, until the top of the cheese just melts. Scrape the melted cheese onto the prepared plates and serve at once. Return the unmelted cheese to the broiler and continue melting and scraping onto the plates.

SUBSTITUTIONS

■ While nothing quite compares to Swiss raclette, which is available in some cheese shops, Austrian Fontina and Gouda are good substitutes. Camembert and Brie, albeit very different in flavor, also work well in this recipe.

■ In place of the Bundnerfleisch, domestic bresaola, an Italian-style air-dried beef, is a good choice. You can also use German-style Lachsschinken, prosciutto, or just about any smoked ham.

■ As for the acidic little European cornichons, any sour pickle can be used as a substitute.

OVEN ROASTING & BAKING

Roasted Cod with New Potatoes and Aioli, page 215

ROASTS ARE FOR ENTERTAINING AND FOR LEISURELY WEEKENDS, RIGHT? WRONG. We had that notion, too, until a fellow food writer (with a seven-year-old son) told us that she always makes a roast early in the week. If the cut is on the small side, so that it doesn't have to cook too long, a roast is perfect for a week-night meal. Preparation is minimal, and leftovers give you a head start on a soup, salad, or sandwich for another night. The same, of course, goes for roast-ed chicken and fish. That being said, we should add that the majority of recipes in this chapter aren't for whole roasts at all. You'll find new ways to prepare fish fillets and chicken breasts, as well as baked dishes such as the irre-sistible savory bread pudding on page 229.

ROASTED COD WITH NEW POTATOES AND AIOLI

Cod fillet is browned in a frying pan to crisp the outside, and then finished in a hot oven alongside the roasting potatoes and onions. Garlicky aioli lends spirit to the mild fish and potatoes.

WINE RECOMMENDATION
This dish, potent with garlic, works nicely with a straightforward, slightly acidic Oregon pinot gris.

SERVES 4

1½ pounds small red new potatoes, cut into quarters, or larger potatoes cut into about 1½-inch chunks

2 onions, each cut into 8 wedges

1 cup plus 3 tablespoons olive oil

1¼ teaspoons salt

Fresh-ground black pepper

1 large egg

4 cloves garlic, minced

1½ pounds cod fillet, about ¾ inch thick

1 teaspoon minced fresh rosemary (optional)

1. Heat the oven to 450°. In a large roasting pan, toss together the potatoes, onions, 2 tablespoons of the oil, ¾ teaspoon of the salt, and ¼ teaspoon pepper. Roast, stirring occasionally, until the potatoes are tender, about 35 minutes.

2. Meanwhile, put the egg, half of the garlic, ¼ teaspoon of the salt, and a pinch of pepper in a food processor. With the food processor running, add ¼ cup of the oil very slowly, and then ¾ cup in a thin stream. The mixture will thicken as you add the oil.

3. In a large nonstick frying pan, heat the remaining 1 tablespoon oil over moderately high heat. Cut the cod into 4 pieces and season with ⅛ teaspoon pepper and the remaining ¼ teaspoon salt. Add the cod to the pan and cook until browned, about 3 minutes. Flip the fish, sprinkle with the rosemary and the remaining garlic, and cook 1 minute longer.

4. Push the potatoes and onions to one side of the roasting pan. Add the cod and roast just until done, about 5 minutes. Serve with the aioli.

ROASTED FISH WITH BALSAMIC GLAZE

The glaze that's drizzled around the fish couldn't be simpler: balsamic vinegar, simmered with thyme until syrupy and then slightly sweetened with a bit of brown sugar. It's a successful imitation of well-aged, $100-a-pint balsamic vinegar. The contrast of the mild fish and pungent sauce is exceptional.

WINE RECOMMENDATION
The simplicity of this fish and its hint of sweetness make it easy to match with a full-bodied white wine. Try a chardonnay from California or a white Burgundy (made from chardonnay).

SERVES 4

½ cup balsamic vinegar

3 sprigs fresh thyme, or ¼ teaspoon dried

½ teaspoon brown sugar, more if needed
   Salt

1 tablespoon olive oil

1½ pounds firm white fish fillets, such as striped bass, red snapper, grouper, or halibut, about ¾ inch thick

¼ teaspoon fresh-ground black pepper

2 tablespoons chopped fresh parsley

1. Heat the oven to 450°. In a small, stainless-steel saucepan, bring the vinegar and thyme to a simmer. Simmer the vinegar until reduced to 3 tablespoons, about 5 minutes. Remove the thyme sprigs, if using. Add the ½ teaspoon brown sugar and a pinch of salt. Taste the sauce. You may need to add more sugar, depending on the acidity of the vinegar. The sauce should taste acidic with just a hint of sweetness.

2. Meanwhile, oil a roasting pan or baking sheet. In a large nonstick frying pan, heat the 1 tablespoon oil over moderately high heat. Season the fish with ¼ teaspoon salt and the pepper. Put the fish, skin-side up, in the frying pan and cook until browned, about 3 minutes. Put the fish, browned-side up, into the prepared roasting pan and cook in the preheated oven until just done, about 6 minutes depending on the thickness of the fish. Put the fish on plates, drizzle the sauce around it, and sprinkle with the parsley.

VARIATION

Add 1½ tablespoons butter to the reduced balsamic sauce and whisk over low heat until just melted. The butter mellows the sauce and gives it a satiny finish—irresistible.

ROASTED MONKFISH WITH GREMOLATA BROWN BUTTER

This succulent, lobster-like fish is delicious when marinated, roasted, and served with a brown-butter sauce seasoned with lemon, parsley, and garlic. Skip the sauce if you prefer; the fish will still be full of flavor.

WINE RECOMMENDATION
A lean, brisk white will cut through the richness of the sauce. Try a dry-as-a-bone French chenin blanc from an appellation such as Vouvray or Anjou in the Loire Valley.

SERVES 4

3 tablespoons olive oil

5 cloves garlic, minced

1½ teaspoons grated lemon zest

1 teaspoon chopped fresh rosemary, or ½ teaspoon dried, crumbled

1¼ teaspoons salt

½ teaspoon fresh-ground black pepper

2 pounds monkfish fillets, about 1 inch thick, membranes removed and fish cut into 4 pieces

¼ pound butter

¼ cup chopped flat-leaf parsley

½ teaspoon lemon juice

1. In a shallow glass dish or stainless-steel pan, combine the oil, a third of the garlic, 1 teaspoon of the lemon zest, the rosemary, ¾ teaspoon of the salt, and ¼ teaspoon of the pepper. Add the monkfish and turn to coat. Let marinate at least 20 minutes. Heat the oven to 450°.

2. In a small frying pan, melt the butter over low heat. Cook, stirring, until the butter is golden brown, about 5 minutes. Remove from the heat and let cool slightly. Add the remaining garlic and cook, stirring, for 30 seconds. Add the remaining ½ teaspoon lemon zest, ½ teaspoon salt, and ¼ teaspoon pepper, the parsley, and the lemon juice.

3. Put the fish in a roasting pan or on a baking sheet and roast in the oven until just done, about 8 minutes.

4. Bring the sauce to a simmer and pour it over the fish.

TEST-KITCHEN TIP

If you find that your monkfish fillets curl during cooking, you can stick a metal skewer through them lengthwise and then remove it once they're cooked. Or you can score the fillets at 1-inch intervals.

Lime-Marinated Chicken Breasts

The marinade will flavor the chicken in just 20 minutes, but for an even more intense taste, you can leave it for up to 2 hours. For a crisp, golden skin, the chicken breasts are run under the broiler after baking. Corn Salad, page 255, is the perfect side dish.

WINE RECOMMENDATION
The flavors to match here are the lime, cumin, and coriander. Try a full-bodied, acidic white, such as a riesling from Alsace in France or a sauvignon blanc from California.

SERVES 4

6   tablespoons cooking oil

¼   cup lime juice (from about 2 limes)

2   teaspoons ground cumin

1   teaspoon ground coriander

¼   teaspoon cayenne

4   unboned chicken breasts (about 2¼ pounds in all)

¼   teaspoon salt

1. In a shallow glass dish or stainless-steel pan, combine the oil, lime juice, cumin, coriander, and cayenne. Add the chicken; turn to coat. Let marinate at least 20 minutes.

2. Heat the oven to 375°. Sprinkle the chicken with the salt. Put in a roasting pan, skin-side up, and bake until just done, about 30 minutes.

3. Heat the broiler. Just before serving, broil the chicken until the skin is brown and crisp, about 2 minutes.

Variations

■ For a milder version, use paprika in place of the cayenne.

■ If you prefer dark meat, use whole chicken legs instead of the chicken breasts. Add about 10 minutes to the cooking time.

■ Instead of baking the chicken, grill it for about 18 minutes.

MAPLE-BRINED CHICKEN

Soaking chicken in a maple-syrup brine keeps it moist and gives it a delicious cured flavor and a lovely golden-brown color. Here we suggest chicken breasts because they need to soak for only 30 minutes, but you can make a whole chicken this way, too. Add another cup of water to the brine and let the chicken soak for about 2 hours.

WINE RECOMMENDATION
The mild, salty flavor of the chicken will go nicely with any number of full-bodied white wines. Try an Alsatian pinot blanc or a white Côtes-du-Rhône, both from France.

SERVES 4

- 3 cups water
- ½ cup maple syrup
- ⅓ cup salt
- 2 bay leaves, crumbled
- ½ teaspoon peppercorns
- 4 unboned chicken breasts (about 2¼ pounds in all)
- 1 tablespoon butter, cut into small pieces

1. In a small saucepan, combine 1 cup of the water, the maple syrup, salt, bay leaves, and peppercorns. Bring to a boil, stirring until the salt dissolves. Pour into a large bowl. Add the remaining 2 cups water and let cool.

2. Heat the oven to 450°. Add the chicken breasts to the brine and let soak for 30 minutes. Remove and pat dry.

3. Put the chicken breasts in a roasting pan, skin-side up. Dot each one with butter and roast until just done, about 25 minutes.

BROWN-SUGAR VARIATION

If you don't have any maple syrup on hand, you can use ⅓ cup dark-brown sugar instead.

TIME-SAVER

To hasten the cooling of the brine, use 2 cups of ice water (mostly ice) in place of the plain water. If the brine's still warm, put it in the freezer for a few minutes.

ROASTED CHICKEN WITH ONIONS AND GARLIC

Crisp, golden chicken legs taste wonderful with soft, mellow cloves of roasted garlic. Squeeze the garlic out of its skin and eat a little bit with each bite of chicken. You might serve this with Mashed Potatoes, page 260, or Polenta with Parmesan, page 272.

WINE RECOMMENDATION
Look for a full-bodied white wine without too much personality to pair with this dish. Try a pinot blanc from France's Alsace region or a non-oaky California chardonnay.

SERVES 4

2 onions, chopped

3 tablespoons olive oil

4 chicken thighs

4 chicken drumsticks

2 heads garlic, cloves separated

½ teaspoon salt

¼ teaspoon fresh-ground black pepper

1. Heat the oven to 450°. Put the onions in a large roasting pan. Add 1 tablespoon of the oil and toss. Spread the onions in an even layer.

2. Toss the chicken and garlic with the remaining 2 tablespoons oil, the salt, and the pepper. Arrange the chicken pieces, skin-side up and about 1 inch apart, on top of the onions. Scatter the garlic cloves around the chicken pieces.

3. Roast in the oven until the chicken is just done and the skin is crisp and brown, about 40 minutes.

HERB VARIATION

Add about 2 teaspoons dried herbs, such as oregano, marjoram, or crumbled rosemary, to the oil before tossing with the chicken.

JERK CHICKEN

Tangy with citrus, hot and spicy with Tabasco and allspice, this marinated chicken is a favorite in Jamaica. If you prefer less heat, add only half the Tabasco. Serve the dish with biscuits, pita, or crusty rolls.

WINE RECOMMENDATION
Plenty of liquid will be needed to chase the heat of this dish, and the best choice is probably a lighter-style beer. If you want to drink wine, try a very light, very cold bottle of pinot blanc from the Alsace region of France.

SERVES 4

 3 scallions including green tops, chopped

 2 cloves garlic, chopped

 ¼ cup cooking oil

 ½ teaspoon grated orange zest

2½ tablespoons orange juice

 2 tablespoons lime juice

 2 teaspoons soy sauce

 2 teaspoons Tabasco sauce

 1 tablespoon dried thyme

 1 tablespoon ground allspice

 1 tablespoon five-spice powder*

 1 teaspoon salt

 1 teaspoon fresh-ground black pepper

 4 chicken thighs

 4 chicken drumsticks

*Available at Asian markets and some supermarkets, or see page 197 for homemade

1. In a blender or food processor, puree all the ingredients except the chicken.

2. Put the chicken in a large, shallow glass dish or stainless-steel pan. Rub the chicken all over with the pureed spice mixture. Let marinate for about 30 minutes.

3. Heat the oven to 450°. Put the chicken in a large roasting pan and cook in the upper third of the oven for 20 minutes. Cover with aluminum foil and cook until just done, about 12 minutes longer. The chicken will be very dark.

VARIATIONS

■ If you prefer chicken breasts, use them in place of the legs. Just reduce the cooking time by about 5 minutes.

■ Do as the Jamaicans do and use pork chops as well as or instead of the chicken. Bake the chops in the upper third of the oven, uncovered, until just done, about 20 minutes. You can also jerk pork tenderloin, turkey breast, and shoulder lamb chops.

CHICKEN WITH LEMON AND THYME

Roasted with lemon and thyme and then briefly broiled, this quartered chickens is flavorful, juicy, and crisp.

WINE RECOMMENDATION
This is a versatile dish that will be fine with your favorite everyday white. If you're choosing a wine just for this dish, make it a citrusy chardonnay from California or (if you prefer more oak flavor) from Australia.

SERVES 4

1 chicken (3 to 3½ pounds), quartered
4 teaspoons olive oil
1 teaspoon dried thyme
1 tablespoon lemon juice
½ teaspoon salt
⅛ teaspoon fresh-ground black pepper

1. Heat the oven to 375°. Coat the chicken with 3 teaspoons of the oil and arrange the pieces, skin-side up, in a large roasting pan. Sprinkle the chicken with the thyme, lemon juice, salt, and pepper. Drizzle with the remaining 1 teaspoon oil.

2. Cook until the breasts are just done, about 30 minutes. Remove and continue to cook the legs until done, about 5 minutes longer. Remove from the oven and put the breasts back in the pan.

3. Heat the broiler. Broil the chicken until the skin is golden brown, about 2 minutes. Serve with the pan juices.

VARIATIONS

■ Use dry vermouth or dry white wine in place of the lemon juice. Lime juice works well, too.

■ You can use other dried herbs, such as oregano or marjoram, in place of the thyme.

CURRY-ROASTED CHICKEN WITH LIME JUS

Basted with curry-and-garlic-flavored butter, this roasted chicken develops a crisp, golden-yellow skin. The sauce, made from the pan juices flavored with lime, adds a pleasant tang. Rice Pilaf with Carrots and Ginger, page 271, or plain rice is the perfect accompaniment.

WINE RECOMMENDATION
The mild curry and subtle lime flavors of this dish work well with a simple, fruity white wine such as a Côtes-de-Gascogne from France or another wine made from the ugni blanc grape.

SERVES 4

- 4 tablespoons butter
- 1 tablespoon curry powder
- 1 clove garlic, minced
- 1 chicken (3 to 3½ pounds)
  Salt and fresh-ground black pepper
- ½ cup water
- ½ teaspoon lime juice

1. Heat the oven to 425°. In a small pot, melt the butter with the curry powder and garlic.

2. Sprinkle the cavity of the chicken with ¼ teaspoon salt and ⅛ teaspoon pepper. Twist the wings behind its back and tie the legs together. Put the chicken, breast-side up, on a rack in a roasting pan. Sprinkle the chicken with ¼ teaspoon salt and ⅛ teaspoon pepper. Brush with the curry butter.

3. Roast the chicken until done, about 50 minutes, brushing with the curry butter several times. Cover loosely with aluminum foil during the last 10 minutes. Transfer the bird to a carving board and leave to rest in a warm spot for about 15 minutes.

4. Meanwhile, pour off the fat from the roasting pan. Set the pan over moderate heat and add the water. Bring to a boil, scraping the bottom of the pan to dislodge any brown bits. Boil until reduced to 3 tablespoons, about 4 minutes. Add any accumulated juices from the chicken. Add the lime juice and a pinch each of salt and pepper. Carve the bird and serve with the lime jus.

ROASTED CORNISH HENS WITH CARAWAY

Rubbing Cornish hens with paprika, mustard, and caraway, and roasting them over diced carrots and potatoes is a wonderful way to maximize your time. Everything cooks at once, and the hens' juices flavor the vegetables.

 WINE RECOMMENDATION
The succulent, gamey flavor of the hens with the mustard, caraway seeds, and garlic is an ideal partner for a hearty, full-bodied red wine such as a Côtes-du-Rhône from France.

SERVES 4

1¼ pounds new potatoes, cut into ½-inch dice

6 carrots, cut into ½-inch slices

4 tablespoons butter, melted

2 teaspoons salt

¼ teaspoon fresh-ground black pepper

2 cloves garlic, smashed

2 tablespoons grainy mustard

1 tablespoon paprika

2 teaspoons caraway seeds

4 Cornish hens

1. Heat the oven to 425°. In a roasting pan, toss the potatoes and carrots with 2 tablespoons of the butter, 1 teaspoon of the salt, and ⅛ teaspoon of the pepper. Roast the vegetables for 15 minutes.

2. Meanwhile, in a small bowl, combine the garlic with the remaining 1 teaspoon salt. Mash together with a fork to make a paste. Add the remaining 2 tablespoons butter, the mustard, paprika, caraway seeds, and the remaining ⅛ teaspoon pepper. Twist the wings of each hen behind its back and tie the legs together. Spread the paste all over the hens.

3. Remove the roasting pan from the oven and stir the vegetables. Set the hens, breast-side down, on top of the vegetables. Return the pan to the oven and roast for 30 minutes.

4. Remove the pan from the oven. Stir the vegetables and turn the birds breast-side up. Return the pan to the oven and cook until the hens are golden brown, about 30 minutes.

5. To serve, remove the strings from the birds. With a slotted spoon, put the vegetables on a platter or on individual plates and nest the hens on top.

—KATHERINE ALFORD

225

CORNISH HENS WITH PRUNES AND COGNAC

This simple main dish requires almost no preparation. With its quick, brandy-flavored sauce, it's perfect for a special weeknight dinner.

WINE RECOMMENDATION
A pinot noir from California or a reasonably priced "Bourgogne Rouge" from Burgundy in France (made from pinot noir) is a delightful match for both the mild hens and the deep, rich-flavored prunes.

SERVES 4

- 4 Cornish hens
- ¾ teaspoon salt
  Fresh-ground black pepper
- 2 tablespoons butter, cut into small pieces
- ¼ cup cognac or other brandy
- 1 cup water
- 24 pitted prunes
- 1 tablespoon chopped fresh parsley (optional)

1. Heat the oven to 450°. Twist the wings of each Cornish hen behind its back and tie the legs together. Put the hens, breast-side up, on a rack in a roasting pan. Sprinkle the hens with ½ teaspoon of the salt and ¼ teaspoon pepper. Dot with the butter. Roast the hens until just done, 40 to 45 minutes.

2. Meanwhile, put the cognac, water, and prunes in a small saucepan, bring to a simmer, cover, remove from the heat, and let steep while the hens cook.

3. When the hens are done, transfer them to a large plate and put in a warm spot. Pour off the fat from the roasting pan. Set the pan over moderate heat and add the prune mixture, the remaining ¼ teaspoon salt, and ⅛ teaspoon pepper. Bring to a boil over moderately high heat, scraping the bottom of the pan to dislodge any brown bits.

4. Continue boiling until the liquid is reduced to about ½ cup, about 8 minutes. Add the parsley. Remove the strings from the birds. Spoon the prunes and sauce over the hens.

—STEPHANIE LYNESS

LEMON AND GARLIC TURKEY BREAST

Make roast turkey in under an hour. This boneless breast is so tasty, you may find yourself using the recipe for the holidays, too.

WINE RECOMMENDATION The gentle garlic flavor and hint of lemon in this succulent turkey breast are a good match with the citrus notes and full body of a chardonnay from California.

SERVES 4

- 4 tablespoons butter, at room temperature
- 3 cloves garlic, minced
- ¾ teaspoon grated lemon zest
- ¾ teaspoon salt
- ½ teaspoon fresh-ground black pepper
- 1 2-pound boneless turkey breast, with the skin
- ¾ cup Chicken Stock, page 303, or canned low-sodium chicken broth

1. Heat the oven to 450°. In a small bowl, combine the butter, garlic, lemon zest, salt, and pepper. Spread the mixture all over the turkey breast.

2. Set the turkey breast, skin-side up, on a rack in a roasting pan. Roast for 20 minutes, basting occasionally. Reduce the oven temperature to 375° and continue roasting the turkey breast until just done (165°), 20 to 25 minutes longer. Transfer the turkey breast to a carving board and leave to rest in a warm spot for about 10 minutes.

3. Meanwhile, pour off the fat from the roasting pan. Set the pan over moderate heat and add the stock. Bring to a boil, scraping the bottom of the pan to dislodge any brown bits that cling to the bottom. Simmer until reduced to ½ cup, about 3 minutes. Cut the turkey breast into slices and serve with the pan juices.

DARK-MEAT VARIATION

Supermarkets now sell turkey parts throughout the year. Boneless breast is the easiest to serve since carving is a breeze, but if you prefer dark meat, roast whole legs instead. The cooking time will be a little longer and the internal temperature should be 15 degrees higher than for the breast.

Sausage and Smoked-Mozzarella Bread Pudding

This dish is a wonderful way to use up leftover meats or vegetables. Substitute roast chicken, veal, pork, or beef for the sausage. You can also add carrots, peppers, or ratatouille.

WINE RECOMMENDATION

An easygoing, fruity Italian red wine is perfect with this hearty dish. Look for a Dolcetto from the Piedmont or a Valpolicella from the Veneto region.

SERVES 4

- 2 tablespoons cooking oil
- ½ pound mild Italian sausage, casing removed
- 4 scallions including green tops, chopped
- 1 green bell pepper, cut into ½-inch pieces
- 4 eggs, beaten to mix
- 2 cups milk
- ½ cup grated Parmesan cheese
- ¾ teaspoon salt
- ½ teaspoon fresh-ground black pepper
- ⅛ teaspoon grated nutmeg
- 4 cups ½-inch cubes of good-quality white bread
- ½ pound smoked mozzarella cheese, cut into ½-inch cubes

1. Heat the oven to 350°. Butter a 1½-quart gratin dish. In a large frying pan, heat 1 tablespoon of the oil. Add the sausage and cook, breaking up the meat with a fork, until no longer pink, about 3 minutes. Remove the sausage with a slotted spoon. Add the remaining 1 tablespoon oil to the pan. Add the scallions and bell pepper and cook, stirring occasionally, until soft, about 5 minutes.

2. In a large bowl, whisk together the eggs, milk, Parmesan, salt, black pepper, and nutmeg.

3. Spread the sausage in the bottom of the prepared gratin dish. Top with the scallion and bell-pepper mixture, the bread, and the mozzarella. Pour the custard over all, and press the bread into the liquid, making sure that the bread is well moistened.

4. Bake the bread pudding for 20 minutes. Raise the oven temperature to 400° and bake until puffed and browned, about 18 minutes longer.

—Paul Grimes

SALT-AND-PEPPER-CRUSTED ROAST BEEF

A coating of coarse salt and crushed peppercorns makes a delicious crust that flavors the meat within. Roasted Vegetables, page 249, Sautéed Potatoes with Lemon and Parsley, page 259, Roasted Brussels Sprouts, page 239, Butternut Squash Baked with Olive Oil and Sage, page 247, and Peas with Scallions and Herbs, page 243, would all be excellent alongside.

 WINE RECOMMENDATION
What could be simpler or easier to match with a favorite full-bodied red wine than this? Try a cabernet sauvignon from California.

SERVES 4

¼ cup cracked black pepper

2 tablespoons coarse salt

1 2½-pound sirloin roast

1 tablespoon cooking oil

½ cup water

1. Heat the oven to 350°. In a small bowl, combine the pepper and salt. Rub the roast all over with the oil. Press the salt and pepper all over the surface of the meat. Put the meat on a rack in a roasting pan.

2. Cook the roast until done to your taste, about 50 minutes for medium rare (140°). Transfer to a carving board and leave to rest in a warm spot for about 15 minutes.

3. Pour off the fat from the roasting pan. Set the pan over moderate heat and add the water. Bring to a boil, scraping the bottom of the pan to dislodge any brown bits. Strain if necessary. Cut the roast into thin slices and serve with the jus.

VARIATIONS

■ For a sauce similar to that of steak au poivre, add 2 tablespoons brandy to the pan along with the water.

■ Try another cut, such as eye of round or rib roast.

TEST-KITCHEN TIP

If you don't have a pepper grinder with a coarse setting, put the peppercorns in a plastic bag and crush them with the bottom of a small heavy pot, a wine bottle, or a rolling pin.

PORK TENDERLOINS WITH WHITE WINE AND PRUNES

Everyone loves this very tender, juicy cut of pork, especially when it's served with a white-wine cream sauce and plump prunes.

WINE RECOMMENDATION
The pork and the sweetness of this dish will go nicely with the soft and slightly sweet red-fruit notes of a pinot noir from California or a red Burgundy (made from pinot noir) from France.

SERVES 4

- 2 pork tenderloins, about ¾ pound each
- 1 teaspoon salt
- ¾ teaspoon fresh-ground black pepper
- 1 tablespoon olive oil
- 1 cup dry white wine
- ½ cup Chicken Stock, page 303, or canned low-sodium chicken broth
- 12 pitted prunes, halved
- ⅓ cup heavy cream

1. Heat the oven to 325°. Sprinkle the tenderloins with ½ teaspoon of the salt and ½ teaspoon of the pepper.

2. In a small, heavy roasting pan or ovenproof frying pan, heat the oil over moderately high heat. Add the tenderloins and brown well on all sides, about 5 minutes.

3. Cook the tenderloins in the oven until done to medium, about 20 minutes.

Transfer to a carving board and leave to rest in a warm spot for about 5 minutes.

4. Set the pan over moderate heat and add the wine and stock. Bring to a boil, scraping the bottom of the pan to dislodge any brown bits. Add the prunes and the remaining ½ teaspoon salt. Boil until the liquid is reduced to about ¾ cup, about 8 minutes.

5. Add the cream and boil the sauce until slightly thickened, about 3 minutes longer. Add the remaining ¼ teaspoon pepper.

6. Cut the pork into thick slices. Serve with the sauce.

—Susan Shapiro Jaslove

STUFFED PORTOBELLO MUSHROOMS

These large, meaty mushrooms are perfect for stuffing. Here, ground pork is flavored with plenty of onion, garlic, and parsley. A quick tomato sauce complements the dish, and buttered pasta would round out the meal nicely.

WINE RECOMMENDATION
A dense but fruity, rustic red wine is perfect with these meat-filled mushrooms. Try a zinfandel from California or a Côtes-du-Rhône from the South of France.

SERVES 4

- 3 tablespoons butter
- 1 large onion, chopped fine
- 4 cloves garlic, minced
- 1½ cups canned crushed tomatoes
- 1 cup water
- 1 bay leaf
- Salt
- ¾ pound ground pork
- 1 egg, beaten to mix
- ½ cup plus 3 tablespoons dry bread crumbs
- 4 tablespoons chopped flat-leaf parsley
- Fresh-ground black pepper
- 4 portobello mushrooms (about 1½ pounds in all), stems removed

1. Heat the oven to 375°. In a medium saucepan, heat 2 tablespoons of the butter over moderately low heat. Add the onion and garlic and cook, stirring occasionally, until the onion is translucent, about 5 minutes. Remove all but ⅓ cup of the onion mixture and put in a medium bowl. Add the tomatoes, water, bay leaf, and ¾ teaspoon salt to the saucepan. Bring to a boil. Reduce the heat and simmer for 20 minutes.

2. Meanwhile, oil a baking sheet. Add the pork, egg, the 3 tablespoons bread crumbs, 2 tablespoons of the parsley, ¾ teaspoon salt, and ¼ teaspoon pepper to the onion in the bowl and mix until thoroughly combined. Sprinkle the mushrooms with ¼ teaspoon salt and ⅛ teaspoon pepper and arrange on the prepared baking sheet. Fill each mushroom with a quarter of the stuffing.

3. In a small bowl, combine the remaining ½ cup bread crumbs and 2 tablespoons parsley with ⅛ teaspoon salt and a pinch of pepper. Sprinkle over the stuffing. Cover the mushrooms with aluminum foil and bake for 15 minutes. Uncover and bake until the stuffing is cooked through, 12 to 15 minutes longer.

4. Remove the bay leaf from the sauce. Use the sauce as is or puree in a food processor or blender until smooth. Reheat and stir in the remaining 1 tablespoon butter. Serve the mushrooms with the sauce.

VEGETABLES & SALADS

Radicchio and Romaine Salad with Walnuts, page 253

DO YOU CONCENTRATE ON THE MAIN COURSE and make the same accompanying tossed salad or boiled vegetables every night? Well, frankly, so do we. But sometimes, when you're doing something dead easy, like grilling a steak or sautéing a chop, it's nice to include a side dish with character. These recipes are so simple that you may be tempted to vary your repertoire or at least add a method—perhaps roasting, which we find often not only produces tastier vegetables but does so with even less effort than boiling or steaming.

ROASTED ASPARAGUS WITH HAZELNUT SAUCE

Roasted until golden and then drizzled with a chunky hazelnut and brown-butter sauce, asparagus spears make a luxurious side dish. With a squeeze of lemon, the combination is magic. You may want to serve the roasted asparagus without the sauce sometimes; it's delicious on its own.

SERVES 4

⅓ cup hazelnuts

2 pounds asparagus

2 tablespoons olive oil

½ teaspoon salt

Fresh-ground black pepper

¼ pound butter, cut into pieces

½ teaspoon lemon juice

1. Heat the oven to 350°. Put the hazelnuts on a large baking sheet and toast in the oven until the skins crack and loosen and the nuts are golden brown, about 15 minutes. Wrap the hot hazelnuts in a kitchen towel and firmly rub them together to remove most of the skins. Discard the skins. Let the nuts cool and then chop them.

2. Raise the heat to 450°. Snap off the tough ends of the asparagus and discard them. On the baking sheet, toss the asparagus with the oil, ¼ teaspoon of the salt, and ¼ teaspoon pepper. Spread the asparagus out on the baking sheet and roast until just tender, 5 to 7 minutes for thin spears, 8 to 10 minutes for medium, or 10 to 12 minutes for thick spears.

3. Meanwhile, in a small frying pan, melt the butter over low heat. Add the toasted hazelnuts and the remaining ¼ teaspoon salt. Cook, stirring, until the butter is golden brown, about 5 minutes. Add the lemon juice and ⅛ teaspoon pepper. Pour the sauce over the asparagus.

PECAN VARIATION

Use pecans instead of hazelnuts. Since there are no skins on pecans, simply toast them in a medium frying pan over moderately low heat, stirring frequently, until golden brown, about 6 minutes. Or toast them in a 350° oven for about 8 minutes.

GREEN BEANS WITH SLICED GARLIC AND ANCHOVY

Green beans never had it so good. Garlic and anchovy add great flavor without overwhelming the beans. In fact, if you didn't know about the anchovy paste, you probably wouldn't be able to tell just what was making the beans so tasty. They're as good at room temperature as they are hot.

SERVES 4

1½ pounds green beans

¼ cup water

¼ teaspoon salt

2 tablespoons olive oil

3 cloves garlic, cut lengthwise into thin slices

1½ teaspoons anchovy paste dissolved in 1½ teaspoons warm water

1. Put the green beans in a large frying pan. Add the water and sprinkle with the salt. Bring to a boil over moderately high heat. Cover the pan and cook for 6 minutes.

2. Uncover the pan and cook until all the water evaporates. Stir in the oil and sauté the beans, stirring occasionally, for 2 minutes. Add the garlic and cook, stirring, just until it begins to turn golden, 1 to 2 minutes longer. Stir in the dissolved anchovy paste and cook 1 minute longer.

BROCCOLI OR CAULIFLOWER VARIATION

Omit the green beans. Cut 1½ pounds of broccoli or cauliflower into florets. Cook as for the green beans, adding ⅓ cup water to the cauliflower.

ROASTED BRUSSELS SPROUTS

Even those who usually like to stay as far away from Brussels sprouts as possible will enjoy these. They're tossed in melted butter and cooked in a hot oven until lightly caramelized. This cooking method adds a touch of sweetness to counteract their slight bitterness.

SERVES 4

1½ pounds Brussels sprouts, cut in half from top to stem end

3 tablespoons butter, melted

½ teaspoon salt

⅛ teaspoon fresh-ground black pepper

1. Heat the oven to 450°. On a baking sheet, toss the Brussels sprouts with 1 tablespoon of the butter, the salt, and the pepper. Arrange the sprouts cut-side down.

2. Roast the Brussels sprouts until they begin to brown, about 10 minutes. Stir and cook until just tender, about 5 minutes longer. Transfer to a bowl and stir in the remaining 2 tablespoons butter.

VARIATIONS

■ Use olive oil instead of butter.

■ Add a squeeze of lemon juice or a little balsamic vinegar to the cooked Brussels sprouts.

■ Sprinkle grated Parmesan cheese over the sprouts before serving.

■ Cut a bell pepper into 1-inch pieces and roast along with the Brussels sprouts. The sweetness of red or yellow pepper makes an especially good complement.

■ Toss the Brussels sprouts with ½ teaspoon of a dried herb such as thyme, sage, or marjoram before roasting.

Golden Cauliflower with Parmesan and Lemon

Bring out the best in this tasty but often maligned vegetable by cooking it in olive oil until golden brown. Lemon, Parmesan, and parsley give it a zesty Italian flavor that's hard to resist.

SERVES 4

1 large head cauliflower (about 3 pounds), cut into small florets

3 tablespoons olive oil

1¼ teaspoons salt

¼ teaspoon fresh-ground black pepper

3 tablespoons dry vermouth or dry white wine

1½ tablespoons lemon juice

½ cup grated Parmesan cheese

¼ cup chopped flat-leaf parsley

1. Heat the oven to 450°. In a medium, shallow baking dish or stainless-steel roasting pan, combine the cauliflower and oil. Sprinkle with the salt and pepper, and mix well. Spread the cauliflower in an even layer. Cover with aluminum foil.

2. Cook the cauliflower in the oven for 15 minutes. Remove the foil and cook for 20 minutes longer. Stir and continue cooking for 15 minutes longer.

3. Add the vermouth, lemon juice, Parmesan, and parsley, and mix well. Continue cooking until the cauliflower is tender and golden brown, about 5 minutes longer.

GRATINEED SWISS CHARD

Tossed with sautéed onions, topped with Gruyère, and broiled, tender Swiss chard (either red or green) is quick and irresistible.

SERVES 4

2   tablespoons olive oil

1   onion, chopped

1½   pounds Swiss chard, leaves and stems cut into 1-inch pieces and washed well

¾   teaspoon salt

⅛   teaspoon fresh-ground black pepper

3   ounces Gruyère cheese, grated (about ¾ cup)

1. In a large pot, heat the oil over moderately low heat. Add the onion and cook, stirring occasionally, until translucent, about 5 minutes.

2. Add the chard, with the water that clings to the leaves, and the salt. Raise the heat to moderately high and cook, stirring frequently, until the chard is tender, about 15 minutes. Stir in the pepper.

3. With a slotted spoon, transfer the chard to a medium gratin dish and spread it in an even layer. If any liquid remains in the pot, cook it over moderate heat until reduced to 2 tablespoons, about 3 minutes. Pour the liquid over the chard.

4. Heat the broiler. Top the Swiss chard with the Gruyère and broil until the cheese is bubbling and golden brown, about 3 minutes.

VARIATIONS

■ Replace the Gruyère with a different cheese. Be sure to choose one that melts smoothly, such as Fontina or cheddar.

■ Use 1½ pounds kale in place of the Swiss chard. Add ⅓ cup water to the pot with the kale. Cover and cook for 20 minutes instead of 15.

GRILLED CORN WITH EXTRA-VIRGIN OLIVE OIL

When grilled, corn takes on a mildly smoky flavor that's so good you'll be tempted to cook it this way every time. Served with extra-virgin olive oil instead of the usual butter, this quintessential American favorite becomes appealingly different.

SERVES 4

4 ears of corn, in their husks

¼ cup extra-virgin olive oil

   Salt

   Fresh-ground black pepper (optional)

1. Light the grill. Peel the corn husks about a third of the way down. Pull off the tassels with as much of the silk as possible. Press the husks back in place, enclosing the corn. Soak the corn in a large bowl of water for 5 minutes.

2. Drain the corn and grill, turning, until tender, 20 to 25 minutes. The husks will blacken.

3. To serve, peel the husks off the corn and remove any remaining silk. Serve the corn with the oil, salt, and pepper.

FLAVORED-OIL VARIATIONS

■ **Garlic:** Put the oil in a small saucepan. Smash 2 large garlic cloves and add them to the oil. Heat just until the garlic begins to brown. Let sit while you grill the corn.

■ **Fresh Herb:** Add a tablespoon of your favorite chopped fresh herbs, such as basil, parsley, chives, or cilantro, to the oil and let sit while you grill the corn.

■ **Garlic and Dried Herb:** Make the garlic oil as directed above. When it is cool, add the fresh herbs.

PEAS WITH SCALLIONS AND HERBS

If you happen to have an herb garden, then it's easy and inexpensive to pick a few sprigs of different herbs to chop and toss into a vegetable dish such as this; but it's not always worth it to buy three or four bunches of fresh herbs only to have them shrivel and dry out in the refrigerator. So, if you don't have fresh herbs on hand, buy just one variety that you know you'll use in other dishes too, or try dried herbs.

SERVES 4

1   10-ounce package frozen peas

2   tablespoons water

1½   tablespoons mixed, chopped fresh herbs, such as tarragon, chives, and parsley, or 1½ teaspoons dried herbs

2   tablespoons butter

2   scallions including green tops, chopped

¼   teaspoon salt

⅛   teaspoon fresh-ground black pepper

1. In a medium saucepan, combine the peas, water, and dried herbs, if using. Bring to a simmer over moderate heat. Cover and cook for 4 minutes.

2. Add the butter, scallions, fresh herbs, if using, salt, and pepper. Cook for 1 minute longer.

VARIATIONS

■ Replace the frozen peas with frozen lima beans, sugar snap peas, or snow peas. Prepare a 10-ounce box of frozen vegetables as directed on the package; include the dried herbs, if using. Drain if necessary and proceed to step 2 of the recipe.

■ Substitute fresh sugar snap peas or snow peas for the frozen peas. If using snap peas, cook them in a pot of boiling, salted water for 2 minutes and drain. If using snow peas, add to boiling, salted water, bring back to a boil, and drain. Finish the recipe as directed in step 2, using either fresh or dried herbs.

ZUCCHINI AND SUMMER SQUASH WITH FRESH OREGANO

Zucchini and yellow summer squash make an attractive pair. They're delicious, too, cut into sticks and sautéed. You can serve these with almost anything. Here they're shown with a Turkey Cutlet with a Parmesan Crust, page 174.

SERVES 4

- 2 tablespoons olive oil
- 1 pound zucchini (about 2), cut into approximately 2-by-½-inch sticks
- 1 pound yellow summer squash (about 2), cut into approximately 2-by-½-inch sticks
- ¾ teaspoon salt
- ⅛ teaspoon fresh-ground black pepper
- 1 clove garlic, minced
- 1½ teaspoons chopped fresh oregano, or ½ teaspoon dried

1. In a large frying pan, heat the oil over moderately high heat. Add the zucchini, summer squash, salt, and pepper, and cook, stirring occasionally, until the squash begins to brown and is almost tender, about 5 minutes.

2. Add the garlic and dried oregano, if using, and cook the squash, stirring, for 1 minute. Stir in the fresh oregano, if using.

ZUCCHINI WEDGES WITH PARMESAN

Sprinkling liberal amounts of Parmesan over steamed wedges of zucchini is a great way to feature summer's bounty. Cooking the squash over steam until just done preserves its flavor and bright-green color—and couldn't be simpler. The zucchini is also good when served at room temperature, but don't wait to sprinkle on the Parmesan; you want the heat of the zucchini to melt it.

SERVES 4

- 1½ pounds zucchini (about 3), quartered lengthwise
- 3 tablespoons grated Parmesan cheese
  Large pinch fresh-ground black pepper

1. In a large pot with a steamer basket, bring about 1 inch of water to a boil. Put the zucchini in the basket, cover, and steam until just done, about 12 minutes.

2. Remove the zucchini and sprinkle with the cheese and pepper.

ROASTED ITALIAN PEPPERS STUFFED WITH MOZZARELLA

Mild, pale-green Italian peppers, roasted to a golden brown, burst with melting mozzarella in this easy and satisfying dish. Serve the peppers with plain grilled or roasted meats or poultry, such as Skirt Steak with Rosemary and Garlic, page 203, or Chicken with Lemon and Thyme, page 223.

SERVES 4

- 4 large Italian peppers
- ½ pound salted fresh mozzarella cheese, cut into four 3-inch lengths, about 1 inch wide
- 2 tablespoons olive oil
- ¼ teaspoon salt
- ¼ teaspoon fresh-ground black pepper

1. Heat the oven to 450°. With a small knife, make a slit down the length of each pepper. Open the peppers just enough to remove the seeds.

2. Stuff each pepper with a piece of the cheese. Close the peppers as much as possible. Coat them with the oil and sprinkle with the salt and pepper.

3. Put the peppers in a roasting pan and cook until tender and brown, about 20 minutes. Check the peppers after 15 minutes and cover with a piece of aluminum foil if they are browning too quickly.

VARIATIONS

■ Fold 4 thin slices of prosciutto and stuff one into each pepper with the cheese.

■ Stuff 8 sun-dried tomatoes into the peppers along with the cheese.

■ Use another cheese in place of the mozzarella, such as feta, goat cheese, or provolone.

BUTTERNUT SQUASH
BAKED WITH OLIVE OIL AND SAGE

Laborious peeling followed by boiling is the norm for butternut-squash prepa-rations, but here we cut the work and get even better flavor by baking the squash as you would acorn.

SERVES 4

1   small butternut squash (about 2¼ pounds), cut lengthwise into quarters and seeded

1   tablespoon olive oil

¼   teaspoon dried sage

⅛   teaspoon salt

⅛   teaspoon fresh-ground black pepper

1. Heat the oven to 425°. Put the squash, skin-side down, on a baking sheet and coat with the oil. Sprinkle with the sage, salt, and pepper.

2. Bake the squash until golden brown and tender, about 50 minutes.

VARIATIONS

You can use other dried herbs, such as thyme or marjoram, in place of the sage. Or omit the herb altogether; the squash is delicious with nothing more than salt, pepper, and olive oil.

TEST-KITCHEN TIP

For even more moistness and flavor, brush the cooked squash with extra olive oil.

BROILED TOMATOES
WITH PESTO AND OREGANO

Ripe red tomato halves broiled with oregano and topped with pesto make a colorful and appetizing side dish that is ready to serve in minutes. The tomatoes are a natural with lamb and steak and also go well with poultry.

SERVES 4

4 medium tomatoes (about 1½ pounds), cut in half horizontally

1 tablespoon olive oil

1 teaspoon ground oregano

½ teaspoon salt

⅛ teaspoon fresh-ground black pepper

1 tablespoon butter

3 tablespoons store-bought pesto

1. Heat the broiler. Coat the tomato halves with 2 teaspoons of the oil and put them on a broiler pan or baking sheet, cut-side up. Sprinkle them with the oregano, salt, and pepper. Drizzle with the remaining 1 teaspoon oil and dot with the butter.

2. Broil the tomatoes, 6 inches from the heat if possible, until golden brown, about 5 minutes. Divide the pesto among the tomato halves and spread it in an even layer. Broil for 1 minute longer.

HERB VARIATIONS

■ Use another ground, dried herb, such as sage or thyme, in place of the oregano.

■ Omit the pesto; the oregano adds enough flavor to make the tomatoes delicious on their own.

■ For a Provençal version, omit the pesto and use 1½ teaspoons herbes de Provence in place of the oregano.

ROASTED VEGETABLES

Eggplant, bell pepper, onion, garlic, fennel, and potatoes—roasted at a high temperature to intensify their flavors—are delectable together. Rounded out with thyme, Parmesan, and balsamic vinegar, they make a sumptuous and colorful side dish that's perfect with just about any roasted or grilled meat, fish, or poultry. Double the recipe for a great vegetarian main dish.

SERVES 4

1 red onion, cut into 1-inch pieces

1 head garlic, cloves separated

1 fennel bulb, cut into 8 wedges

1 red or green bell pepper, cut into 1½-inch squares

1 small eggplant (about 1 pound), cut into 1½-inch cubes

¾ pound small red new potatoes, halved, or larger ones cut into chunks

¼ cup olive oil

1 tablespoon chopped fresh thyme, or 1 teaspoon dried

1¼ teaspoons salt

¼ teaspoon fresh-ground black pepper

3 tablespoons grated Parmesan cheese

3 tablespoons chopped flat-leaf parsley

1 tablespoon balsamic vinegar

1. Heat the oven to 450°. In a large roasting pan, combine the vegetables and oil. Sprinkle the vegetables with the dried thyme, if using, the salt, and the pepper, and mix well. Spread the vegetables in an even layer.

2. Roast the vegetables in the middle of the oven for 25 minutes. Add the fresh thyme, if using. Stir the vegetables and turn the pan so that they cook evenly. Roast 15 minutes longer.

3. Add the Parmesan, 2 tablespoons of the parsley, and the vinegar, and mix well. Continue roasting until the vegetables are well browned, 5 to 10 minutes longer. Serve topped with the remaining 1 tablespoon parsley.

VARIATION

For variety and to feature what's in season, substitute one or more of the following vegetables:

Yellow bell pepper, cut into 1½-inch squares

Corn on the cob, cut into 1½-inch rounds

Thick asparagus spears, cut into 1½-inch lengths

You'll need about 8 cups of vegetables in all. If you include asparagus spears, add them after the first 25 minutes of cooking.

Broccoli Salad with No-Egg Caesar Dressing

Tossed with a dressing redolent of garlic, anchovies, and Parmesan cheese, cold broccoli makes a tasty salad that can be prepared in minutes. This dish is also delicious hot.

SERVES 4

1¼ pounds broccoli
    No-Egg Caesar Dressing

1. Cut the broccoli stalks into about eight branches. In a large pot with a steamer basket, bring about 1 inch of water to a boil. Put the broccoli in the basket, cover, and steam until just done, about 7 minutes.

2. Remove the broccoli and let cool. Toss with the dressing.

Test-Kitchen Tip

Be sure to remove the broccoli from the pot as soon as it's cooked so that its bright green won't fade to olive drab.

No-Egg Caesar Dressing

MAKES ABOUT ½ CUP

3 anchovy fillets, or ¾ teaspoon anchovy paste
2 teaspoons capers
1 small clove garlic, chopped
1 teaspoon Dijon mustard
1½ tablespoons grated Parmesan cheese
1 tablespoon parsley leaves
⅓ cup olive oil
2 tablespoons lemon juice
⅛ teaspoon salt
⅛ teaspoon fresh-ground black pepper

Puree all of the ingredients in a blender.

GRATED CELERIAC SALAD

The French usually cut this bulbous relative of the familiar green stalk celery into matchstick strips for salad, but grating is easier, especially with a food processor.

SERVES 4

- 4 teaspoons white-wine vinegar
- 1 tablespoon Dijon mustard
- ½ teaspoon salt
- ⅛ teaspoon fresh-ground black pepper
- ¼ cup plus 1 tablespoon cooking oil
- 2 tablespoons mayonnaise
- 1 pound celeriac (about 2 bulbs), peeled and grated coarse

1. In a large bowl, whisk together the vinegar, mustard, salt, and pepper. Add the oil slowly, whisking. Whisk in the mayonnaise.

2. Stir the celeriac into the dressing. Serve at room temperature or slightly chilled.

—STEPHANIE LYNESS

TEST-KITCHEN TIP

Buy smallish bulbs that look fresh—hard and unwrinkled. Old celeriac is spongy and woody.

JICAMA AND CARROT SALAD WITH LIME

Jicama is a root vegetable that has the fine, crunchy texture of a water chestnut but is sweeter. It can be cooked, but it's especially good raw in salads.

SERVES 4

- 1½ pounds jicama (about 1 small), peeled and cut into 1½-inch-long matchstick strips
- 4 carrots, grated (about 1½ cups)
- 6 tablespoons olive oil
- 3 tablespoons lime juice
- ½ jalapeño pepper, ribs and seeds removed, minced
- ¾ teaspoon salt

In a large bowl, combine all the ingredients. Serve at room temperature or chilled.

—STEPHANIE LYNESS

VARIATION

Replace the jalapeño with ½ teaspoon black pepper, and the lime juice with 2½ tablespoons lemon juice.

RADICCHIO AND ROMAINE SALAD WITH WALNUTS

The mellow taste of sherry vinegar goes particularly well with the walnuts and mildly bitter radicchio. If you can't find sherry vinegar, balsamic also works well.

SERVES 4

- 1 tablespoon sherry vinegar or balsamic vinegar
- 1 teaspoon Dijon mustard
- 1/8 teaspoon salt
- 1/8 teaspoon fresh-ground black pepper
- 1/4 cup cooking oil
- 1/2 head romaine lettuce, cut crosswise into 1/2-inch strips (about 3 cups lightly packed)
- 2 heads radicchio, cut into 1/2-inch strips (about 3 cups lightly packed)
- 1 scallion including green top, chopped
- 1/3 cup chopped walnuts

1. In a large bowl, whisk together the vinegar, mustard, salt, and pepper. Add the oil slowly, whisking.

2. Add the romaine, radicchio, scallion, and walnuts to the dressing and toss.

—STEPHANIE LYNESS

WATERCRESS, ENDIVE, AND TOMATO SALAD

Readily available but lesser-used greens make a change from the usual lettuce salad. We call for cherry tomatoes because they're good year-round.

SERVES 4

- 1 tablespoon red- or white-wine vinegar
- 1/4 teaspoon salt
- 1/4 teaspoon fresh-ground black pepper
- 3 tablespoons olive oil
- 1 bunch watercress (about 5 ounces), tough stems removed
- 3 cups cherry tomatoes, cut in half
- 2 heads Belgian endive, cut crosswise into 1-inch strips

1. In a large bowl, whisk together the vinegar, salt, and pepper. Add the oil slowly, whisking.

2. Add the watercress, tomatoes, and Belgian endive to the dressing and toss.

253

TOMATO SALAD WITH FETA, BASIL, AND BALSAMIC VINAIGRETTE

Few salads are quicker or easier than this delicious combination of sliced tomatoes, onion, feta cheese, and basil topped with olive oil and balsamic vinegar. It's pretty, too, and makes a perfect side dish during the summer months when tomatoes are at their peak.

SERVES 4

1½ pounds tomatoes (about 3), cut into ¼-inch slices

½ teaspoon salt

⅛ teaspoon fresh-ground black pepper

1 red onion, chopped

3 ounces feta cheese, crumbled (about ¾ cup)

2 tablespoons chopped fresh basil

6 tablespoons olive oil

2 tablespoons balsamic vinegar

1. Arrange the tomatoes on a platter. Sprinkle with the salt and pepper and top with the onion, feta, and basil.

2. Pour the oil and then the vinegar over the tomatoes. Let the salad sit for a few minutes, basting several times with the oil and vinegar before serving.

VARIATIONS

- In place of the basil, use 3 tablespoons chopped flat-leaf parsley or another fresh herb, such as tarragon or oregano.

- Balsamic vinegar reinforces the tart/sweet appeal of the tomatoes, but wine vinegar is fine, too.

Corn Salad

The lime juice and cumin make this tasty salad the perfect match for Lime-Marinated Chicken Breasts, with which it's shown on page 219. You'll find you want to serve the salad with a range of dishes, though, from hamburgers to pork chops to steaks.

SERVES 4

4 tablespoons olive oil

3 cups fresh (cut from about 5 ears) or frozen corn kernels

1 teaspoon salt

¼ teaspoon ground cumin

½ cup chopped red bell pepper

⅓ cup chopped red onion

3 scallions including green tops, sliced

2 tablespoons chopped flat-leaf parsley

1 tablespoon plus 2 teaspoons lime juice

1. In a large frying pan, heat 2 tablespoons of the oil over moderate heat. Add the fresh corn, if using, and ½ teaspoon of the salt and cook, stirring, for 5 minutes. Add the cumin and cook 1 minute longer. Transfer to a large bowl and let cool. If using frozen corn, you'll need to cook it only 1 minute with the ½ teaspoon salt and the cumin.

2. When the corn has cooled, stir in the bell pepper, onion, scallions, parsley, the remaining 2 tablespoons oil, the lime juice, and the remaining ½ teaspoon salt. Serve at room temperature.

Grilled-Corn Variation

Before cutting off the kernels, grill the whole ears of corn as directed in the recipe for Grilled Corn with Extra-Virgin Olive Oil, page 242. Finish the salad as for frozen corn.

Variations

- Add ¼ teaspoon dried oregano.
- Use cilantro in place of the parsley.
- Add 1 minced jalapeño pepper, ribs and seeds removed.

POTATOES, PASTA, GRAINS & BEANS

Rice Pilaf with Carrots and Ginger, page 271

WE'RE ADMITTED STARCH LOVERS. In restaurants, we sometimes order a main dish mainly for its accompaniment—the roast chicken because it comes with garlic mashed potatoes, the veal chop for its polenta. At home, though, we're all too likely to make side dishes that are so familiar that we risk dozing off while cooking them. What we've included in this chapter are some essentially basic side dishes, but with an interesting addition or two. Sautéed potatoes with lemon and parsley or rice with mustard seeds makes a tempting change with only a tiny bit more effort.

SAUTEED POTATOES WITH LEMON AND PARSLEY

Crisp, golden-brown chunks of potato flavored with lemon zest and parsley make a tempting and delicious year-round side dish. They're great with just about any grilled, roasted, or sautéed meat, fish, or poultry.

SERVES 4

- 2 tablespoons olive oil
- 2 pounds baking potatoes (about 4), peeled and cut into 1½-inch chunks
- ¾ teaspoon salt
  Pinch fresh-ground black pepper
- 1 teaspoon grated lemon zest
- 1 tablespoon chopped flat-leaf parsley

1. In a large nonstick frying pan, heat the oil over moderate heat. Add the potatoes, salt, and pepper, and cook, stirring occasionally, until golden brown and tender, about 25 minutes.

2. Stir in the lemon zest and parsley and continue cooking for 30 seconds longer.

TEST-KITCHEN TIP

Be sure to dry the potato chunks with paper towels. That way the oil won't spatter you when you add the potatoes to the pan.

VARIATIONS

■ In place of the chopped parsley, use 1½ teaspoons chopped fresh mint, thyme, or dill.

■ To flavor the potatoes with just a touch of garlic, add 1 peeled garlic clove to the oil along with the potatoes. Discard the garlic when the potatoes are cooked.

MASHED POTATOES

Few side dishes are as comforting as perfect mashed potatoes. To speed the cooking process, we call for cut-up, unpeeled new potatoes. Of course, you can use peeled baking potatoes, cut into 2-inch chunks, instead. For uncommonly delicious mashed potatoes, try the flavored variations.

SERVES 4

2 pounds new potatoes (about 6), cut into chunks

¾ teaspoon salt

Pinch fresh-ground black pepper

4 tablespoons butter, at room temperature

½ cup heavy cream, light cream, or milk

1. Put the potatoes in a medium saucepan of salted water. Bring to a boil, reduce the heat, and simmer until tender, about 15 minutes.

2. Drain the potatoes and put them back into the saucepan along with the salt and pepper. Mash the potatoes over very low heat, gradually incorporating the butter and cream.

TEST-KITCHEN TIP

Before draining the potatoes, reserve some of the cooking liquid. It's flavorful, and handy for making final adjustments in the texture of the potatoes. You can even use it as the only liquid.

VARIATIONS

- **Herb:** Add ¼ cup chopped fresh herbs at the end.

- **Sour Cream and Scallion:** Save ¼ cup of the potato water before draining. Use ¾ cup sour cream in place of the cream and add the potato water. Chop 2 scallions including the green tops, and stir them in at the end.

- **Yogurt and Scallion:** Save 2 tablespoons of the potato water before draining. Use ½ cup plain yogurt in place of the cream and add the potato water. Chop 2 scallions including the green tops, and stir them in at the end.

- **Parmesan, Garlic, and Parsley:** Add 2 tablespoons grated Parmesan cheese, 1 minced garlic clove, and 1 teaspoon chopped parsley to the finished mashed potatoes.

GRILLED RED POTATOES

As long as you're grilling meat, fish, or poultry, why not cook everything on the grill, including the potatoes? You parboil them in their jackets, toss them with olive oil, and grill them to a golden brown—simple and tasty.

SERVES 4

2 pounds small red new potatoes

1 tablespoon olive oil

¾ teaspoon salt

⅛ teaspoon fresh-ground black pepper

1. Light the grill. Put the potatoes in a large saucepan of salted water. Bring to a boil and simmer until almost tender, about 10 minutes. Drain the potatoes.

2. In a large bowl, toss the potatoes with the oil, salt, and pepper. Grill over moderate heat, turning, until tender and golden brown, about 15 minutes.

VARIATIONS

■ **Sweet Potato:** Use unpeeled sweet potatoes, cut into 1½-inch chunks, in place of the new potatoes. Reduce the boiling time to 7 minutes.

■ **Herb:** Add about 1 teaspoon of chopped fresh herbs such as rosemary, thyme, or oregano to the oil before tossing the potatoes.

■ **Flavored Oil:** If you have a flavored oil on hand, such as garlic, basil, or rosemary, try it instead of the olive oil.

ROASTED NEW POTATOES WITH ROSEMARY

New potatoes roasted in their skins with a little olive oil, salt, and rosemary are a welcome side dish any time of year. You can use boiling potatoes instead; just cut them into quarters. Covering the potatoes for part of the time helps the rosemary flavor to permeate them.

SERVES 4

2 pounds small new potatoes, cut in half, or boiling potatoes, cut into quarters

1½ tablespoons olive oil

2 tablespoons chopped fresh rosemary, or 2 teaspoons dried, crumbled

½ teaspoon salt

Pinch fresh-ground black pepper

1. Heat the oven to 400°. In a large roasting pan, combine all the ingredients. Arrange the potatoes skin-side down so that they won't stick to the pan. Cover with aluminum foil.

2. Roast the potatoes for 15 minutes. Remove the foil and stir. Cook the potatoes, uncovered, stirring once, until golden brown and tender, about 15 minutes longer.

VARIATIONS

■ **Thyme and Garlic:** Use thyme in place of the rosemary. Add another ½ tablespoon oil and 1 head garlic cloves, separated but unpeeled. Roasting makes the garlic soft and delicious. Serve the cloves along with the potatoes and press out the flesh at the table.

■ **Bay Leaf:** Use 5 bay leaves in place of the rosemary. Remove before serving.

INDIAN-SPICED POTATOES AND CAULIFLOWER

Bright yellow from the turmeric, fragrant with ground coriander, and spicy from the cayenne, this potato and cauliflower combination is terrific with simply prepared meats and chicken.

SERVES 4

1 pound boiling potatoes (about 3), peeled and cut into ¾-inch chunks

1 small head cauliflower (about 2 pounds), cut into small florets

2 tablespoons butter

1 onion, chopped

¾ teaspoon ground coriander

½ teaspoon turmeric

Pinch cayenne

¾ teaspoon salt

½ cup water

1. Put the potatoes in a large saucepan of salted water and bring to a boil. Reduce the heat and simmer the potatoes for 4 minutes. Add the cauliflower and cook until tender, about 5 minutes longer. Drain.

2. In a large frying pan, heat the butter over moderately low heat. Add the onion and cook, stirring occasionally, until translucent, about 5 minutes. Add the cauliflower and potatoes and cook over moderate heat until beginning to brown, about 3 minutes.

3. Add the spices, salt, and water and cook, scraping the bottom of the pan, until the water evaporates, 3 to 5 minutes. The potato chunks will begin to fall apart.

VARIATIONS

■ **Cumin:** Use cumin in place of the coriander, or use a mixture of both.

■ **Herb:** Stir in about 2 tablespoons chopped cilantro or parsley at the end.

Sweet-Potato Wedges with Cayenne

These roasted potatoes with a touch of cayenne taste sweet, spicy, and irresistible. While they don't get as crisp as regular potatoes, they do turn a tempting golden brown. Delicious as an accompaniment to steaks, they're ideal with Skirt Steak with Rosemary and Garlic, page 203.

SERVES 4

2 pounds sweet potatoes (about 3), each cut lengthwise into 6 wedges

2 tablespoons olive oil

¾ teaspoon salt

Large pinch cayenne

1. Heat the oven to 425°. On a baking sheet, toss the potatoes with the oil, salt, and cayenne.

2. Spread the potatoes, cut-side down, on the baking sheet. Bake, turning once or twice, until golden brown and tender, about 20 minutes.

Mashed Sweet Potatoes with Apple Cider

The cider takes the place of cream in these mashed potatoes, adding subtle apple flavor and additional sweetness.

SERVES 4

3 pounds sweet potatoes (about 5), peeled and cut into 1-inch chunks

1 cup apple cider or juice

½ teaspoon salt

2 tablespoons butter

⅛ teaspoon fresh-ground black pepper

1. Put the potatoes, cider, and salt in a large pot. Bring to a boil. Reduce the heat, cover, and simmer, stirring once, until the potatoes are tender, 25 to 30 minutes.

2. Mash the potatoes with the cider until smooth. Add the butter and pepper and heat just until the butter melts.

Sweet-Potato Hash Browns

Sweet and golden brown, these hash browns are ideal with pork, such as Pork Chops with Red Cabbage, Apples, and Currants, page 177; with ham; or really with almost any meat or poultry. They're shown with a grilled steak on page 200.

SERVES 4

3 tablespoons cooking oil

3 tablespoons butter

1 onion, chopped

2 pounds sweet potatoes (about 3), peeled and cut into ½-inch cubes

¾ teaspoon salt

1. In a large nonstick frying pan, heat the oil and butter over moderately low heat. Add the onion and cook, stirring occasionally, until translucent, about 5 minutes.

2. Stir in the potatoes and salt. Reduce the heat to low and cook for 15 minutes. With a wide spatula, turn the potatoes in sections as they begin to brown. Pack them down. Cook until the potatoes are tender and golden brown all over, about 10 minutes longer.

VARIATIONS

■ Use half sweet potatoes and half baking potatoes. Because bakers get crisper than sweet potatoes, you'll have crunchier hash browns.

■ For regular hash browns, use baking potatoes in place of the sweet potatoes.

■ The flavor of bacon is delicious with hash browns. If you have any leftover bacon fat, use it in place of the butter or the butter and oil. Or, fry 4 strips of bacon until crisp. Use the bacon fat to cook the potatoes, and crumble the bacon over the potatoes before serving.

Orzo with Grape-Leaf Pesto

Serve alongside Lamb Kabobs with Lemon, Port, and Oregano, page 208, for a Greek-inspired feast. If you want a milder brine flavor, rinse the grape leaves.

SERVES 4

½ pound orzo

2 ounces bottled grape leaves, drained and chopped coarse (about ½ cup lightly packed)

6 tablespoons olive oil

1 teaspoon grated Parmesan cheese

½ teaspoon wine vinegar

1 teaspoon dried oregano

¼ teaspoon sugar

Pinch cayenne

¼ cup walnuts

1. In a pot of boiling, salted water, cook the orzo until just done, about 12 minutes. Drain.

2. Meanwhile, put all the remaining ingredients except the walnuts in a food processor and whir until chopped fine. Add the walnuts and pulse two or three times.

3. Toss the orzo with the grape-leaf pesto and serve.

Orzo with Garlic and Parmesan

Garlic butter and mixed herbs flavor this rice-shaped pasta. If you don't have many herbs on hand, use just parsley—or omit the herbs altogether.

SERVES 4

2 tablespoons butter

1 clove garlic, minced

¾ teaspoon salt

⅛ teaspoon fresh-ground black pepper

½ pound orzo

3 tablespoons mixed, chopped fresh herbs, such as parsley, chives, and tarragon

2 tablespoons grated Parmesan cheese (optional)

1. In a small saucepan, heat the butter, garlic, salt, and pepper over low heat just until the garlic softens, about 1 minute. Remove from the heat.

2. In a large pot of boiling, salted water, cook the orzo until just done, about 12 minutes. Drain.

3. Stir the butter, herbs, and Parmesan cheese into the orzo.

PEPPERED PASTA SHELLS

We like the way the curves of the shells hold the creamy sauce, but use whatever pasta shape you happen to have on hand. Add more or less fresh-ground pepper depending on your taste.

SERVES 4

½ pound medium pasta shells
2 tablespoons butter
½ teaspoon salt
¼ teaspoon fresh-ground black pepper
2 tablespoons sour cream
2 tablespoons grated Parmesan cheese

1. In a large pot of boiling, salted water, cook the pasta until just done, about 10 minutes. Reserve 2 tablespoons of the pasta water. Drain the pasta.

2. Put the butter, reserved pasta water, salt, and pepper in the pot and heat until the butter melts. Stir in the sour cream, pasta, and Parmesan.

VARIATIONS

■ Add about 1 tablespoon chopped chives or scallion tops.

■ Add about 1 tablespoon mixed, chopped fresh herbs, such as thyme, basil, and parsley.

■ Use light or heavy cream in place of the sour cream.

RICE WITH MUSTARD SEEDS

A small addition makes a big difference in this steamed rice. The tiny mustard seeds pop pleasantly in your mouth with every bite.

SERVES 4

1	tablespoon butter
1	tablespoon cooking oil
1	onion, chopped
1½	tablespoons mustard seeds
1½	cups rice
1¼	cups Chicken Stock, page 303, or canned low-sodium chicken broth
1½	cups water
1	teaspoon salt
¼	teaspoon fresh-ground black pepper

1. In a large, deep frying pan, melt the butter with the oil over moderate heat. Add the onion and cook, stirring occasionally, until golden, about 5 minutes. Add the mustard seeds and cook, stirring, for 1 minute.

2. Stir in the rice and cook for 30 seconds. Stir in the stock, water, and salt. Bring to a simmer. Cover, reduce the heat, and simmer until all the liquid is absorbed and the rice is done, about 20 minutes. Stir in the pepper and fluff with a fork.

VARIATIONS

■ Stir in about 2 tablespoons chopped parsley at the end.

■ Add 1 teaspoon ground cumin with the mustard seeds.

■ For aromatic rice, add one 3-inch cinnamon stick, 6 cloves, and 2 bay leaves to the rice with the water.

RICE PILAF WITH CARROTS AND GINGER

A brief sauté in butter and olive oil keeps the grains of rice separate as well as adding flavor. The pilaf is great with just about any grilled or sautéed meat, fish, or poultry.

SERVES 4

1 tablespoon butter

1 tablespoon olive oil

1 onion, chopped

2 carrots, grated

1½ cups rice

1½ teaspoons ground ginger

2¾ cups Chicken Stock, page 303, or canned low-sodium chicken broth

½ cup currants or raisins

1¼ teaspoons salt

Pinch fresh-ground black pepper

1 bay leaf

1. In a large, deep frying pan, melt the butter with the oil over moderately low heat. Add the onion and carrots and cook, stirring occasionally, until the onion is translucent, about 5 minutes. Add the rice and ginger and cook, stirring frequently, for 3 minutes.

2. Add the stock, currants, salt, pepper, and bay leaf. Bring to a simmer. Cover, reduce the heat, and simmer until all the liquid is absorbed and the rice is done, about 20 minutes. Remove the bay leaf.

VARIATIONS

■ **Thyme and Parsley:** For a basic pilaf, omit the carrots, ginger, and currants. Reduce the salt to ½ teaspoon. Make the rice as directed, adding ¾ teaspoon dried thyme and 3 parsley stems to the rice with the stock. Discard the parsley stems and bay leaf before serving.

■ **Almond:** If you like, stir in ½ cup toasted, sliced, or slivered almonds at the end.

POLENTA WITH PARMESAN

A soft and creamy cornmeal favorite from northern Italy, polenta makes a great accompaniment to Sautéed Chicken Breasts with Garlic and Herbs, page 167, as well as other poultry and meat.

SERVES 4

4½   cups water

1½   teaspoons salt

1⅓   cups coarse or medium cornmeal

3   tablespoons butter or olive oil

⅓   cup grated Parmesan cheese

1. In a medium saucepan, bring the water and salt to a boil. Add the cornmeal in a slow stream, whisking constantly. Reduce the heat and simmer, stirring frequently with a wooden spoon, until the polenta is very thick, about 20 minutes.

2. Stir in the butter and Parmesan cheese and serve.

TEST-KITCHEN TIP

This soft polenta is usually served at once; it begins to firm up the minute you take it from the heat. To hold it for a bit, stir in 1 tablespoon extra olive oil. Press plastic wrap onto the surface. Cover the pan and let sit for up to 20 minutes. Reheat, stirring, over moderate heat until smooth and hot, about 5 minutes.

TOPPINGS

The polenta is extra special when served with either of these:

Gorgonzola Cheese

As you serve the polenta, top it with 1½ ounces crumbled Gorgonzola (about ⅔ cup). The cheese will melt with the heat of the polenta.

Sautéed Mushrooms, Garlic, and Parsley

2   tablespoons olive oil

1½   pounds mushrooms, sliced

¼   teaspoon salt

1   clove garlic, minced

2   tablespoons chopped flat-leaf parsley

⅛   teaspoon fresh-ground black pepper

1. In a medium frying pan, heat the oil over moderate heat. Add the mushrooms and salt and cook, stirring, until brown, about 5 minutes.

2. Add the garlic, parsley, and pepper, and cook, stirring, for 30 seconds. Serve over the polenta.

Kasha with Sauteed Shiitakes

One of the quickest-cooking grains, kasha (also called buckwheat groats) has a nice nutty flavor. Chopped parsley brightens this less-than-colorful dish, but you can omit the herb if you like.

SERVES 4

- 2 tablespoons butter
- 2 onions, chopped
- 1 tablespoon chopped fresh thyme, or 1 teaspoon dried
- ¾ pound shiitake mushrooms, stems removed and caps sliced
- 1 cup kasha
- 1 egg, beaten to mix
- 2 cups Chicken Stock, page 303, or canned low-sodium chicken broth
- ¾ teaspoon salt
- 3 tablespoons chopped flat-leaf parsley (optional)

Test-Kitchen Tip

Because shiitake and portobello mushroom stems are woody, cut them off and use only the caps in the recipe. But don't throw the stems away. Freeze them and add to a pot of stock for extra flavor.

1. In a large frying pan, heat the butter over moderately low heat. Add the onions and thyme and cook, stirring occasionally, until the onions are translucent, about 5 minutes. Raise the heat to moderate, add the sliced mushrooms, and cook, stirring occasionally, until golden, about 5 minutes.

2. Put the kasha in a bowl and stir in the egg. Add to the mushroom mixture and cook, stirring, until all the kernels are dry and separate, about 2 minutes. Stir in the stock and salt. Cover and cook over moderately low heat until fluffy, 7 to 9 minutes. Stir in the parsley.

REFRIED BLACK BEANS WITH SCALLIONS, QUESO FRESCO, AND SALSA

A natural with spicy Mexican dishes, these beans also complement grilled steaks, pork, chicken, and full-flavored fish. Because we call for canned beans and store-bought salsa, you can have this side dish on the table in about 15 minutes. If you like, use Guacamole, page 187, instead of the salsa.

SERVES 4

- 3 tablespoons olive oil
- 2 19-ounce cans black beans, drained and rinsed (about 1 quart in all)
- ½ cup water
- ½ teaspoon salt
- ⅛ teaspoon fresh-ground black pepper
- 2 scallions including green tops, chopped
- 2 ounces queso fresco* or feta cheese, crumbled (about ½ cup)
- 1 cup store-bought salsa, for serving

*Available at Spanish markets

1. In a large, heavy frying pan, heat the oil over moderate heat. Add half the black beans and ¼ cup of the water and cook, mashing with a potato masher, for 5 minutes. Add the remaining beans and ¼ cup water and the salt. Continue cooking, mashing, until the beans thicken, about 5 minutes longer. Stir in the pepper.

2. Spoon the refried beans onto plates and top with the scallions and cheese. Serve with the salsa.

VARIATIONS

■ **Cumin:** Add ¾ teaspoon ground cumin to the frying beans.

■ **Pumpkin Seed or Pine Nut:** In place of the scallions, use shelled pumpkin seeds or pine nuts. Toast them in a 350° oven until golden brown, about 6 minutes.

■ **Smoky Spice:** Stir in 2 teaspoons minced canned chipotles in adobo sauce, available at Spanish markets, or a few drops liquid smoke and a big pinch of cayenne with the pepper.

CHICKPEAS WITH CUMIN AND PARSLEY

Chickpeas survive the high heat of the canning process better than any other legume. The taste of this recipe reminds us of the flavor of hummus—and, in fact, you can turn it into a quick version of hummus easily. Serve with grilled chicken or lamb.

SERVES 4

3	tablespoons olive oil
1	small onion, chopped
½	teaspoon ground cumin
2	19-ounce cans chickpeas, drained and rinsed (about 1 quart in all)
1	teaspoon salt
¼	teaspoon fresh-ground black pepper
	Pinch cayenne
¼	cup warm water
2	scallions including green tops, chopped
2	tablespoons chopped flat-leaf parsley
1	tablespoon lemon juice

1. In a medium saucepan, heat the oil over moderate heat. Add the onion and cook, stirring, until golden, about 5 minutes. Add the cumin and cook about 30 seconds longer.

2. Add the chickpeas, salt, black pepper, cayenne, and water and heat until warmed through. With a potato masher, mash about half of the chickpeas. Stir in the scallions, parsley, and lemon juice.

HUMMUS VARIATION

Because it's made without tahini, this chickpea spread isn't strictly authentic. Nevertheless, it's delicious and those who aren't keen on the slight bitterness of tahini may prefer it. Use 1 chopped garlic clove in place of the onion and scallions. Increase the olive oil to ¼ cup and use cold water instead of warm. Puree all the ingredients in a food processor. Serve the hummus with pita.

DESSERTS

Peach and Raspberry Sundae, page 287

TO TELL THE TRUTH, we don't usually make desserts on weeknights. But we figure some people do, and so here are nineteen of the quickest sweets we know— simple fruit desserts, sundaes, mix-in-the-pan cakes, slice-and-bake cookies that you can keep on hand in the freezer. More power to those who can afford the calories of a dessert every night; the rest of us can save these recipes for the weekend.

PEARS AND PRUNES POACHED IN SPICED RED WINE

Pears and prunes complement each other perfectly. The compote tastes great when it's just made and is also delicious on the second day, when the pears take on a lovely, deep-burgundy color from the wine. If you don't have time to let the compote chill, serve it warm, either plain or with ice cream.

SERVES 4

12 pitted prunes

2 cups red wine

1 cup water

¾ cup sugar

2 3-inch strips lemon zest

1 cinnamon stick

4 peppercorns

3 cloves

4 pears, peeled, cut in half, and cored

1. In a medium stainless-steel saucepan, combine the prunes, wine, water, sugar, lemon zest, cinnamon stick, peppercorns, and cloves. Bring to a simmer over moderately high heat. Reduce the heat and simmer, partially covered, for 5 minutes.

2. Add the pears and bring back to a simmer over moderately high heat. Reduce the heat and simmer just until the pears are tender when pierced, 10 to 12 minutes. If the pears were hard to begin with, they'll probably need about 5 minutes longer. Transfer the fruit and poaching liquid to a medium glass or stainless-steel bowl. Let cool and then chill.

VARIATIONS

■ If you like, add up to ½ cup of an additional dried fruit, such as cherries, raisins, or cranberries.

■ Try different spices, such as star anise or pink peppercorns.

TEST-KITCHEN TIP

Wine and other acidic ingredients react badly with aluminum to produce a truly foul flavor. That's why we always call for a stainless-steel pan and a stainless or glass bowl in recipes such as this. Enamel-coated cast-iron pans and crockery bowls work fine, too.

PEARS BAKED WITH LEMON, BROWN SUGAR, AND WALNUTS

Baked pear halves with crunchy walnuts and a brown-sugar sauce are a lovely autumn dessert. The sauce makes itself as the pears bake; what could be easier? We think the warm fruit is especially delicious served with vanilla ice cream.

SERVES 4

2 pears, peeled, cut in half, and cored

⅓ cup chopped walnuts

¼ cup brown sugar

2 tablespoons water

1 teaspoon lemon juice

¼ teaspoon grated nutmeg

2 tablespoons unsalted butter, cut into small pieces

1. Heat the oven to 350°. Put the pears, cut-side up, in a baking dish just large enough to hold them. Fill the cored centers of the pears with the walnuts. Sprinkle with the brown sugar, water, lemon juice, and nutmeg. Dot with the butter.

2. Bake until the pears are tender and the walnuts are golden brown, about 20 minutes. Serve with the brown-sugar sauce that forms in the bottom of the baking dish.

VARIATIONS

■ Use whatever nuts you have on hand. Pecans or almonds work well, or try hazelnuts or macadamia nuts.

■ This recipe is also a good one for apples. Use bakers such as Golden Delicious, Rome Beauty, or Cortland; Rome Beauty is our favorite. Peel the top third of 4 apples and core them to within ½ inch of the bottom. Sprinkle the apples with the brown sugar, lemon juice, and nutmeg. Put the butter in the hollow centers. Add ¼ cup brown sugar and ¼ cup water to the baking dish. Bake 25 minutes. Fill the apple centers with the nuts and bake until tender and golden, 40 to 50 minutes.

Warm Baked Apples "Tatin"

If you love French *tarte Tatin* but never get around to making it, we have the perfect solution: Forget the crust and bake the apples whole in the same rich, buttery caramel sauce. They're delicious served plain, but topped with a scoop of ice cream or a dollop of crème fraîche or whipped cream, they are sublime.

SERVES 4

4 large Golden Delicious apples (about 2 pounds)

1 cup sugar

¼ pound cold unsalted butter

1. Heat the oven to 400°. With an apple corer, core the apples. Peel the bottom halves only.

2. In a medium, heavy saucepan, heat the sugar over moderately high heat, stirring occasionally, until it begins to melt around the edges, about 5 minutes. Reduce the heat and continue cooking, stirring, until the sugar turns a light-brown caramel color and all of the sugar crystals dissolve. Remove from the heat. Add the butter in one piece and, with a whisk planted in the butter, stir in a circular motion. The butter will melt into the sugar. Put the pot back on the heat and cook, whisking, until the caramel sauce is smooth.

3. Into a deep baking dish just large enough to fit the apples, pour enough of the hot caramel sauce to just cover the bottom.

4. Working quickly, put the apples in the baking dish, peeled-side down, and pour caramel into the hollow centers. Drizzle the apples with the remaining caramel, covering as much of them as possible.

5. Bake the apples on the bottom rack of the oven for 40 minutes. Using two spoons, gently turn the apples over. Continue baking, basting occasionally, until tender and medium brown, about 20 minutes longer. Let cool to warm, about 20 minutes.

6. To serve, put the warm apples onto plates, peeled-side up. Pour the sauce over.

Test-Kitchen Tip

Golden Delicious are the apples most often used in France for *tarte Tatin*. They're sweet and juicy and hold their shape when baked. Or, we should say, 99% of the time they hold their shape. Once in a blue moon, you'll get some that have been hanging around in cold storage and become mealy. They're likely to fall apart during cooking, and there's not much you can do except keep a sharp eye on them. If they begin to split, reduce the baking time to about 50 minutes. They won't look perfect but will still taste wonderful.

VANILLA APPLE COMPOTE

For a different take on the standard applesauce, large chunks of apple are poached in light vanilla-flavored syrup until they're falling-apart tender. The combination of apples and vanilla is a favorite in France and one that we think is delicious.

SERVES 4

4   Golden Delicious apples, peeled, cored, and quartered

¾   cup sugar

2   cups water

½   vanilla bean, or 1½ teaspoons vanilla extract

1   3-inch strip lemon zest

1. Put the apples, sugar, water, the vanilla bean, if using, and the lemon zest in a medium saucepan and bring to a simmer over moderately high heat. Stir. Reduce the heat and cook at a bare simmer, partially covered, until the apples are tender, translucent, and just beginning to fall apart, 20 to 25 minutes. Avoid stirring or the apples will break up too much.

2. Transfer the apples and syrup to a medium bowl and let cool. Gently stir in the vanilla extract, if using. Chill for at least 30 minutes. Spoon the apples and syrup into bowls and serve.

VARIATIONS

■ **Lime:** Gently stir about 1 tablespoon lime juice into the cooked compote.

■ **Cranberry:** Add ½ cup dried cranberries to the apples about 5 minutes before they're done cooking.

TIME-SAVER

To speed up the cooling process, spread out the apple compote in a shallow dish, cool slightly, and then refrigerate.

TEST-KITCHEN TIP

Golden Delicious apples are the perfect choice for this compote. They're perfumed and sweet, and they hold up during cooking. If you like, try another variety with similar characteristics, such as Gala.

STRAWBERRY AND RHUBARB COMPOTE

Tangy rhubarb and sweet, juicy strawberries make a perfect match in this simple yet superb, rosy-red baked compote. Serve it warm, room temperature, or chilled, with or without a scoop of vanilla ice cream.

SERVES 4

1 pound rhubarb, cut into 1-inch pieces
1½ pints strawberries, hulled and halved
½ cup sugar

1. Heat the oven to 350°. In a 2-quart baking dish, combine the rhubarb, strawberries, and sugar.

2. Cover the dish with aluminum foil and bake until the rhubarb is tender, about 45 minutes. Don't stir or the rhubarb will fall apart.

TEST-KITCHEN TIP

Spring marks the beginning of rhubarb season. You can find rhubarb through August, but toward the end of summer, what's available is often older and rather tough. For the tastiest and tenderest rhubarb, look for narrow stalks, about one inch in diameter.

VARIATIONS

■**Low-Fat:** To dress up the dessert but still keep it low-fat, serve the compote with vanilla yogurt or frozen yogurt. Or, to highlight the strawberries, serve it with strawberry sorbet. Also, a plate of gingersnaps would go well here.

■**Off-Season:** You can use frozen rhubarb with fresh or frozen strawberries. All you need to do is thaw the fruit; no need to halve the frozen strawberries. If you use all frozen fruit, even though it's been thawed, add another 15 minutes to the cooking time.

PEACH AND BLUEBERRY CRISP

Crisps are just as appealing as pies and much quicker to put together. Here a buttery brown-sugar crumb mixture touched with nutmeg tops fresh peaches and blueberries. The fruit gives up plenty of sweet juice, making a delicious sauce. A scoop of ice cream wouldn't be amiss.

MAKES ONE 9-INCH CRISP

1	cup plus 1 tablespoon flour
$\frac{1}{2}$	cup brown sugar
$\frac{1}{2}$	teaspoon grated nutmeg
	Salt
6	tablespoons unsalted butter, at room temperature
$1\frac{1}{2}$	pounds peaches (about 4), peeled, pitted, and cut into $\frac{1}{2}$-inch wedges
1	cup blueberries
$1\frac{1}{2}$	tablespoons lemon juice

1. Heat the oven to 400°. In a medium bowl, combine the 1 cup flour, all but 2 tablespoons of the brown sugar, the nutmeg, and $\frac{1}{4}$ teaspoon salt. Add the butter and rub it into the flour mixture until it forms large crumbs.

2. In a large bowl, combine the peaches, blueberries, the remaining 2 tablespoons brown sugar and 1 tablespoon flour, the lemon juice, and a pinch of salt. Transfer the fruit to a 9-inch glass pie plate.

3. Top the fruit with the crumb mixture. Bake for 25 minutes. Reduce the oven temperature to 350° and bake until the peaches are tender and the topping has browned, 15 to 20 minutes longer. If the topping browns too quickly, cover loosely with aluminum foil.

VARIATIONS

■ Add cinnamon or allspice to the topping along with the nutmeg.

■ Add chopped nuts of almost any kind to the topping.

■ Try a different fruit. Replace the peaches with nectarines. Use mixed berries, rhubarb, or cranberries—with additional sugar for the last two. Apples and pears also work well but require a longer cooking time.

PINEAPPLE, RUM, AND RAISIN SUNDAES

Most supermarkets carry peeled and cored pineapple. Sautéed with brown sugar, rum, and raisins, then poured over vanilla ice cream, it makes a luscious dessert that's welcome year-round. For an added tropical sensation, serve the pineapple topping with coconut ice cream or sorbet.

SERVES 4

2 tablespoons butter

½ peeled and cored pineapple, cut in quarters lengthwise, then cut crosswise into ¼-inch slices (about 2 cups)

¼ cup brown sugar

2 tablespoons raisins

2 tablespoons rum, preferably dark

2 tablespoons water

1 pint vanilla ice cream

MANGO AND BANANA VARIATIONS

You can use 1 mango or 3 bananas in place of the pineapple. However, because they have less juice than pineapples, cook them over moderate heat rather than moderately high. And, for the bananas, reduce the cooking time to about 2 minutes in all.

1. In a large nonstick frying pan, melt the butter over moderately high heat. Add the pineapple and cook, stirring, for 4 minutes. Add the brown sugar, raisins, rum, and water, and cook, stirring, until the sugar dissolves and the sauce thickens slightly, about 1 minute.

2. To serve, scoop the ice cream into bowls or sundae glasses and pour the hot pineapple mixture over it.

PEACH AND RASPBERRY SUNDAES

A sundae of frozen yogurt topped with sliced peaches and raspberry sauce is bound to please all ages. It's pretty, and is both refreshing and satisfying. Of course, you can use vanilla ice cream in place of the yogurt.

SERVES 4

6 ounces raspberries (about 1½ cups)

3 tablespoons sugar, or more to taste

¼ teaspoon lemon juice

1 pint vanilla frozen yogurt

1 pound peaches (about 3), peeled, pitted, and cut into ¼-inch slices

1. In a food processor or blender, puree the raspberries. Strain through a medium or fine sieve and press the puree firmly to get all the fruit. Stir in the sugar and lemon juice and let sit for about 20 minutes to dissolve the sugar.

2. To serve, scoop the frozen yogurt into sundae glasses or bowls. Top with the peaches and pour on the raspberry sauce.

TIME-SAVER

Use superfine sugar in the raspberry sauce. Because it dissolves instantly, you can skip the 20-minute wait for regular granulated sugar to melt.

FROZEN-RASPBERRY VARIATION

You can make a delicious raspberry sauce using frozen raspberries. In fact, it tastes remarkably like the fresh version. Simply measure the same amount of frozen berries, let them thaw, and then proceed with the recipe.

MINT CHOCOLATE SUNDAES

A luscious dark-chocolate sauce infused with fresh mint covers vanilla ice cream, making a delicious sundae with a flavor reminiscent of after-dinner mints. For a double-chocolate dessert, serve the sauce over chocolate ice cream or sorbet. You can serve the sauce warm or at room temperature; it will thicken only slightly as it cools.

SERVES 4

½ cup chopped fresh mint, or ⅓ cup dried

½ cup unsweetened cocoa powder

6 tablespoons sugar

1 cup heavy cream

1½ pints vanilla ice cream

1. Put all the ingredients except the ice cream into a medium saucepan and bring to a simmer, stirring. Strain. Let cool to warm.

2. To serve, scoop the ice cream into bowls or sundae glasses and pour the chocolate sauce over the top.

TEST-KITCHEN TIP

Make a double batch of the chocolate sauce and store it in a glass jar; it keeps for weeks in the refrigerator. To serve, simply let the sauce come to room temperature. Or, heat the sauce by setting the jar in a pot of simmering water; stir occasionally until warm.

CAFFE AFFOGATO

Picture ice cream drowning in hot coffee: The name of this heavenly Italian dessert means just that. To make Caffè Affogato, pour hot espresso over vanilla ice cream. The espresso melts the ice cream slightly, and the sweet cream blends into the coffee, making a delicious sauce.

SERVES 4

⅔ cup ground espresso beans

¾ cup water

1½ pints vanilla ice cream

1. Using a drip coffee maker, make coffee with the ground espresso and the water. You should have ½ cup strong espresso. Alternatively, make ½ cup espresso using an espresso machine.

2. Scoop the ice cream into each of four bowls or parfait glasses. Pour 2 tablespoons of espresso over each serving of ice cream.

VARIATIONS

■ **Mocha:** Use chocolate ice cream in place of the vanilla.

■ **Double Coffee:** Use coffee ice cream in place of the vanilla.

TEST-KITCHEN TIPS

■ If your coffee maker won't make such a small amount of coffee, we recommend using an individual filter cone. Put a coffee filter in the cone, fill it with the ground espresso, set it over a cup, and pour in the boiling water. Or, put a coffee filter in a sieve and set it over a bowl.

■ You can use espresso from a coffee bar instead of making your own. Simply reheat it until very hot. Avoid simmering the espresso, which can give it a bitter taste.

MELON WITH LEMON SORBET AND MINT

Melon balls tossed with mint and topped with lemon sorbet look as light and refreshing as they taste. To make this easy dessert even quicker, you can just cut the melon into cubes. Either way, it's ideal for a hot summer evening.

SERVES 4

1 cantaloupe or 1 small honeydew melon, seeded

1½ teaspoons sugar

1 teaspoon lemon juice

2 teaspoons chopped fresh mint

1 pint lemon sorbet

1. Using a melon baller, scoop out rounds of the melon. You should have about 2 cups. In a medium glass or stainless-steel bowl, combine the melon balls, sugar, lemon juice, and mint. Let sit for at least 5 minutes. Chill until ready to serve.

2. To serve, put the melon balls into bowls or stemmed glasses. Top them with the lemon sorbet.

VARIATIONS

■ Use lime juice in place of the lemon juice.

■ Use 1 cup blueberries, raspberries, strawberries, sliced peaches, or halved green grapes in place of 1 cup of the cantaloupe. Or, omit the cantaloupe altogether and use one or a mixture of the other fruit. Add more sugar to taste if necessary.

■ Add a liqueur to taste. Midori melon liqueur is great with the cantaloupe or honeydew, as is grappa. Grand Marnier and kirsch work well with almost any fruit, and Whidbeys (made from loganberries) or framboise is delicious with berries.

■ For an all-citrus variation, use orange or grapefruit sections, or a combination of the two.

STRAWBERRY AND BALSAMIC FOOL

Two classic combinations—strawberries with cream, and the Italian mix of strawberries and balsamic vinegar—meet in this summertime dessert. The quantity of vinegar is just enough to add a new dimension without overpowering the flavor of the berries.

SERVES 4

1   pint strawberries, hulled

2   teaspoons balsamic vinegar

1   cup heavy cream

6   tablespoons sugar

1. In a food processor or blender, puree 1 cup of the strawberries with the vinegar. Chop the remaining strawberries into approximately ¼-inch pieces and add to the fruit puree.

2. In a medium bowl, whip the cream and sugar until the cream holds firm peaks when the beaters are lifted. Fold in the puree mixture. Chill until ready to serve. Spoon into bowls or dessert goblets.

VARIATIONS

■ If you don't have balsamic vinegar on hand, try a teaspoon or two of lemon or lime juice.

■ Fresh or frozen peaches would be a good alternative to the strawberries, as would blackberries and raspberries. Rhubarb, blueberries, and quince also make excellent fools; just cook these fruits until tender, cool, and puree.

TEST-KITCHEN TIP

Balsamic vinegars vary widely. If the flavor doesn't come through, don't hesitate to add a bit more.

Bittersweet-Chocolate-Truffle Cake with Walnuts

Amazingly easy to make, this cake is sure to become a favorite of any chocolate lover. It's rich and silky smooth like chocolate truffles but has a subtle crunch of walnuts in every bite.

MAKES ONE 8-INCH CAKE

- 10 ounces bittersweet chocolate, chopped
- 1/2 pound cold unsalted butter, cut into 1/2-inch pieces
- 1 1/4 cups confectioners' sugar, sifted
- 2 large eggs
- 3 large egg yolks
- 2 teaspoons brandy (optional)
- 3/4 cup chopped walnuts
- Unsweetened cocoa powder, for dusting

1. Heat the oven to 325°. Line the bottom and sides of an 8-inch round cake pan with a piece of aluminum foil. Make sure not to pierce the foil. Melt the chocolate and half the butter in a double boiler, stirring frequently, until smooth. Remove from the heat and whisk in the remaining butter.

2. Add the confectioners' sugar gradually, whisking. Whisk in the eggs one by one. Add the egg yolks and the brandy and whisk until smooth. Stir in the chopped walnuts.

3. Pour the batter into the prepared pan. Bake in the middle of the oven until the cake is set about 1 1/2 inches around the edge but the center still moves when the pan is jiggled, about 30 minutes.

4. Cool on a rack for 30 minutes. Freeze for 1 hour and then refrigerate until firm, about 30 minutes. Unmold onto a serving plate. Peel off the aluminum foil. Some bits of butter may show on the surface. Dust the cake with cocoa. Chill until ready to serve.

VARIATIONS

- Out of cocoa powder? Dust the top of the cake with confectioners' sugar.

- For an ultra-simple and elegant version, leave out the nuts altogether.

- Add 3/4 cup raisins or other dried fruit, such as cherries or strawberries.

- Omit the walnuts and add 1/2 cup crystallized ginger chopped fine, rinsed to remove the sugar granules, and dried. (If you leave the sugar on the ginger, it gets into the batter and makes the cake gritty rather than smooth.)

- You can use various liqueurs in place of the brandy, such as framboise, crème de menthe, or Frangelico.

APPLE SPICE CAKE WITH BROWN-SUGAR GLAZE

We can't say enough about this wonderful, moist spice cake filled with tart apples and glazed with brown sugar. Because you mix all the ingredients together at once, it's quick and easy to make. The cake is delicious warm or at room temperature, with or without a scoop of vanilla ice cream.

MAKES ONE 9-INCH CAKE

- ¾ cup granulated sugar
- ¼ cup dark-brown sugar
- ¾ cup cooking oil
- 2 large eggs
- 1½ cups flour
- 1½ teaspoons baking soda
- 1½ teaspoons cinnamon
- ¼ teaspoon grated nutmeg
- ⅛ teaspoon ground cloves
- ¼ teaspoon salt
- 1 pound tart apples (about 2), such as Granny Smith, peeled, cored, and cut into 1-inch chunks
- ½ cup chopped walnuts
- 1 tablespoon vanilla extract
  Brown-Sugar Glaze

1. Heat the oven to 350°. Butter a 9-inch springform pan. Put all the ingredients except the glaze into the bowl of a mixer, preferably with a paddle attachment. Beat on the lowest speed until the apples are in ¼-inch chunks and their juice has thinned the batter slightly, about 3 minutes. Alternatively, use a hand-held mixer and beat the batter at the edges of the bowl before moving into the center. That way, the juice from the apples will begin to thin the batter before you beat it at the deepest point, thus avoiding strain on your mixer.

2. Pour the batter into the prepared pan and smooth the top. Bake in the middle of the oven until a toothpick stuck in the center comes out clean, about 50 minutes.

3. Let the cake cool slightly. Unmold and pour the glaze over the warm cake, letting the excess run down the sides.

BROWN-SUGAR GLAZE

- ¼ cup unsalted butter
- ¼ cup granulated sugar
- ¼ cup dark-brown sugar
- ¼ cup heavy cream

Put all the ingredients in a small saucepan and bring to a simmer, stirring, over low heat. Simmer until the sugar dissolves, about 1 minute. Let cool until slightly thickened, about 5 minutes.

Mix-in-the-Pan Chocolate Cake

Before we tried it, we were skeptical about mixing and baking the cake in the same pan, but it works beautifully—no butter to cream nor eggs to beat. This is a chocolatey cake; it's great on its own and even better with one of the toppings suggested below. If you don't have a springform pan, mix the cake in a bowl and pour it into a 9-inch square cake pan. In any case, serve the cake when it's still slightly warm if you can.

MAKES ONE 9-INCH CAKE

1½ cups flour

1⅓ cups sugar

½ cup plus 2 tablespoons unsweetened cocoa powder

1½ teaspoons baking soda

½ teaspoon salt

½ cup very hot water

¼ pound unsalted butter, melted

2 large eggs, beaten to mix

1 teaspoon vanilla extract

1 cup buttermilk or low-fat plain yogurt

1. Heat the oven to 350°. Butter a 9-inch springform pan. Cover the bottom with a round of waxed paper. Butter the paper.

2. Put the flour, sugar, cocoa, baking soda, and salt in the prepared pan. Whisk just to mix. Whisk in the hot water, butter, eggs, and vanilla. Whisk in the buttermilk or yogurt. With a rubber spatula, scrape around the bottom edge of the pan to incorporate all of the ingredients.

3. Bake the cake in the middle of the oven until a toothpick stuck in the center comes out clean, about 40 minutes. Cool in the pan for about 10 minutes. Unmold the cake and peel off the waxed paper. Serve warm or at room temperature.

Toppings

■ Dust the top of the cake with unsweetened cocoa powder, confectioners' sugar, or a combination of the two.

■ Whip ¾ cup heavy cream with 2 teaspoons granulated sugar until the cream holds stiff peaks. Spread on top of the cake and top with sliced bananas, strawberries, or raspberries.

■ Melt 4 ounces chopped bittersweet or semisweet chocolate with 4 tablespoons unsalted butter. Spread the mixture on the top and sides of the cake and leave to set.

STICKY TOFFEE PUDDING

Studded with dates and served warm with Toffee Rum Sauce, this moist, spice-cake-like English pudding is a luscious cold-weather treat. For the full effect, be sure to pour plenty of sauce over each serving. And to really indulge, add a scoop of vanilla ice cream or a dollop of whipped cream.

SERVES 6

- 1 cup water
- 1 cup chopped dates
- 6 tablespoons unsalted butter, at room temperature
- ¾ cup dark-brown sugar
- 2 large eggs, at room temperature
- 1 teaspoon vanilla extract
- 1½ cups flour
- ¼ teaspoon salt
- 1 teaspoon baking soda
  Toffee Rum Sauce, opposite page

1. Heat the oven to 350°. Generously butter an 8-inch-square cake pan. Bring the water to a boil. Add the dates and set aside.

2. Using an electric mixer, cream the butter with the brown sugar until fluffy, about 5 minutes. Beat in the eggs one at a time and then the vanilla. Add the flour and salt and mix until combined. The batter will be thick.

3. Stir the baking soda into the date and water mixture. Pour into the cake batter and mix until well combined. Pour the batter into the prepared pan.

4. Bake the pudding in the middle of the oven until a toothpick stuck in the center comes out clean, 40 to 45 minutes.

5. Pour ½ cup of the warm toffee sauce over the top of the pudding and bake for 30 seconds longer.

6. To serve, cut squares of the warm pudding and pour some of the Toffee Rum Sauce over each piece. Pass the remaining sauce at the table.

RAISIN VARIATION

In a pinch, you can use raisins in place of the dates. Though not so good as dates for this dessert, they do make a tasty pudding.

TOFFEE RUM SAUCE

Dark with brown sugar and rich with butter and cream, this sauce is positively addictive. If you like, use 1 teaspoon vanilla extract in place of the rum. It's good, but we think the rum is better yet.

MAKES ABOUT 3 CUPS

¼ pound unsalted butter

1½ cups dark-brown sugar

1½ cups heavy cream

2 tablespoons dark rum

Melt the butter in a medium saucepan over moderately high heat. Stir in the brown sugar and then the cream. Bring to a boil, reduce the heat, and simmer for 4 minutes, stirring occasionally. Stir in the rum. Let cool slightly. Serve warm.

TOFFEE-RUM-SAUCE VARIATIONS AND TIPS

■ For a wickedly delicious dessert, serve this sauce over ice cream, such as vanilla, coffee, chocolate, or coconut.

■ Make the sauce even better by adding a handful of raisins with the cream—they'll plump during cooking.

■ Drizzle the sauce over sliced fresh mangoes, bananas, peaches, or pineapple. Or, make a parfait with the fruit, ice cream, and sauce.

■ The sauce keeps well. Refrigerate in a glass jar.

ALMOND BUTTER COOKIES

In this homemade version of slice-and-bake cookies, ground unblanched almonds impart flavor, and their skins add attractive flecks to the finished cookies. Rolling the dough in crystallized ginger or spiced sugar before slicing gives the cookies a sweet, crunchy edge.

MAKES ABOUT 30 COOKIES

⅓ cup whole unblanched almonds

½ cup confectioners' sugar

¾ cup flour

⅛ teaspoon salt

¼ pound unsalted butter, at room temperature, cut into pieces

2 large egg yolks, at room temperature

⅓ cup finely chopped crystallized ginger, or ¼ cup granulated sugar mixed with ½ teaspoon cinnamon, allspice, or nutmeg

1. In a food processor, grind the almonds to a powder with the confectioners' sugar. Add the flour, salt, and butter, and pulse until combined. Add the egg yolks and pulse until the dough comes together into a ball.

2. Shape the dough into two logs, each 1½ inches in diameter. Wrap tightly in plastic and chill in the freezer until firm, about 25 minutes.

3. Heat the oven to 325°. Butter two baking sheets. Roll the logs in the crystallized ginger or the spiced sugar.

4. Cut the dough into slices, between ¼ and ½ inch thick, and put the slices about 1 inch apart on the prepared baking sheets. Bake until golden, about 18 minutes. Transfer the cookies to a rack to cool.

VARIATIONS

Consider this a basic cookie dough that can be modified to your taste.

■ If you prefer a stronger almond flavor, add a few drops of almond extract.

■ Replace the almonds with a different nut, such as pecans or hazelnuts.

■ Flavor the dough with ½ teaspoon grated orange or lemon zest or ¼ teaspoon of a spice like cinnamon, nutmeg, allspice, or cloves.

DOUBLE-CHOCOLATE CINNAMON WAFERS

Test-kitchen observation: Biting into a just-baked homemade cookie never fails to bring a smile. Make this dough in minutes in the food processor and keep a roll of it in the freezer so that you can slice off a few cookies to bake as smiles are needed. The cookies, pictured on page 298, are also terrific for making ice-cream sandwiches.

MAKES ABOUT 36 COOKIES

1 cup flour

5 tablespoons unsweetened cocoa powder

½ cup plus 2 tablespoons granulated sugar

¼ cup brown sugar

½ teaspoon cinnamon

½ teaspoon baking soda

¼ teaspoon salt

¼ pound unsalted butter, at room temperature, cut into pieces

1 egg, at room temperature, beaten to mix

4 ounces bittersweet or semisweet chocolate, chopped

1. Put the flour, cocoa, ¼ cup plus 2 tablespoons of the granulated sugar, the brown sugar, cinnamon, baking soda, and salt in a food processor and pulse once or twice to mix.

2. Add the butter and pulse until incorporated. Add the egg and pulse until the dough is thoroughly combined, about 10 seconds. Put the dough in a bowl and stir in the chopped chocolate.

3. Shape the dough into two logs, each 1½ inches in diameter. Wrap tightly in plastic and chill in the freezer until firm, about 25 minutes.

4. Heat the oven to 325°. Butter two baking sheets. Roll the logs in the remaining ¼ cup granulated sugar.

5. Cut the dough into slices, between ¼ and ½ inch thick, and put the slices about 1 inch apart on the prepared baking sheets. Bake until done, about 18 minutes. Transfer the cookies to racks to cool.

TEST-KITCHEN TIP

Roll the log of dough a quarter turn or so after each slice to keep it round.

TIME-SAVER

If you don't want to wait for the logs of dough to chill, simply drop tablespoonfuls onto the prepared baking sheets.

MOCHA PUDDING

In this adult version of chocolate pudding, instant coffee lends an intense flavor. You can top the pudding with a dollop of fresh whipped cream if you like.

SERVES 4

- 2 cups milk
- 1 cup heavy cream
- 4 teaspoons instant coffee
- 4 large egg yolks
- 1/3 cup sugar
- 1/4 cup cornstarch
  Pinch salt
- 4 ounces bittersweet chocolate, chopped

1. In a medium stainless-steel saucepan, bring the milk and 2/3 cup of the cream to a boil. Stir in the coffee.

2. In a medium bowl, whisk the egg yolks, sugar, cornstarch, and salt until pale yellow. The mixture will be very thick at first, but will become thinner as you whisk.

3. Pour the hot coffee mixture into the egg yolks, whisking. Pour back into the pan and cook over moderate heat, whisking constantly, until the mixture comes to a boil, about 6 minutes. Boil, whisking, for 30 seconds. Remove from the heat.

4. Add the chocolate and whisk until melted and smooth. Stir in the remaining 1/3 cup cream. Pour the pudding into individual bowls, cover, and chill.

VARIATION

For old-fashioned chocolate pudding, omit the instant coffee. Bring the milk mixture to a boil and make the pudding as directed. Stir in 1 teaspoon of vanilla extract with the final 1/3 cup cream.

THE PERFECT PANTRY

It's amazing what you can make out of nothing. Well, seemingly nothing—actually the magic act is built on a well-stocked kitchen. We haven't listed absolute basics here, like flour and sugar, but instead offer a catalog of all the extras that we think make our own quick cooking a pleasure. You can pick and choose among our staples to make your own perfect pantry.

CUPBOARD

- artichoke hearts
- beans, canned— black, kidney, white, chickpeas
- bread crumbs
- chicken broth, low-sodium
- clam juice
- coconut milk, unsweetened
- coffee, instant
- cornmeal
- couscous
- grits
- honey
- lentils
- liquid smoke
- mushrooms, dried wild
- olive oil
- oyster sauce
- pasta, various
- peppers, roasted red
- pimientos
- rice—short- and long-grain
- soy sauce
- tomatoes—canned and sun-dried
- tuna, packed in oil
- Tabasco sauce
- tapenade
- vinegar—balsamic and red wine

SPICE SHELF

- allspice
- bay leaves
- caraway seeds
- cayenne
- chili powder
- cinnamon
- cloves
- coriander
- cumin
- curry powder
- dill
- fennel seeds
- ginger
- herbes de Provence
- marjoram
- mustard—seeds and ground
- nutmeg
- oregano
- paprika
- peppercorns
- red-pepper flakes
- rosemary
- sage
- thyme
- turmeric

REFRIGERATOR

- anchovies—fillets and paste
- capers
- chutney, mango
- dates
- fish sauce, Asian (nam pla or nuoc mam)
- horseradish
- mustard—Dijon and grainy
- olives—Kalamata or Niçoise
- Parmesan cheese
- pickled vegetables
- prunes
- raisins
- salsa
- sesame oil, Asian

FREEZER

- bacon
- bread
- chicken stock
- coffee
- frozen vegetables— corn, lima beans, peas, spinach
- nuts, various
- poppy seeds
- sesame seeds
- tortillas—flour and corn

LIQUOR CABINET

- cognac or other brandy
- Grand Marnier
- port
- sherry
- vermouth, dry white
- wine—dry white and dry red

CHICKEN STOCK

The one item in our Perfect Pantry that you make yourself is chicken stock. It's a great all-purpose stock that you can use in fish and meat dishes as well as chicken recipes, so make plenty while you're at it. Boil it down to half or even less, freeze in small containers, and reconstitute as needed. You can keep the stock in the refrigerator for up to a week or freeze it almost indefinitely.

MAKES ABOUT 1½ QUARTS

- 4 pounds chicken carcasses, backs, wings, and/or necks, plus gizzards (optional)
- 2 onions, quartered
- 2 carrots, quartered
- 2 ribs celery, quartered
- 8 parsley stems
- 5 peppercorns
- 2 quarts water

1. Put all the ingredients in a large pot. Bring to a boil and skim the foam that rises to the surface. Reduce the heat and simmer, partially covered, for 2 hours.

2. Strain. Press the bones and vegetables firmly to get all the liquid. Skim the fat from the surface if using immediately. If not, refrigerate for up to a week or freeze. Scrape off the fat before using.

INDEX

Page numbers in **boldface** indicate photographs

A

Aegean Pita Pizza, 44
Aioli, Roasted Cod with New Potatoes and, **214**, 215
Almond Butter Cookies, **298**, 299
ANCHOVY, 109
Green Beans with Sliced Garlic and Anchovy, 238
No-Egg Caesar Dressing, 250
Antipasto Caesar Salad with Parmesan Croûtes, 81
APPLE CIDER
Chicken Sauté with Apple Cider and Thyme, 173
Mashed Sweet Potatoes with Apple Cider, 265
APPLE(S), 280, 284
Apple Spice Cake with Brown-Sugar Glaze, 294
Chicken Sauté with Apple Cider and Thyme, 173
Green Salad with Chicken Livers, Apples, and Bacon, 71
Pork Chops with Red Cabbage, Apples, and Currants, **176**, 177
Spinach and Red-Cabbage Salad with Smoked Trout and Apples, **60**, 61
Vanilla Apple Compote, 282
varieties, 281, 282
Warmed Baked Apples "Tatin," 281
Arroz con Pollo, 134
ARTICHOKES
Bow Ties with Salami and Artichoke Hearts, **100**, 101
Sausage, Artichoke, and Mushroom Stir-Fry, 157
ARUGULA
Cheese-and-Salami-Salad Sandwiches, 56
Jerk-Steak Sandwiches with Chutney, **48**, 49
Soft-Shell-Crab Sandwiches, 38

ASPARAGUS, 149, 249

ASPARAGUS, 149, 249
Lemon Risotto with Asparagus and Shiitake Mushrooms, **130**, 131-32
Roasted Asparagus with Hazelnut Sauce, **236**, 237
Spaghettini with Asparagus and Walnut Brown Butter, 102
Stir-Fried Tofu, Shiitakes, and Asparagus, 153
AVOCADOS, 80
BLT Burritos, **54**, 55
Cobb Salad, **66**, 67
Goat-Cheese and Chicken Quesadillas with Guacamole, 42-43
Grilled-Shrimp Tostadas, **186**, 187
Grilled Swordfish with Orange and Avocado Salsa, 189
Guacamole, 187
Shrimp Gazpacho, 16

B

BACON
Black-Eyed-Pea Risotto with Red Wine and Bacon, 126
BLT Burritos, **54**, 55
Cobb Salad, **66**, 67
Fettuccine with Peas and Bacon, 98
Green Salad with Chicken Livers, Apples, and Bacon, 71
Shrimp and Cheese Grits, 119
Soft-Shell-Crab Sandwiches, 38
Baked main dishes, 212-33
Baked Penne with Eggplant, Red Pepper, and Three Cheeses, 104-5
BALSAMIC VINEGAR, 291
Basil Vinaigrette, 191
Marinated Pork Tenderloin with Napa Cabbage, 204
Roasted Fish with Balsamic Glaze, 216
Sherry Balsamic Vinaigrette, 61

Steak-and-Cheese Sandwiches with Balsamic Mayonnaise, 46-47
Strawberry and Balsamic Fool, 291
Tomato Salad with Feta, Basil, and Balsamic Vinaigrette, 254
Bananas, 285
Barbecued Pork Ribs, 205
BASIL, 180. *See also* **Pesto**
Basil Vinaigrette, 191
Grilled Tuna with Tomato-Basil-Salad Sauce, 192
Penne with Eggplant, Fennel, Smoked Mozzarella, and Basil, 106
Pizza Margherita, **108**, 109
Summer Pasta with Grilled Shrimp, 88
Tomato Salad with Feta, Basil, and Balsamic Vinaigrette, 254
BEANS, CANNED. *See also* **Lentils**
Chickpea Salad with Shrimp and Feta Cheese, 65
Chickpeas with Cumin and Parsley, 275
Grilled-Shrimp Tostadas, **186**, 187
Grilled Turkey with Corn, Thyme, and Black-Bean Salsa, 198
Indian Chili, 28
Lamb Stew with Couscous, 122
One-Pot Chicken Couscous with Bell Peppers and Chickpeas, 121
Pork and Sausage with Black Beans, 33
Refried Black Beans with Scallions, Queso Fresco, and Salsa, 274
Rice and Black Beans, 137
Smoky Pork Chili, 26
Sourdough Panzanella with Tuna, White Beans, and Rosemary, 63
Two-Bean Chili with Smoked Ham, 27
White-Bean Soup with Tiny Meatballs, 21
BEAN SPROUTS
Cold Sesame Noodles with Chicken, Bean Sprouts, and Scallions, 93

C

M

N

2

Contributors

Katherine Alford is a food writer and cooking instructor in New York City.

Jim Flint is an international consultant whose travels influence his cooking.

June Greenwald is an avid home cook.

Paul Grimes is a chef, cooking teacher, and food stylist in New York City.

Susan Shapiro Jaslove is a food writer and recipe developer in New York City.

Marcia Kiesel is the associate director of FOOD & WINE magazine's test kitchen and co-author of *Simple Art of Vietnamese Cooking* (Prentice Hall).

Peter Klein is the chef at El Teddy's in New York City.

Stephanie Lyness is a food writer, recipe developer, and author of the forthcoming *Cooking with Steam* (Morrow).

Alvio Renzini is an astronomer and an enthusiastic cook.

Judith Sutton is a food writer and freelance chef in New York City.

Thanks To

Christofle Silver Inc. 373 Park Avenue South, 4th floor, New York, NY 10016: Flatware, cover and pages 22, 30, 60, 100, 124, 200, 214, and 292.

Léron 750 Madison Ave., New York, NY 10021: Napkin, page 78.

The Pfaltzgraff Co. 140 East Market St., York, PA 17401: Pitcher, cover; bowl, page 66; dinner plate, page 124.

Riedel Crystal of America Inc. 24 Aero Rd., Bohemia, NY 11716: Glasses, cover and pages 30, 78, 108, and 200; decanter, page 60.

Wedgwood 1330 Campus Pkwy., Wall, NJ 07719: Open vegetable dish and dinner plates, cover; rimmed soup, page 18; rimmed soup and plate, page 22; dinner plates, pages 176, 200, 214, and 244; salad/dessert plates, pages 182 and 292; soup/cereal bowls, page 270.

Wolfman-Gold & Good Company 117 Mercer St., New York NY 10012: Bowl, page 140.